D1563592

PARTY PLURALISM OR MONISM

Social Movements and the Political System in Yugoslavia 1944-1949

Vojislav Koštunica
and
Kosta Čavoški

EAST EUROPEAN MONOGRAPHS, BOULDER
DISTRIBUTED BY COLUMBIA UNIVERSITY PRESS, NEW YORK

1985

EAST EUROPEAN MONOGRAPHS, NO. CLXXXIX

Copyright © 1985 by Vojislav Koštunica and Kosta Čavoški
Library of Congress Catalog Card Number 85-70778
ISBN 0-88033-082-1

Printed in the United States of America

TABLE OF CONTENTS

INTRODUCTORY NOTE

As is usually the case in other societies, the historical development of Yugoslav society, has also followed a very uneven course. The decisive events which formed its basic institutions and determined the nature of its system took place within relatively short periods of time followed by longer intervals in which essentially nothing changed. That is also the reason for the varying interest of historians in some periods of the post-war development.

Guided by this orientation toward what is essential, the writers of this study have taken the political development of Yugoslavia from 1944 to 1949 as the subject of their research. That was the formative period of the new political system in which far-reaching changes were carried out and whose results and consequences have accompanied us to the present day. For, in the development of a society moments when the creative role of political skill is indeed at work are relatively rare. This is the period which immediately follows coups and revolutions when those at the center of political power have much greater freedom of choice in forming basic social and political institutions than they otherwise have in everyday, ordinary conditions. Such exceptional freedom is a consequence of the fact that the equilibrium of the order of things is fundamentally disrupted and its pivotal point undermined thereby opening the way for more significant and even more radical changes. In the jargon of the realpolitik of revolutionary Machiavellism, which sees the midwife of new forms of order only in violence, this is usually termed a change in the balance of forces which sooner or later leads to a final settling of accounts. But in order for these new forms to be introduced and consolidated it is first necessary to uproot the existing institutions and traditions. This sort of radical change is not only an act of creating the new but also destroying the old.

The period from 1944 to 1949, but particularly the first three years (1944-1946), represents precisely this kind of creative time in our recent history. During it a new order of things took root and was formed as an attempt at realizing the Communist idea in its Bolshevik variant. The years since then and periodical changes in current policy have changed its surface forms to a certain extent but ultimately have not reached to its very roots. That is why an examination of this formative period of our current history constitutes a return to our deepest roots and an attempt to answer the question: how did all of this come to pass?

Naturally it is up to the readers to judge how far the authors of this work have succeeded in this. Nevertheless, it should be pointed out that to a certain extent reality differs from a collection of facts and events and always represents something more than them. This is so because the person who reports on what has been and is taking place always tells a story, *his own* story, in which individual facts are cited, linked and explained according to his own understanding and selection of what is essential. Aware of this limitation, the authors at least hope that they have demonstrated sufficient balance and objectivity in their presentation and conclusions and that they have sought out the truth free from any sort of self-interest in thought or judgment. This is particularly reflected in the review of the conflict between the party which became hegemonistic and the other parties which, by defending the independence of their continuing existence, defended the existing party pluralism. The authors have endeavored to show the views and aspirations not only of the ruling party, as is mostly done today, but also conformed to the well-known dialogical principle that it is also necessary to hear the other side. For this reason many of the considerations in this study are of an antithetical nature.

A certain deficiency in this study results from limiting its subject matter to questions of the party-system in that crucial period of our recent history. Although today many political thinkers consider that the character of the party system is the best yardstick in evaluating the nature of a modern political system and the best guarantee of basic citizens' rights, other important factors in a given political system are nevertheless lost from view with this approach. In our particular case these are, for instance, elements of the civil war which were the inseparable accompaniment to the liberation war against the foreign invader, then the multinational character of our state and the disputes over the new federal structure, and particularly the way in which the organs of state coercion and the newly established courts operated. Some of these questions—federalism, for example—would require going beyond the context of the party system at that time, whereas others, such as political trials, are only touched upon because of the impossibility of inspecting court archives. This is so because as is usually the case in these kinds of historical studies, the object and method of the research depend not only on previously adopted plans but also on available historical sources.

The scheme of presentation itself and the basic approach in this study are the result of an agreement between both authors. Similar cooperation existed also during the composition of individual chapters but the writing itself was divided in an appropriate manner. Thus, Vojislav Koštunica wrote the first and third parts and Kosta Čavoški the second, fourth and fifth parts. Both writers joined together in writing the introductory and concluding remarks.

This monograph forms part of the project on "Industrialization and Emancipation" by the Center for Philosophy and Society Theory at the Institute of Social Sciences. The project was financed by the Republican Science Community of Serbia. In its final form this monograph contains an introductory treatise and an extensive collection of selected documents concerning the political development of Yugoslavia in the period between 1944 and 1949, a total of around 750 typescript pages. However, as the funds allocated were insufficient for the publication of such a voluminous manuscript, we decided to publish at this time just the introductory treatise, under the title "Party Pluralism or Monism," as a first volume. We are doing this in the hope that next year we shall also be able to publish the second volume of documents with corresponding comments and explanations.

CHAPTER I

THE CHARACTER OF SOCIAL MOVEMENTS
AND THE PARTY SYSTEM

1. Social Movements and the Popular Front

The study of the social movements and the political system of Yugoslavia in our project is connected with one particular period of time, the period from 1944 to 1949. This was the revolutionary period, a period of the establishment of a particular form of political pluralism which from the beginning showed a tendency toward party monism. In our study, however, the relations between the political parties are examined within the context of the broader social movements to which these parties belonged. Therefore, in this investigation of the postwar political development of Yugoslavia is not only considered through the prism of inter-party relations, that is, the decline of party pluralism and the establishing of party monism. Rather, party life and political life in general are considered within the context of the broad social movements in which the post-war political parties operated, not only after the liberation of the country but also during the war and in the period between the two wars. *Social movements and political parties,* therefore, constitute the framework for this investigation of the post-war system and the political development of Yugoslavia.

1

In the post-war political arguments and debates between the Communist Party and the opposition parties we discuss *political questions* in the strictest sense of the word, questions of democracy, elections, the role of political parties and so forth. All of these questions were raised in the debates on political laws in Parliament. We have not gone into the controversies in other areas of social life (the economy, culture, and the like). The chief aim of this study is to reconstruct as faithfully as possible the relationship between a liberal and a basically Bolshevik variant of the Communist idea in post-war Yugoslavia, in the formative period of the new political system.

The post-war party system as it existed in Yugoslavia immediately after the liberation cannot be studied if, in addition to the parties as organized social formations, social movements too are not taken into consideration as collective efforts to provoke greater changes in social institutions or even create a completely new order. In this connection, despite the close interdependence and mutual influence of the social movements and the political parties, the differences between the parties and movements remain essential. Although social movements contain within their ranks certain formally organized groups, movements do not constitute organized groups. A degree of organization appears in social movements, but movements never have the full character of formally organized groups. Social movements which become more and more bureaucratized and institutionalized lose at one stage their original, authentic character and cease to be social movements.[1]

The post-war political parties, particularly the five big parties (the Democratic Party, the Radical Party, the Agrarian Party, the Croatian Republican Peasant Party and the Indepedent Democratic Party), represented in Yugoslavia between the two wars parts of the broader social movements which since 1919 had fought for a change in the political set up. Mutually antagonistic, these movements under King Alexander's personal regime proclaimed on 6 January 1929, began to come together more and more in the common struggle against an authoritarian regime. This convergence of the different social movements (the Croatian side focused on the struggle against unitarism and the Serbian part centered on the struggle against the authoritarianism of the current regime and against its party blocs) gradually led to the rapprochement of these movements and their merging into one, though not united, movement. The rapprochement of these movements was best expressed in the formation of the United Opposition before the elections of 1935, as well as in the formation of the National Agreement Bloc in 1937.

In his basic discussion of the draft Constitution of 1946, in the Constituent Assembly, Dragoljub Jovanović, General Secretary of the People's Peasant Party, recalled the fact that in Yugoslavia movements had existed since 1919 which aimed at changing the governmental structure of the country. In it, he emphasized that at the root of "the national opposition movement, dating from 1919" there had been a different concept of the unity of Yugoslavia from that of the ruling regime and dynasty: "all those who fought against the old state of King Alexander and the Vidovdan Constitution agreed that they wanted Yugoslavia as a state entity but under a different leadership."[2] The relationship between that social movement and the parties within its framework was far from being one of unity. Disputes, conflicts and even dissesion among the political parties themselves were often serious. On the other hand, the political parties did not keep pace with the currents or mood of the moment in the movements. Nevertheless, there were times when there was essentially a rapprochement between these movements and the political parties in opposition.

From 1935, when the United Opposition was formed prior to the assembly elections, one political party did come foreward with a new concept of social movement.[3] This refers, of course, to the illegal Communist Party of Yugoslavia (CPY) which, after the decisions reached at the Seventh Congress of the Comintern, held in Moscow from 25 July to 20 August 1935, began, like other sections of the Communist International, to advocate the concept of a broad social movement of all the anti-fascist and democratic social forces, that is, the concept of a *Popular Front*.

Thus, in the proclamation of the Communist Party of Yugoslavia entitled "For the Unity of the Working Class! For a Popular Front of Freedom!", printed in 2,000 copies and published on 9 August 1935, a positive assessment was made of the parties in the United Opposition, but it was also emphasized that these parties did not represent all of the people's forces. Therefore, the authors of this proclamation advocated that the working class should also be represented in an organized form within the framework of a "broader united opposition," and that the organization, that is, the party of the working class within this collective movement of all progressive and democratic forces, should have the leading role. To put it more precisely, the aforementioned proclamation states:

> The political groupings of the United Opposition (the Croatian Pea-
> sant Party, the Agrarians, the Davidović followers [Democratis—
> authors' note], the Independent Democrats, the Left-wing Fed-
> eralists [Montenegro Party—authors' note]) are rally around them-
> selves a large section of the people from all regions who are really
> prepared to fight for their freedom. Nevertheless, these groupings
> do not embrace all the progressive people's forces, nor do they pre-
> sent a united front which would, regardless of political programmes,
> mobilise all freedom fighters and lead them into the common strug-
> gle . . . . The working class has hitherto been and still is in the front
> ranks of all actions conducted by the United Opposition for national
> liberties, but it has not participated in those struggles as an organised
> and equal unit like the rest of the groupings in the United Opposi-
> tion because it has not been mobilised and united into its own
> workers' party which would lead it in that struggle and represent
> its interests. The broad people's freedom front is still to mobilise
> workers, peasants and all progressive democratic elements, and the
> working class must play a decisive role in rally those forces.[4]

In an attempt to have the working class participate in the movement of the United Opposition as an "equal and organized unit," the Communist Party had been taking certain steps in the direction of setting up a unified workers' party (under the name of the United Workers' Party in 1935 and of the Party of the Working People in 1937), and had negotiated with the Socialists about this. However, there was no agreement reached between the Communists and the Socialists and in the efforts to create a unified workers' party the regime also sensed the Communists' striving to win for themselves the character of a legal party organization.

The Ribbentrop-Molotov pact in 1939 brought a halt to activity aimed at forming the Popular Front, and in the Resolution of the Fifth Confer-ence of the CPY in 1940 this appraisal was made of that activity:

During the time of the formation of the Popular Front from 1935 to 1939 our party did not succeed in reaching an agreement with the top echelons of a single political party or group, except with some petit-bourgeois political groups in Slovenia. Nor did it succeed in reaching agreement on a unified front of the working class with the leadership of the Social Democrats who sabotaged that unity. However, the Conference concludes that the tactics of forming a unified popular front have brought notable results...with joint large-scale demonstrations under the leadership of the Communists ...at the time of Munich, the Anschluss, the occupation of Czechoslovakia...at the time of the struggle against the notorious Stojadinović regime and for an agreement and resolution on the Croatian national question...with numerous momentous and massive strikes by workers in the course of the last few years...with mass demonstrations against the imperialist war in the Autumn of 1939, with mass demonstrations in support of co-operation with the USSR.[5]

On the basis of this appraisal the Communist Party can be considered to have operated within the framework of the opposition movements. In spite of opposition from the organizers, the Democrats and the Agrarians, the Communists also made speeches at the famous Kragujevac rally on 25 August 1935 in which 30,000-40,000 people took part. During 1935 and 1936 in the region of Vojvodina alone, Dragoljub Jovanović, one of the fiercest advocates of the inclusion of the Communists in the movement of the United Opposition, organized around 30 different rallies and meetings at which the Communists also spoke side by side with him. Conflict arose at the rally in Petrovgrad (Zrenjanin) on 10 November 1935 between the United Opposition on the one hand, and Dragoljub Jovanović and the Communists on the other hand. On the eve of this rally, the United Opposition issued a leaflet criticizing Dragoljub Jovanović for his policies and removing him from the ranks of the opposition.[6]

Dragoljub Jovanović also popularized abroad the idea of the necessity for the United Opposition also the encompass representatives of the Communist Party. Thus, in a statement for the French paper *Populaire,* Jovanović said:

There is enough time until the autumn for the United Opposition to consolidate itself and to admit to its ranks in the form of a Popular Front the rest of the opposition forces which want nothing else than to assist unselfishly in the overthrow of the existing regime. The Popular Front which we are setting up at present, uniting us on the left wing of the opposition with the socialists, republicans and representatives of the working class who consider themselves Communists, is in no way aimed against the United Opposition nor even against its insufficiently active leadership: this is how much we are interested in a grouping of all democratic and left-wing elements.[7]

Nevertheless, the formation of this kind of Popular Front did not materialize in the direct negotiations between the Communists and the leaders of the other political parties. In Serbia, the Democratic Party and the Agrarian Party were against this idea of a Popular Front and support was given only by factions of these parties, that is, by the small political parties: by Socialists, Republicans, left-wing Agrarians and left-wing Democrats. In Croatia the Croatian Peasant Party rejected the idea of a Popular Front. The reasons against the formation of a Popular Front by the three main parties of the United Opposition (the Democrats, the Agrarians and the Croatian Peasant Party) were the same and could be summed up by the following position: the Popular Front which the Communists advocated was to be realized through the very existence of the United Opposition, which already comprised an anti-fascist front and a front against the dictatorship, that is, a freedom front. This opposition or lack of interest from the United Opposition toward co-operation with the Communists can be explained by the fact that these parties already enjoyed broad, mass support and so did not have to bother about co-operating with a small (at the time of the negotiations), cadre-led, illegal party, and above all a party which represented only a section of the Comintern. Similarly, the concept of a Popular Front in which the working class must have a major role would have been acceptable to followers of certain ideological orientations following from the Marxist concept of the historical mission of the proletariat, but this idea was alien to members of other parties, especially in an industrially under-developed country where the peasantry was numerically predominant.

On the basis of everything stated here, it can be concluded that the idea of a Popular Front was accepted chiefly by some factions of the large parties, and by small political parties: Socialists, Republicans, left-wing Agrarians and left-wing Democrats. The leadership of the large parties considered, however, that the unification and agreement between the opposition parties, parties which fought against the regime of the dictatorship and its protagonists made the idea of a Popular Front superfluous. Some leaders of these parties showed a certain tolerance toward the speeches and activity at their own meetings and in the press of these individuals whom they knew, or could have supposed to be members or sympathizers of the illegal Communist Party.

But not even the political parties and groups which supported the idea of a Popular Front looked upon this formation in the same way. The first thing which struck the members of these parties was the readiness of the Communists to co-operate with followers of those ideological orientations with which until recently they had refused any form of co-operation. Thus, suddenly, not only other workers' parties prior to then deemed "socio-fascist," but also bourgeois parties became desirable partners. Many of the small political parties mentioned here did not concern themselves overmuch with this turnabout in the tactics of the Communist Party, proceeding from the view that changing circumstances imposed a change in means of the struggle and in the modes of operation by the political parties. Besides that, the idea of rallying and linking democratic and anti-fascist forces corresponded to the spirit of the times and to the mood of the public at large. To a certain extent the concept of a Popular Front was imposed on the Communist parties by the masses and it was only later that these parties were to develop their plan for such a Front more thoroughly and try to impose it on the masses.

Some parties or their leaders, nevertheless paid attention to this change in tactics by the Communist parties. Thus the Republican Vladimir Simić pointed to the existence of a "twofold Communist concept."[8] According to Simić, in the Soviet Union itself there prevailed the concept of the regime of the dictatorship of the proletariat which was introduced through revolution and civil war, whereas outside the borders of the Soviet Union the democratic principle was supported by the Comintern. Revolutionary changes in the Soviet Union had led to the abandonment of the slow course of democratic evolution and thereby to the annulment of all democratic values and to the acceptance of political tactics which were, according to Simić, anti-democratic. On the other hand, "in countries with highly developed capitalist production (that is, in countries in which Communist parties were not in power but in opposition—authors' note), the position of democratic evolution and its mechanism for resolving political and economic problems in society was adopted." According to Simić, such a turnabout in the tactics of the Comintern contained an inner contradiction:

> To proclaim the regime of the dictatorship of the proletariat as the basis of political life in one country, but to advocate the struggle for the principles of democracy and for social and economic progress by way of democratic evolutionin countries where, in the distribution of forces, the Communist orientation represents the minority, is, to put it very mildly, such a clear programmatic contradiction that it is immediately noticeable.[9]

This change in the tactics of the Communist parties, according to Simić, can be interpreted in several ways. First of all, it could be said that the change in tactics of the Communist parties, which tried to conceal the revolutionary character of their policies, was to deceive the bourgeoisie and the advocates of democratic evolution and to win over their adherents so that, at a convenient moment, by making use of the existing power, they could carry out a revolutionary coup, "to establish the regime of the dictatorship of the proletariat and do away with all democratic values in society." Secondly, it could be said that the change was objectively caused; that it was the result of changing social circumstances and not the consequence of the Party will. And thirdly, it would be possible to describe it as purely battlefield tactics imposed by the immediate danger from fascism.

After pointing out the twofold Bolshevik concept of political development—the difference between the regime of the dictatorship of the proletariat and the democratic regime—and also the possibility of explaining the changes in the Comintern's tactics, Vladimir Simić himself made a sudden turnabout, abandoning any deeper investigation of the "secret of this about-face." He now maintained that any conclusion in this context was problematical and that matters should be accepted as they really were, regardless of motives. "Such a state of affairs," according to Simić, "points to what is most important in practical political life, namely, that a political action, even by a political opponent, has to be taken into account and judged according to the real facts and views at the moment of that action itself, or in the duration of that action and that its vital force has to be utilized in case its immediate targets coincide with one's own political aims."[10] This is even more applicable to circumstances in which "those who have been outstanding representatives of the anti-democratic systems also accept the path of democratic evolution;" according to Simić, acceptance of the principle of democratic evolution by the Communist parties, regardless of their real motives, testifies to the "victory of universal democratic principles."

The political parties which supported the idea of a Popular Front had different views of the character of inter-party relations in this political formation. The majority of these parties believed that the existence of a broad national movement meant giving priority to common aims, but not to the extent that the existing parties should renounce their own identity. This concept was best expressed in the famous words of the Democrats' leader, Ljubomir Davidović, at the Kragujevac rally in August 1935: "I am inviting you, not to the Democratic Party but, under the banner of democracy, to a broad national movement!" In contrast to this kind of coalitionist Popular Front, the democratic left (a faction of the Democratic party) advocated the national movement of the United Opposition as a unified organization. Thus, the Democratic left, led by Ivan Ribar, Života Milojković, Dragoslav Smiljanić and Čedomir Plećević, was virtually advocating the same concept of a Popular Front which the Communist Party was to present when it acquired and consolidated political power. The memorandum, which the leadership of the democratic left sent to the leadership of the United Opposition in connection with this in March 1938, stated, among other things, that:

> the United Opposition is a unified political grouping, composed of parties, groups and individuals, who agree to fight with united forces, in harmony and shoulder to shoulder against the dictatorship of 6th January 1929 in all its forms and stages, and to work toward replacing it with a democratic government, i.e., a government by the

majority of the people for the benefit of the majority of the people.
. . . As a general national movement, the United Opposition must
have, besides a single leadership, a single programme, united tactics
and a single organisation.[11]

However, in reply to the democratic left's memorandum on the United
Opposition as a single organization, Ljubomir Davidović, drew attention to
the fact that the democratic left's proposals were to lead to the abolition
of party pluralism and thereby open the door to a one-party dictatorship.
The polemic between the democratic left and the leadership of the Democratic Party is interesting insofar as it recalls the polemic between the
leadership of the Communist Party and certain leaders of the opposition
parties after the war. On both occasions one side supported a Popular
Front in which party pluralism would be protected (Davidović before the
war and the opposition parties after the war), while the other side defended
the concept of a Popular Front as a homogeneous formation developing
from a unified organization into the organization of an avant-garde political party. In a letter which he sent on behalf of the Main Committee of
the Democratic Party, Davidović pointed out that under the guise of
organizing unified action by the United Opposition the democratic left
advocated the position that:

> there are no more parties and only the people exist, which is what
> the present rulers have been saying since 6th January. . . . Every
> sensible person will understand without any further arguments that
> pulverisation of the people would help the forces of reaction. Parties
> exist, Democratic, Radical and Agrarian, and they are a guarantee
> for the disciplined work determined by the responsibilities of each
> individual in each group. Today they are acting in close partnership
> as the United Opposition; they have a definite programme, set out
> in the act of the National Agreement, which the parties of the Na-
> tional Agreement Bloc are continuing to develop in the same spirit
> and in the hope that this programme is suitable for the situation.
> . . . It must be clear even to small children that now, on the eve of
> the great battle facing democracy, the way to unity cannot lead
> through the destruction of the political parties, which during all this
> time have staged the struggle, but through discipline, with an estab-
> lished leadership of the parties and party bloc.[12]

More than the disputes over the formation of a Popular Front after 1935—disputes provoked by the decision of the Comintern—it was further political development, particularly after the war, which pointed to the existence of two different concepts of social movements. The opposition parties in Yugoslavia between the two wars more or less explicitly accepted social movements as largely informal and only partially organized collective bodies, although some of these movements were better organized (the movement around the Croatian Peasant Party) than others (the movement around the Serbian United Opposition). At the end of the the 1950s the Popular Front, in whose formation toward the end of the war and after it the Communist Party played a leading role, moved farther and farther away from this concept of movements and increasingly toward the *Bolshevik concept* which said the *organization* (the Communist Party) was something completely different and above the mass *movement*. Lenin probably best expressed this concept of the relationship between the organization and movements in his paper *What is to be done?* As it was pointed out, under the influence of this concept of a social movement, at the end of the 1950s the Popular Front was turning into "an organization for summoning the workers to work and carrying out voluntary mass actions," that is, into an "organization for the mobilization of the physical labor."[13]

Besides the existence of two different viewpoints on the nature and tasks of social movements, in the post-war political development of Yugoslavia it is also necessary to point out the existence of two different concepts of political parties and party systems. The system of political parties which evolved in Yugoslavia in the period from 1944 to 1949 was marked by two completely different concepts of democracy and the role of political parties. The traditional liberal concept was confronted by the orthodox, Bolshevik concept of democracy, parties and the parliamentary system. Setting aside for the moment the greater or lesser differences between the opposition parties which in the period before the war often led to divisions between parties with the same attitude to democracy, the majority of the opposition parties in the post-war period proceeded from one and the same viewpoint on democracy. That identical view consisted of the acceptance and justification of the values of a liberal, pluralistic or competitive, democracy. Differences between the opposition parties in this period were reduced and identical points became apparent sooner or later because for the first time these parties were up against a strong ideological and political opponent which held the reins of power. Except for those opposition parties or party leaders who renounced their former party identities either during the war or immediatley after the liberation, all the parties and their individual followers were facing a political opponent who had little in common with their political world. This confrontation of two worlds, liberalism and Bolshevism, came to the fore primarily in the disagreement over the concepts of democracy and the role of political parties.

The liberal concept, as is well-known to all, says there is no democracy without a contest between political parties in which the difference between the majority and the minority is crystallized. In the democratic system, the rules of the political game are such as to enable the minority freely to set forth and spread its views, argue it case, attempt to influence the policy of the governing party and, in a peaceful manner, via parliamentary elections, to attain power itself. In order to be able to counter successfully the arguments of the majority with its own arguments, the minority must have at its disposal those means of persuading the public, those political weapons which the majority also possess: a party organization and the possibility of association, freedom of public assembly and speech and freedom of the press. In a contemporary, developed society, people of the same political persuasion can hope for success only if they act in an organized manner, relying on their own party, associations and press. To equate democracy and party pluralism does not mean, according to the liberal standpoint, to close one's eyes to the shortcomings of party pluralism. As Harold Laski wrote, political parties suffer from the evils of group separatism and distort and pervert the issues they create, they produce artificial divisions in the electoral body, they build about persons allegiance which should go to the ideas, in their activity they manipulate the opinions of people, but, nevertheless, they are of vital importance for the preserving and functioning of the democratic process. They are not perfect but they still represent the most effective safeguard against the danger of dictatorship.[14]

The liberal viewpoint that there is no political democracy without political pluralism, and that there is no political liberalism without party pluralism, also implies that there is no democracy where party monism holds sway. The original idea of the party system implies the existence of more than one party; each party represents a part of society, as the name itself indicates. In essence any party means *belonging* to a particular organization and *separation* from other organizations by means of a special program. The system of political parties implies a set of relations between parties as well as the relations between them and their environment (political system). Where there is but one political party there is neither a party system nor a political party. A single-party system is a *contradiction in adiecto*. A single-party system negates the original meaning and purpose of a political party; the ruling party resists the existence of other parties. Instead of acknowledging and accepting its own *partiality,* which is the basic characteristic of a party's essence, the one and only party emphasizes its totalitarian nature; other political parties are not permitted. In this manner also, torn from its natural context in the democratic system, the political party ceases to be one of the participants in the discussion or debate conducted in the public view.[15]

Particularly characteristic of the liberal concept of democracy and of especially significance for the subject of our investigation is the notion of the protection of minority rights. In this connection, that tendency in the political thought of liberalism which constantly emphasized the danger that government by the majority, as the basis of democracy, might itself degenerate into the tyranny of the majority is important. This is the idea that any tyranny is evil and that the tyranny of the majority, because the resistance of the minority is made even more difficult and hopeless. Developed from this in an inspired form is the concept that it is necessary to protect the rights of the minority:

> Liberalism is that principle of political rights, according to which the public authority, in spite of being all-powerful, limits itself and attempts even at its own expense, to leave room in the State over which it rules for those to live who neither think nor feel as it does, that is to say, as do the stronger, the majority . . . . It announces the determination to share existence with the enemy; more than that, with an enemy which is weak.[16]

This attitude that the essential characteristic of democracy and party pluralism is to protect the rights of the minority was advocated by representatives of the opposition parties in the post-war parliamentary debates and in the press. Aleksa Tomić, one of the leaders of the Republican Party,

expressed this liberal standpoint on party pluralism in a particularly strik-
ing form:

> A *party is only one part of a greater whole.* This means that a party
> contains within itself the consciousness of only one part of the
> people and it should never, under any circumstances, equate itself
> with the people and the state. If, nevertheless, a party does do this,
> then it also overrates itself, overrates its own strength, and, in addi-
> tion, does injustice on other parts by doing so, it can ruin itself, the
> people and the state . . . . No party which wishes well for itself and
> the community can live only for itself, just as no individual can. A
> party can only develop and improve itself more and more if it also
> has alongside it an opposition party. Therefore, it is a justified opin-
> ion that if there is no opposition it is necessary to create it, in order
> that affairs should run in the way that is necessary for the general
> good of the people and the state.[17]

In contrast to this concept of democracy, the Bolshevik type of organization advocates a completely different concept, by proceeding from
Lenin's and Stalin's teaching about the dictatorship of the proletariat,
which amounts to the rule of one—Communist—party as the basic leading
force of the proletariat, this implies the party does not share, nor can
share, the leadership with other parties.[18] According to the orthodox
Bolshevik concept, which was set out theoretically by Georg Lukács, in
order for the revolutionary working movement to separate itself from the
roots of capitalism, it must also distance itself from party life and from the
spirit characteristic of it. According to Lukács, as long as the proletariat
operated within the framework of the party system:

> the location, type and scope of operations descended to the level of
> party conflicts, that is, to a level which brought with it uncertainty,
> compromise and opportunism. Furthermore, as a consequence of
> operating within the organizational frameworks of a party, it also
> meant that the party of the proletariat was forced to acknowledge
> the form of a capitalist society. In vain did it criticize that form in
> word and deed because it participated in the elections and in parlia-
> mentary life. In fact, it acknowledged capitalist society. Hence that

deep gulf between words and deeds which has characterized the movement in recent years.[19]

In 1919 during the Hungarian revolution, Lukács pointed out in his writing the difference between the Social-Democratic and Communist parties in Hungary and elsewhere:

> The Social-Democratic Party is founded on the assumption that the proletariat itself is still not in a position to take over power and to impose its will on the whole of society. Therefore, the Social-Democratic Party was just one party among other parties. That whole world in which the Social-Democratic Party operated as one among many is annihilated by the dictatorship of the proletariat becoming a fact.[20]

When the Social-Democratic party in Hungary accepted the Communist program, with the establishment of the dictatorship of the proletariat, Lukács pointed out the significance of the great difference which arises when only one workers' party, the Communist Party, emerges and operates on the scene:

> *The parties have ceased to exist—now only the united proletariat exists: this is the decisive theoretical meaning of that unification.* If that new unification is termed a party, the word party expresses an entirely different meaning from before. . . . That crisis of socialism manifested in the dialectical contradictions of the party movements is finally at an end. The proletarian movement has at long last stepped into a new phase, into the phase of its own power.[21]

If, therefore, according to the liberal concept, party pluralism is a necessary condition of democracy, then, according to the Bolshevik concept, the absence of party pluralism is a necessary prerequisite of the socialist transformation of society and of the democracy peculiar to it.

Two things must, however, not be overlooked in this context. Firstly, this attitude of the Bolshevik organization to party pluralism manifests itself at the moment when Communist parties are entrenched in power. During the struggle for power, these parties make use of the privileges of party pluralism and of the parliamentary system. In bourgeois states they can even fight for the basic rights of pluralism to be respected and condemn the violation of these rights by the state bureaucracy or reactionary bourgeois social forces and their parties. Even after attaining power, Communist parties in environments in which the roots of party pluralism are deeper can, in the short or long term, maintain illusory forms of party pluralism, as well also be shown in our study.

Secondly, the liberal and Bolshevik concept of democracy and of the position and role of political parties in the form in which they are expressed here, are typical above all of the time with which we are dealing. More substantial changes will arise in the later developments of these two great ideas and movements. Leaving aside those orientations in the Communist movement which have not removed themselves to any considerable extent from the original attitudes, it is the parties in the Communist movement which in their critique of party pluralism today use entirely new arguments, and the parties which publicly declare that party pluralism is compatible with a democratic system and with the socialist transformation of society (for example, Euro-communism) which attract attention. For the purposes of our investigation, it is the ideological and doctrinaire situation such as existed in Yugoslavia after the Second World War which must be borne in mind.

2. Political Parties and the Party System

We turn now to the characteristics of the opposition parties in the post-revolutionary period. While some disputes were important in the political sphere between the two wars, the parties differed in a number of aspects, but primarily in the disputes concerning the form of government (monarchy or a republic, federalism or unitarism, centralization or decentralization and the like). After the war, when many of these disputes became irrelevant it appeared that in the changing circumstances between these parties there was more that brought them together than set them apart. Nevertheless, as regards the concept of political democracy, certain differences between the opposition parties can be observed. The question of political democracy, especially democratic procedure, was the fundamental question in the program and activity of the Democracy Party, whereas the choice between monarchy and republic was of fundamental significance for the Republican Party, overshadowing all other questions of political democracy. While the Democrats emerged in the post-war debates as the most consistent champions of political democracy, by virtue of their program, their tradition and the people which their party attracted, the People's Peasant Party, whose program gave priority to a social question (the position and role of the peasantry in society) approached the problem of political democracy with more reserve and made the issue of democracy relative. Placing the question of ends above that of forms, procedures and means, the People's Peasant Party in the first parliamentary debates came near to the Communist Party, that is, its tactics were somewhat reminiscent of Communist Party tactics.

What were the political aspects and importance of all these non-Communist parties which participated in the post-war parliamentary life? There were nine of them on the post-war political stage (see Table 1).[22] Of these five can be considered large, and more important parties. These were the

TABLE 1

Number of Votes Gained by the Post-War Political Parties in the 1920-1927 Parliamentary Elections

Party	Parliamentary Elections (in %)			
	1920	1923	1925	1927
Radical Party	17.7	25.6	25.6	31.9
Democratic Party	19.9	18.5	11.8	16.6
Independent Democratic Party	––	––	9.2	8.8
Croatian Republican Peasant Party	14.3	21.9	22.4	15.8
Communist Party	12.4	––	––	––
Agrarian Party	7.4	7.0	4.5	6.4
Social-Democratic Party	2.9	2.2	1.0	1.0
Republican Party	1.1	0.9	0.2	0.2

Radical Party, the Democratic Party, the Agrarian Party, the Independent Democratic Party and the Croatian Republican Peasant Party. The Radicals, Democrats and the Agrarians were the three main Serbian parties by their electoral strength and influence, although by the number of votes gained in the elections between the wars the first two were out in front. In parliamentary elections up until 1929, with the exception of 1920, the Radicals represented the strongest party. They obtained their highest share of votes in 1927 (31.9%) and their lowest in 1920 (17.7%). The Democratic Party, ranked second among the Serbian parties, won their largest share of the vote in 1920 (19.9%) and smallest in 1925 (11.8%). In contrast to these two parties, whose origins were older and which, in a certain sense, shared a common geneology (they originated from the Radical and Independent Radical Party), the Agrarian Party was founded in 1919-1920 primarily as a social movement for the advancement of rural areas and agriculture. It was the most successful in the elections, taking 7.4% of the votes. Of the remaining two big parties, one was composed chiefly of Serbs from outside Serbia (primarily in Croatia) and had emerged from a split in the Democratic Party in 1925, while the other, the Croatian Republican Peasant Party was the strongest Croatian party and the second strongest in Yugoslav terms in the elections of 1923 and 1925, and the third strongest in the elections of 1920 and 1927. It obtained its highest number of votes in 1925 (22.4%). After the split with the Democratic Party, the Independent Democratic Party won 9.2% of the vote in the 1925 elections.

In the last elections before the introduction of the 6 January dictatorship, the five big parties took four-fifths of the vote. All these parties, or rather their sections, can be in the main considered democratic because of their opposition to King Alexander's personal regime, and because of the role which they played within the framework of the United Opposition. Two of these parties also voted against the Vidovdan constitution (the Croatian Republican Peasant Party and the Agrarian Party). All of them were represented in the government formed after the coup d'etat of 27 March 1941, and in the governments in exile until the formation of the Šubašić government.

The remaining four parties, which also resumed their activity after the war, did not have great influence in the period between the wars and were not represented in the governments in exile. The two parties with a socialist orientation (the Socialist Party and the Social-Democratic Party) were, in fact, two parts of the same pre-war party which had been obtaining 1.3% of the vote in the elections. Even weaker was the Republican Party with obtained 1.1% of the vote and three deputies in the first elections and none at all afterwards. The last of the parties which participated in post-war events was the People's Peasant Party, the result of a separation of the Agrarian Left, led by Dragoljub Jovanović, from the Agrarian Party in 1940. The electoral potential and parliamentary influence of these parties was slight, though their extra-parliamentary significance and the personal influence of their leaders was substantial (Dragoljub Jovanović, Jaša Prodanović, Nedeljko Divac and others).

This survey of the political parties which participated in the post-war political life up until 1947 shows that two ethnic, that is, confessional groups were not represented through their own parties in the post-war parliament: the Slovenes and the Moslems. Not a single Slovene party participated in the Slovene variant of the Popular Front, the so-called Liberation Front, which had the character of a coalition until 1943, although some twenty groups, some of which were factions of the two main party blocs in pre-war Slovenia (Liberal and Catholic) operated within the Front. The leading Slovene People's Party was represented in the governments in exile. After the Dolomite Declaration by the founding groups of the Liberation Front (the Christian Socialists, members of the Sokol organization and cultural workers) that:

> in keeping with their national, political and social objections, which
> in respect of all fundamental questions are identical with the ob-
> jectives of the Communist Party of Slovenia, they do not feel or
> see any need for separate parties or political organizations.[23]

The elements of institutionalized party pluralism practically disappeared from political life in post-war Slovenia.

Seen overall, it can also be concluded that in its character, in the number of politial parties in pre-war Yugoslavia (around 40 parties in the first parliamentary elections in 1920, including a considerable number of parties of national minorities), in the nature and differences between the parties and in its instability, this system falls into that category of party systems described as *systems of extreme pluralism.*[24]

Thanks to the considerable degree of agreement between the programs of some of the small pre-war parties (the Republican Parties) and the Communist Party, and to the consistent criticism of the bourgeois parties between the wars (the left-wing Agrarians of Dragoljub Jovanović), some of these small parties gained in importance and rank beyond their pre-war significance. This is also seen by the number of deputies who entered the Provisional Assembly with the agreement of the leaders of those parties. With the exception of the Social-Democratic Party, which had one deputy, and the Radicals, who had six (the Radicals did not even fill these seats with their deputies), the rest of the parties, despite earlier differences, were more or less equal in their electoral strength. Not counting the pre-war deputies who entered the Provisional National Assembly because they had been elected in the last parliamentary elections in 1938, the Democratic Party and the Croatian Republican Peasant Party had 13 members each in the post-war parliament, the Agrarian Party 12, the Independent Democrats and the Republic Party 11 and the People's Peasant Party eight.

All pre-war political parties were "legalized" in two ways: by declaring that they were joining the Popular Front, or by applying to the relevant authorities for permission to carry out party activity. With regard to the first condition, all parties joined the Popular Front with the exception of the Democrats and the Radicals (although some members of the rank and file of these parties were in the Popular Front). On the eve of the elections for the Constituent Assembly, one party (the Agrarians) left the Popular Front but a section of the party did stay in this organization. Only one party had its application to join the Popular Front turned down—the Yugoslav National Party. Its application was refused by the Executive Committee of the Popular Front of Serbia, which gave individual members who had acquitted themselves "honorably" during the War the option of joining their organization. Organized as a party which should have given the regime a semblance of democracy after the Constitution of 1931 granted by King Alexander, it split into two parts at the time of the 1938 elections, one part attaching itself to the goverment list of Stojadinović and the other to the opposition list headed by Maček. After this split, the party was represented in the government of 27 March 1941 and in the governments in exile.

In addition to the political parties, one non-party organization, the "Napred" group, also declared itself in favor of joining the Popular Front. The "Napred" group began in January 1937, initially with the publication of the series entitled "Politika i društvo ("Politics and Society"), consisting of minor monthly brochures containing treatises on political, social, economic and cultural affairs. In April 1938, the "Politics and Society" Publishing Co-operative was founded, and in June 1938 it began publishing the newspaper *Napred,* which grew from a monthly to a weekly. Because of its democratic and anti-regime orientation, the paper was often banned, as was the "Politics and Society" series.[25] The first issue of *Napred* stated that it would "defend and disseminate the democratic thought and spirit by standing aside from all political organizations."[26] This orientation bound together the people working in it who had different political convictions and who supported different, though democratic, political parties. In addition to this orientation, in its treatment of the subject matter the paper was also characterized by a high degree of competence on the part of its contributors (the majority were university professors, chiefly from the Law Faculty in Belgrade), and by its effort to write about the most complex themes in a way which was accessible and clear to everybody (in its subtitle, *Napred* carried the legend that it was a "paper for the people"). The Declaration on Political, Social and Economic Questions, published in *Napred* at the beginning of 1940, set out the fundamental direction of its associates and of its writing as follows:

> Democracy, as the basic law of our national life, is the only principle capable of rallying and organizing our national forces for the purpose of building and defending our national community: an agreement between Serbs, Croats and Slovenes, as the basic criterion of our national policy, is the only thing capable of guaranteeing free co-operation by our three fraternal peoples in national and state affairs; federation is the only form of internal state order which can protect, safeguard and strengthen state unity at this point in time; social and economic justice is the basic motivation and cardinal rule of state policies in social relations with the purpose of protecting the socially weak and the economically depressed; the peasantry is the guiding principle of economic, agrarian and educational policy, and this is also indicated by the economic structure of our state itself; collective security and international solidarity is the principle of foreign policy.[27]

The founder and chief editor of the "Politics and Society" series and owner of the paper *Napred,* was Mihailo Ilić, a professor at the Law

Faculty in Belgrade, who spent from November 1941 until March 1944 in the prison camp at Banjica for his democratic and anti-fascist convictions and activities, and who was killed by the Germans at the end of March 1944. The "Napred" group was among the first to decide to join the Popular Front—on 18 November 1944. Milivoje Marković, lecturer at the Law Faculty in Belgrade, read on behalf of the group, the declaration about joining at the First Congress of the Popular Front.

In accordance with the Law on Associations, Assemblies and other Public Gatherings of 1945, all parties, except the Agrarian Party and the Communist Party, submitted applications for permission to engage in party work, though the Democratic Party objected in principle to the requirement "that the old parties, parties with a clean political past and with a long tradition, should register again."[28] Since the majority of the parties submitted their applications during the Constituent Assembly elections, the licences permitting their activity were issued in the Autumn of 1945. The People's Peasant Party resumed its work at the end of 1946, and the Independent Democratic Party at the beginning of 1947.

In post-war political life, the presence of other political parties in addition to the Communist Party, manifested itself in a number of ways. Party representatives were in the Government of Democratic Federal Yugoslavia and the Provisional Assembly. The parties' delegates were in the supreme bodies of the Popular Front. Some political parties also had their own newspapers. Some parties were able to develop their organizational network, a network of local party committees (this applied primarily to the Croatian Republican Peasant Party). Parties in the Popular Front took part in the election campaign, published their own electoral manifestos and put forward their candidates within the framework of the Popular Front's lists. Leaders of these parties issued statements to the foreign press before the elections (D. Jovanović) and afterwards (J. Prodanović), which should have confirmed the democratic nature of the electoral procedure and the reality of the election itself.[29] In the article "Elections at the Right Time," published in two issues of *Glas,* the paper of the Popular Front of Serbia, Dragoljub Jovanović stressed that in Serbia representatives of all parties were distributed in fairly equal numbers on both lists for the Constituent Assembly. In all districts, with one or two exceptions where only one candidate was nominated, there were two, three or even five candidates. The people in Serbia, therefore, according to Jovanović, had the opportunity of not only choosing between persons but also according to party allegiance.[30] Members of different political parties (M. Pijade on behalf of the Communists and D. Jovanović on behalf of the non-Communist parties) participated in drafting the election manifesto of the Popular Front. Lastly, when the first Government of the Federal People's Republic of Yugoslavia was formed, 11 of its 21 ministers were non-Communists. The Premier, J. B. Tito, declared that he had formed the Government in consultation with the representatives of the parties in the Popular Front.[31]

Besides the declarations of loyalty to the new regime which the old parties had made when stating that they were joining the Popular Front, and on other occasions, they also expressed their readiness to co-operate in the new system and in the building of a new society. They dissociated themselves more or less explicitly from the sections of the party leaderships which had remained abroad and which continued to work against the new system and government. Thus, in April 1946, the Socialist Party of Yugoslavia sent a letter to the Italian Socialist Party criticizing it for not having invited the Socialist Party of Yugoslavia to the Italian Party's congress in Florence which Živko Topalović, its former leader, had attended. The Italian party was reminded of the statement published, when the Socialist Party of Yugoslavia joined the Popular Front, about Živko Topalović's expulsion from the Party.[32]

However, the existence of several parties in a political system does not say everything about the character of the party system itself. A party system in which one party stays in power for some time, despite the existence of several parties, is not the same as a system in which different political parties come into power for relatively short periods. Since one party (the Communist Party) has been predominant in the party system in post-war Yugoslavia, the post-war political system of Yugoslavia can be classified in that category of the multi-party systems in which the whole party system is dominated by one political party, despite the existence of several parties.

Maurice Duverger first pointed to the phenomenon whereby one party can be predominant, despite the existence of several parties in the system.[33] In this context, Duverger correctly observed that the concept of a dominant party is somewhat vague. On the one hand, there are countries

in which opposition parties actually exist and obtain a significant number
of votes; their systems are closer to multi-party than to one-party systems.
On the other hand, in other countries the opposition is completely insignificant while the dominant party displays authoritarian tendencies, that is,
there are enough grounds to assume that in the event of the opposition
becoming stronger and posing a threat to the dominant party, the latter
would introduce a pure one-party system.

Giovanni Sartori, whose typology of party systems is of special significance in explaining the nature of the party system in post-war Yugoslavia,
went further in his investigation of the real nature of such systems. Sartori
first of all established that all multi-party systems in which one party
predominantes belongs either to system with an opposition or to opposi-
tionless systems—to competitive or non-competitive systems. The mere
fact of a system having several parties does not mean that it is a system
with an opposition. Where party competition is overshadowed by one
party, two possibilities exist: either the opposition will assume power
sooner or later, despite the predominance of one party, or it has no chance
of doing so. The first group of systems is of a competitive character, the
second group non-competitive. Sartori labelled the first group predomin-
ant-party systems, the second, hegemonic-party systems.[34]

The main features of systems with a predominant party is that in addition to the predominant party, the existence of other parties is also permitted; they are legal and legitimate, though not successful competitors
of the predominant party. Systems with a predominant party are systems
of party pluralism in which power does not change hands for long periods,
but the possibility of such change is not ruled out. There is also the possibility of open disagreement with and opposition to the predominant
party. It follows from this that the predominant party may, by peaceful,
legal means within the framework of the existing rules of the game, cease
to be predominant, and with that the party system changes its nature
(such changes have taken place in several countries recently—Sweden,
Norway, India and Israel).

In contrast to the system with a predominant party in which one party
is stronger than the rest for a long period, yet all of the parties have equal
standing, in systems with a hegemonic party, if not formally but in reality,
the parties are not equal and do not have the same rank. In the center of
the party system is one party, with second-class and subordinate parties on

on 18 March 1944, was signed individually by representatives of the parties and groups which had taken part in the work of the conference. In this way the impression was created that the Popular Front was some kind of coalition of the different parties and groups. However, this impression did not correspond to the actual relations between the Communist Party and other groups but it corresponded only too well to the propaganda needs of the time.

> This coalitionist form expressed in the documents of this conference had primarily a propagandist-political character: its aim was to demonstrate to the public at home and abroad—and this was entirely true—that the Popular Liberation Movement was not represented by Communists only but also that all democratic, anti-fascist and patriotic forces fought alongside and with the Communists, and that *the Communists allowed the work and activity of all parties, organizations and individuals* (authors' italics) which accepted the platform of the Popular Liberation Movement.[39]

That same propaganda aim was also contained in the subsequent letter of the Central Committee of the Communist Party of Croatia of 10 June 1944, in which the area committees were advised that it was necessary "to refute all the slanders of the different enemies of the people, from the occupying forces to Maček and Draža Mihailović, that *the Popular Liberation Movement is fighting for Communism and sovietization.*"[40] Eight months later, Sreten Žujovic-Crni in a similar manner denied the malicious claims that a one-party system was being introduced in the new Yugoslavia:

> It is a totally malicious distortion of facts to identify the living and broad activity of our peoples within the United Popular Liberation Front with a one-party system. *There is no such thing as a one-party system in our country* (authors' italics). . . . The strength of the United Popular Liberation Front lies in the very fact that it can encompass all national strata and that within it there are both individuals and groups and *political parties of different political persuasions* (authors' italics), all of them engaged in the great common work of the liberation and construction of our homeland.[41]

2. Opposition Outside the Popular Front

The public recognition for the legitimacy of the existence of a number of different political parties during the national liberation struggle did not yet constitute sufficiently clearly a definition of the nature of the *permitted* party pluralism. Crucial to this definition was the attitude toward the opposition, since the latter's existence, or non-existence, had a more fundamental influence on the nature of the given party system than the number of parties.

The question of the attitude toward the opposition was raised immediately after Belgrade was liberated and the provisional Yugoslav Government established. The liberation of the whole country then became just a question of time and so almost all the existing political parties, particularly those in Serbia, broadened the field of their activity. They especially attempted to revamp their organization and, following the greater or lesser part they had played in the war effort and in the current preparations for the final liberation, to embark immediately on wide-spread political agitation and recruitment of followers—the customary means in the struggle for power in a system of party pluralism. In such circumstances, the CPY leadership was compelled publicly to state its view and give its answer to three key questions: 1) whether to acknowledge the legitimacy of party pluralism; 2) whether the permitted party pluralism should also include the activity of the opposition and of the parties outside the Popular Front; and 3) whether, while the struggle for liberation was in progress, all parties should be allowed right away to go among the people and recruit followers. We find an answer to the first and third of these questions in J. B. Tito's speech on 28 January 1945:

> There are, unfortunately, similar philanthropists both in London and in America. And they fear for the freedom of the Serbian people and for the freedom of the rest of the peoples of Yugoslavia. Are you afraid that we shall not have democracy? They say: it is necessary to have democracy—one party, that is dictatorship. Under no circumstances one party only. Give freedom to all parties—they say. But what if the people do not want different little parties but one single popular movement?

*I am not in principle against parties because democracy also presup-
poses the freedom to express one's principles and one's ideas* (authors' italics). But to create parties for the sake of parties, now,
when all of us, as one, must direct all of our strength in the direction
of driving the occupying forces from our country, when the homeland has been razed to the ground, when we have nothing but our
awareness and our hands—and not to let agitators loose in every
village and town and say: oneward, old agitators! I, for my part,
would have nothing against their doing this because I know they
would quickly return to Belgrade. But we have no time for that now.
And here is a popular movement. Everyone can be in it—both
Communists and those who were democrats and radicals etc., whatever they were called before. This movement is the force, the only
force which now can lead our country out of this horror and misery
and bring it complete freedom. *And when we are liberated—you can
please yourself! Let us look around then and let us see there, in the
arena, which party shall exist!* (authors' italics).[42]

This interesting speech provides the answer to the first and third questions. First of all, J. B. Tito very explicitly recognized the legitimacy of
the multi-party system when he said: "I am not, in principle, against
parties because democracy presupposes the expression of one's principles
and one's ideas." In other words, this acknowledges that democracy presupposes freedom of opinions and public speaking, and that if men think
freely, they will think differently. And this will ultimately also lead to
their organizing into different political parties which fight for influence
on public opinion and for the greatest possible share in power. The only
thing which was not accepted at that time (January 1945) was that a start
be made *immediately* on forming parties outside the popular movement
(The Popular Front) since the battles for the final liberation of the country were still going on. Consequently, therefore, while *a state of war* still
lasted, freedom to set up political organizations had to be *temporarily*
curtailed. But as soon as the war had finished, the parties could enter the
arena, i.e., they could freely compete for votes and influence, this being
the basic hallmark of the pluralist system.

An explicit answer to the second question about the activity of the opposition, that is, parties outside the Popular Front being permitted, was

given publicly just after the liberation of the entire country. Since some kind of temporary solutions, which would be justified by extraordinary circumstances and the war situation, were no longer possible, and answer in favor of free activity by the opposition quickly followed. At the beginning of June 1945, J. B. Tito declared:

> We are reproached for not being expeditious enough in permitting parties to open shop. I have already said many times that *we are not against parties* (authors' italics), all the more as some are already co-operating usefully in the Popular Front; those outside the Front should also be formally allowed to operate because they are operating anyway. Which are these parties? Groups of men who were leaders before. They think that the people, who at one time followed them, are now awaiting for them alone to appear—but they forget that generals can be left without an army. I think that the time will come when they will be convinced of that. That time will come and *we have no objection to them operating—let them operate, and we shall see who will follow them* (authors' italics). They meet, hold conferences, but they present matters to the international public as if we had banned parties. And why do they not ask to open shop so that *we can give them permission to do so?* (author's italics). We do not want anyone to accuse us of not allowing this.[43]

Immediately after these assurances that opposition parties were allowed to operate outside the Popular Front, J. B. Tito had even been calling on opposition leaders to form such parties:

> *And we say to whoever does not want to be in the Front, whoever wants his own party; go and let him form it* (authors' italics). We shall not hinder him, and I think that we shall not have any difficulty in counting his followers.[44]

What is noteworthy in this message is that not a single party was denied the right to exist and to operate freely. Indeed, those who did not wnat to be in the Front were told to form their own party. This was a clear verbal example of the minimum *tolerance* of political opponents without which a genuine multi-party system was not at all possible.

We also see this readiness to accept the activity of an organized political opposition in subsequent declarations by J. B. Tito during 1945. Of course, he attempted to belittle the existing opposition and to ascribe to it bad intentions and shortsighted reactionary policies. But he nevertheless always maintained that the opposition enjoyed all political freedoms from the freedom of the press to freedom of association, and that, furthermore, it could nominate its own candidates in the elections for the Constituent Assembly: "The opposition too had emerged. *We had no objection to its taking part in the elections* (authors' italics), but it did not want to. At first it had been preparing for them but later it changed its mind because it was aware how it would fare in these elections."[45] Immediately after these first elections, J. B. Tito declared once again that the continuing activity of the opposition would be tolerated:

> I am happy to declare that there will be no sharpening of the attitude toward the opposition, provided its activity remains within the bounds of legality.... Any opposition may freely operate if it uses legal and honest means.[46]

Naturally, these were not the only *public* declarations in favor of the free existence and activity of the opposition. Thus, for example, in his capacity as President of the Legislative Committee of the Provisional Assembly Moša Pijade said on 22 August 1945: "I can say for my part that I am satisfied that we have an opposition."[47]

A more careful study of the political events of that time, however, leads us to the conclusion that the activity of the opposition was not so much a matter of satisfaction for the then leaders of the CPY as a fact which had to be reckoned with through force of circumstances. For, at the moment when the Tito-Šubašić agreement was concluded and when, on the basis of the recommendation of the Crimean Conference of the Great Powers to broaden the Anti-fascist Council of the National Liberation of Yugoslavia (AVNOJ) by including some deputies of the National Parliament of the Kingdom of Yugoslavia elected in 1938, the activity of the opposition represented a calculated risk. The Ministry for the Constituent Assembly, headed by Edvard Kardelj, proposed that 53 former deputies join AVNOJ. According to accessible sources, these 53 deputies were divided into three categories: 1) "the dependables," i.e., people who were bound to the line created by the CPY and the new authority; 2) "the waverers," i.e., members of the Popular Front or those who had supported it but who could, nevertheless, be expected to link up with "reactionary elements"; and 3) "the opponents," i.e., those who had been compromised during the occupation.[48] In addition to this, on the basis of agreement with some parties and political groups, about 70 people were co-opted and thus AVNOJ was increased by 118 new deputies. It was estimated that in this Provisional Assembly the "enemy," that is, the opposition group of deputies, would be no greater than 50-60 members. If this group were to be joined by the "doubtful elements," its number would not exceed 80-100 members.[49] The CPY, therefore, as the leading force in AVNOJ, agreed in practical terms to tolerate the activity of opposition parties outside the Popular Front. Another reason for this tolerance of the CPY toward the non-Communist parties is closely connected with its wartime policy and with the efforts to present the recently ended national liberation struggle to the Western allies in the most favorable light possible. To obtain international recognition for this struggle and its achievements it was necessary to present it to the world as *exclusively anti-fascist* in which the elements of the internal civil war were practically negligible. And to achieve this, it was necessary to convince the world that this struggle was not the matter of only one party but of the entire people, that is, of all the other parties and political groups. Thus it is here that we find yet another reason for the tolerant attitude of the CPY toward party pluralism and the activity of the opposition parties. The future was to confirm whether this tolerance of opposition activity was to be extended over a longer period.

The real scope of this tolerance characteristic of the liberal systems of political pluralism was soon revealed in the case of two opposition groups: a faction of the Croatian Peasant Party and the Democratic Party of Milan Grol, which operated outside the Popular Front. At the end of the war, the Croatian Peasant Party disintegrated into several factions. One of them joined the Popular Liberation Movement and as such enjoyed the support of the CPY and acquired the right to represent the whole party within the framework of the Popular Front. Outside the Popular Front, however, there were several other factions and almost all of the better known leaders of the party. Some of them were prepared to act publicly as political opposition. Such an attempt took place on 20 October 1945 with the publication in Zagreb of the first Croatian opposition newspaper *Narodni glas* as the "organ of Croatian peasant politics." The publisher of this newspaper was Radić's (founder and former leader of the Croatian Peasant Party) widow, Marija, and the chief and responsible editor Ivan Bernadić. In its first issue, *Narodni glas* carried the articles: "Why we are not participating in the elections," "Our first issue," by Marija Radić, "For genuine democracy and the sovereignty of the Croatian People," an article about Maček and the loyalty of the Croatian people to Maček as President of the Croatian Peasant Party, and others. The second issue of *Narodni glas* appeared only two days later as the first had immediately been sold out.[50]

The authorities of the time, were not prepared to tolerate such an opposition paper and it was immediately banned by a decision of the public prosecutor's office in Zagreb. At the same time the People's Printing Works, responding to the decision of the printing union, refused to continue printing the paper.[51] Thus an apparent paradox had arisen. Members of the officially permitted Croatian Peasant Party faction within the framework of the Popular Front, who considered themselves "old Radić followers" and "sincere followers of the teaching of the immortal Radić brothers," enjoyed all the privileges of free public activity, yet the authorities denied Stjepan Radić's widow the right to publish a paper on behalf of the "old Radić followers."

In contrast to this quickly frustrated faction of the Croatian Peasant Party, the opposition activity of Milan Grol's Democratic Party left much deeper traces. The first of the more serious public differences between this party and the ruling majority emerged soon with the transformation of AVNOJ into the Provisional Assembly. Since the deputies of this party (13 of them) often voted against government proposals and on such occasions even managed to rally as many as 17 votes, the ruling majority soon lost its patience. It was no surprise, therefore, that at the session of the Legislative Committee held on 13 August 1945, Moša Pijade, a Communist deputy, issued the following warning to them:

> If these new fellow-travelers of ours, while co-operating with us with such good will, began to set themselves apart so often with their opinions and abstain from voting—after all, I have nothing against that—*one day we may come into open conflict, into a conflict which would perhaps be easier than such co-operation* (authors' italics).[52]

There were indeed prophetic words because the difference between
liberal parliamentarism and the type of political system in which the
principle of tolerance toward political opponents is replaced with open
struggle against them, right up to their liquidation, was very quickly
manifested. Had Moša Pijade and people who thought like him by chance
persisted with a tolerant attitude toward the opposition, and a weak opposition at that, they would have undoubtedly remained great exponents
of the preservation of the most worthwhile achievements of the liberal
democratic tradition, a tradition which new socialist society could also
have taken up with good reason. As has already been shown, liberalism
is a political and judicial principle by which public power, although
dominant, is limited and put to the test, even to its own disadvantage,
by leaving a free place in the state which it governs in order that they who
do not think and feel as it does, might live and work. This is the *right*
which the ruling power, that is the majority, gives a minority with which
it does not agree and which, furthermore, it considers its rival. And since
in 1945 this political opponent was relatively weak and disunited, it was
all the easier to acknowledge and respect this right of the opposition.

But such tolerance was not *typical of* the militant spirits, imbued with
doctrinaire obstinacy, who believed more in other people's fallibility than
in their own. Milan Grol also sensed this when, on behalf of the minority,
he warned:

> The first condition for letting a small group into this house is that it
> may speak here in the manner used in a parliament and that it does
> not have to listen the whole time to such things from its opponents
> as it has to reject with indignation . . . . I cannot run away from
> the truth just because someone will accuse me of telling that truth
> as somebody's agent.[53]

Milan Grol reached this unenviable position of spokesman for the opposition after his resignation from the post of vice-premier on 19 August
1945. The chief reason which made him do this was "the deviation in the
form of the implementation of an exclusive party program,"[54] which, in
his view, was not in line with the assurances given at the time of the
formation of the provisional government and the Tito-Šubašić agreement.
Grol considered that the expansion of AVNOJ, political laws and the

system of freedom were interrelated and that one could not be implemented without the others. And for that an agreement was necessary "on the spirit of these laws and the system in general which had to apply these laws in the pre-election period and at the elections."[55] Grol therefore constantly warned about:

> an agreement by the progressive political parties being possible only if it suits the leading Communist Party, which is to say, if it were prepared to moderate its program and share power with the rest of the political parties which only share responsibility with it now.[56]

According to Grol, he transmitted such a warning to Marshal Tito, but he did not meet with any understanding.[57] Furthermore, Grol discovered in this disinclination to consider other views in the joint government:

> a business-like attitude to basic political questions which is almost identical with the practical implementation of a policy, already thoroughly established and sacrosanct, which excludes any divergence of views.[58]

In fact, the demands which Milan Grol's Democratic Party made in its public activity were relatively measured and in the main amounted to the basic achievements of *liberal* democracy. They were contained in the party's program which proceeded from the democratic principle that the people had to be "the source of all power: legislative power which dispenses justice on the basis of the law."[59] But in order for the people to be the source of all power, their decision-making has to be free from any diktat. Every political freedom is needed for this: freedom of the press, of assembly and of agreement-reaching and of association. The program of the Democrats also contained the principle of the equality of the nationalities, religion, the state and judicial frameworks within which the peoples of Yugoslavia lived, views and feelings, and thus also the principle of social justice which called for the equitable distribution of resources, together with the simultaneous protection of liberty, personal security, property and free initiative. This, according to the Democrats' assertion, demanded the following immediate measures: the nationalization of large natural resources and of large means of production, along with fair compensation; security of land tenure for the farmers; the development of co-operative institutions and free trade union organizations; special social care for the weak, for health, and in particular for mothers and children. With regard to the state system, as far back as 1932 the Democratic Party came out in favor of "federalism of large units and autonomy for the provinces and self-rule for the regions," emphasizing that the

> only requirement in a fully evolved system of relations between the federal units and the autonomous regions, is to preserve the organic whole of a state community, which is indispensible to the natural, economic and cultural development.[60]

In the field of international relations on the other hand, the Democrats advocated close relations with Bulgaria, the expansion of the neighborly co-operation of the peoples in the Balkans, even a confederacy of the Balkan peoples, ties with the Soviet Union, and economic and cultural relations with the countries of the Danube Basin, particularly fraternal Czechoslovakia and the great democratic countries of the West.

The chief stumbling block in the program of the Democratic Party was the liberal concept of freedom. For, in addition to social and national freedom, the Democrats placed particular emphasis on personal, civil, political and moral freedom. From the standpoint of the Democrats' attitude toward the authorities of that time, these were in many respects controversial freedoms because they established the inviolability of the individual while setting certain limits to public power. Thus, for the Democrats, personal freedom meant the absence of any intimidation, coercion, arbitrary arrest and surveillance, while political freedom, as the freedom of thought, speech, association and public avowal of one's principles, was incompatible with absolutist and dictatorial political set-ups.[61] But the real scope of this concept of freedom can be best observed in the criticial attitude of the Democratic Party to the political circumstances and institutions of that time, and particularly toward the existing party system.

The most important difference between the Democratic Party in opposition on the one hand, and some of the non-Communist parties in the Popular Front on the other hand, is in fact reflected in the very concept of the nature and future of the existing party system. The Democrats had asserted (in the second half of 1945) that the existing party pluralism was being transformed into a one-party system, and this at that point was assessed as an obvious untruth by official circles. Thus, according to *Demokratija*, Milovan Djilas decisively refuted the "slanders" about the one-party character of the Popular Front and about the power of one party existing within it. Milan Grol answered him thus:

> We who find ourselves on the other side opposite the Front, are not complaining about this position of the Communists in the Front but about the camouflage of the Front, which deceives no one but which gives the Communists the illusion that such pebbles make the edifice built on sand stronger. This leads them away from the healthy path and healthy ground on which they could contribute to the public benefit and that of their own party.[62]

Milan Grol was only too aware of the role of the Communist Party in the national liberation war and he did not omit to say it in public:

> Because the Communist Party united in that struggle at the same time the general freedom-loving and national liberation interest, it also succeeded in rallying within it other progressive elements, and what was significant in this, was that it mobilized the nationally and territorially divided citizens of Yugoslavia—at that time exposed to the danger of disintegration. The Communist Party as the leading element in the liberation action during the war, draws its fundamental moral and political strength from this championing of state unity.[63]

The first suspicions about the Communist Party appeared, according to Grol, at the moment when the achievements of the liberation struggle began to be presented as the merit of only one party.

> Where and when did the difference arise between myself and my friends—and I hope that some from the other side will remain my friends? When these achievements were understood not as achievements of the peoples but as the achievements of one group. It was when in the press and in speeches, words began to appear indicating

that these were the achievements of one group that disagreements arose.[64]

These words of reproach point forward to the time when all the achievements of the national liberation struggle were soon ascribed to only one party which was to conclude on the basis of this that it was the only party that should exist. Milan Grol, however, was inclined to see in this conclusion a totalitarian tendency:

> The Communist Party shows itself to be unusually sensitive when it and not the Popular Front is singled out in discussion, and even more sensitive to the assertion about *the totalitarian tendencies of the regime, that is, about the tendencies of a one-party system and the uniform moulding of public opinion* (authors' italics). On the one hand, the parties in the Popular Front are obstructed and denied the right to separate party electoral activities, yet on the other, when it is necessary to refute the assertions about a totalitarian regime, party accord and the preserved individuality of parties within the Popular Front is emphasized.[65]

This then is an assertion that the regime of the time was being transformed into a one-party system, which, according to Grol, aimed at totalitarianism. Though many people today believed that to equate a one-party system with totalitarianism is a questionable exercise, it seems that *at that time,* and particularly just before the war, it was more or less customary to do so. Thus we can also find this assertion about a one-party system being a *totalitarian* system in which there can be no democratization of any kind, in the following description of the situation in Yugoslavia in July 1940:

> There can be no question of any democratization. On the contrary, the reaction is growing worse day by day. The present rulers are openly advocating a totalitarian corporate system on the model of Italy and Germany, and in this almost the entire press is helping them. The leadership of the Croatian Peasant Party particularly supports this, as does the Premier, Dragiša Cvetković, and the notorious priest Karošec, who has now been appointed Minister for National Education in order to turn young people into fascists.

However, an agreement will be hard to come by since the Croats will not consent to the new centralism which is a prerequisite for a *totalitarian, one-party system* (authors' italics) such as exists in Italy and in Germany.[66]

True enough in October 1945, Grol did not equate the then party system with totalitarianism but only spoke of the totalitarian tendency toward a one-party system, which could easily be prevented. To achieve this a simple skill was necessary—*tolerance* toward the opposition. Or as Grol advised:

> there is a much simpler way to deny assertions about a totalitarian system and to demonstrate the freedom of different views and parties, and that is *tolerance toward parties outside the Front and their organs* (authors' italics). Especially, as is the case today, when all they amount to is only one paper as opposed to the 130 papers of the Popular Front.[67]

To demonstrate an example of the difference between intolerance and tolerance, Grol mentioned the current attitude toward the paper *Demokratija,* which he himself edited, and to the opposition press in Greece:

> The witch-hunt conduced against *Demokratija,* a witch-hunt not with arguments or words, not even the worst possible words, but a physical witch-hunt by seizing copies from the hands of salesmen, tearing them up, soaking them with petrol, and by burning both the papers and the clothes and hands of those selling *Demokratija*—refutes all declarations and all laws about political freedom. What this intolerance shows will be understood when the situation is compared with that in Greece where, under a reactionary regime of which we have only had bad things to say from the beginning, more opposition papers, among them also Communist ones, are published than government ones.[68]

Of particular interest is Grol's view of the way in which opinion would develop under what he described as the "unform moulding of public opinion." This is a situation with which we have already been confronted on several occasions this century and which can occur only at the cost of neglecting and even rejecting the value of freedom of thought, of public speech and of discussion. Complete unanimity, consequently, is only the reverse side of spiritual servititude. Because if people can think freely, they will also think differently. Grol describes this as "freedom to express different views and to have different parties." If there is uniformity in public, it means only that many different opinions are muzzled and suppressed. Such a spiritual unanimity is a situation which should certainly be avoided.

> A sensible man shudders at the thought of an assembly where all proposals are passed unanimously and with acclamation. There everything seems to go miraculously well, all are in agreement, all are unanimous, and then in a moment everything can be called into question and shown to be unreal.[69]

Lastly, we should also note where Grol saw the basic reason for this tendency toward a unifrom moulding of public opinion: stubborn dogmatism and belief in one's own infallibility:

> Such a policy clearly would not be the policy of today's leading party if it did not consider itself to be self-sufficient, sufficient to itself and to the country, and if it did not believe that the dogmas of its program contain the solutions for all problems of all countries for all time, that is, if the leading party did not adhere to a totalitarian program in all fields of national life (which is not the case with Communist parties in other countries), and if it did not resort to methods which squeeze the life of the people into moulds. Such a program and such methods exclude any examination of suitability, any criticism and change of opinion.[70]

Such dogmatism can only align people into two opposing categories: friends and enemies, believers and heretics, progressives and reactionaries, torchbearers and obscurantists. Who is not with us is against us.

> Any doubt about the infallibility of dogmas, like those of the Church, or any demand not to reject but only to adapt an idea to

reality, is immediately described as heresy and any criticism of what
is introduced into life and the way in which it is introduced as
fascism. People blinded by dogmas and even more by power do not
acknowledge the existence of anything outside Communism and
fascism; they do not want it and they don't stand for it either in
conversation of in the written word.[71]

This perception of the party system at the time and the direction in
which, according to the Democrats, it was tending to go, had as its consequence the resolute refusal of the opposition to participate in the elections for the Constituent Assembly. This attitude of the opposition could
be felt even at the time when the laws on voters' registers and the election
of people's deputies for the Constituent Assemby were being discussed.
Milan Grol, in his capacity as Vice-Premier, warned at that time that to
hold elections they needed the appropriate political laws which ensured
personal freedom, freedom of the press, of assembly, association and of
parties, and which, in addition, contained guarantees that they would indeed by applied in practice. "We know from experience throughout decades how much the regulations on paper mean without full guarantees
for their execution."[72]

In the final decision of the united opposition parties not to participate
in the elections, published on 20 September 1945, the reason put forward
was:

> the restriction of freedom in the laws themselves disqualifying hun-
> dreds of thousands of voters in an arbitrary manner, which has been
> demonstrated from the very beginning, first by striking people off
> voters' registers and, immediately the electoral campaign started, by
> pressure. The tone of this savage campaign is visible from the posters
> and slogans on walls throughout Yugoslavia.[73]

The Democrats saw this as a deliberate witch-hunt against the opposition:
"Hordes of hacks daub insults and threats to the opposition on house walls
and on pavements, next to slogans praising the Front and its leaders."
"Down with Grol," "Down with Grol, the Fascist," "Death to Grol," etc.
Children sing a chorus songs like "Hang Pera (Peter II, Yugoslav king in
exile and formal head of the state at that time—authors' note) and Grol

from the Pole" and others. In Vojvodina, in the Subotica district, groups
of children in the street chant the slogan "a Bullet for Grol."[74]

In the Democrats' judgement, the validity of the elections was also questionable because of the absence of personal security and freedom of public
discussion. "For the elections to be free, the voters too should be able to
choose between several viewpoints. They cannot do so if only one viewpoint is presented to them."[75] This again was a consequence of the fact
that the entire press in the country, with the exception of the short-lived
weekly *Demokratija,* was in the hands of the Government's political
organization. The feeling of personal insecurity was provoked by the fear
prevailing among the followers of the opposition. "That fear," the Democrats had stressed "is real. While it lasts, free nominations, free signing
of candidates' lists, free campaigning are impossible."[76]

These opposition's assessments of the validity of the elections met with
the most severe condemnation by the ruling circles of the time. Thus
Andrija Hebrang explained that the opposition was not participating in
the elections because "it wants to spite us."[77] Moša Pijade maintained
that the opposition, which was calling on the people to abstain was "fright-
ening the people with terror."[78] Even Miloš Moskovljević, one of the
"fellow-travellers" within the set-up of the Popular Front, found it necessary to declare that the introduction of ballot boxes without lists would
ensure the freedom of the elections, so that the opposition would not be
able to say . . . that many of the electorate have not voted for their own
free will but because of this or that, because of pressure—because they,
allegedly, had to vote.[79] On top of that the "fellow-travellers" who published *Slobodni dom* on behalf of the Croatian Peasant Party, declared
that the basic problem of the so-called "whisperers," that is, of the opposition, was not because freedom of opinion, association and choice
had been denied them but because their opinion was dangerous.

> They can join into parties, they can express their views through the
> press, they can meet and come to agreements, but they do not feel
> like doing so. Why? Because what they would say would be their
> death sentence. They would have to acknowledge that they are not
> in favor of the kind of people's freedom and the kind of social
> justice which is sought by the people . . . . Naturally, they did not
> want to do this, they have remained faithful to themselves and con-
> tinued with the policy of whispering: 'There is no freedom, there are

no free elections because only one list exists and thus there is no choice.' This is what the advocates of abstention have said.[80]

Even Dragoljub Jovanović described those who had remained outside the Popular Front as "internal emigres,"[81] and this expression was also to be used much later as a means of stigmatizing those who think differently in some countries of real socialism.

After such fierce condemnation of the opposition, it was quickly demonstrated that the tolerance of the government at that time toward the opposition was short-lived. Thus Moša Pijade's prediction that for the ruling party, the fight against the opposition, a fight to the finish would be easier than any kind of co-operation, very quickly became a reality. Or as Branko Petranović described this struggle: "The CPY did not allow this campaign by the opposition trends to be expanded, to acquire its own mouthpieces and papers, because the country was in a revolutionary process of change and had just emerged from the war."[82] Two basic ways of struggle were employed in this context.

The first was reflected in the attempt to break up the opposition parties from within with the help of some "fellow-travellers." But since this way was not successful enough, other more efficient means had to be resorted to. These amounted to besmirching the leaders of the Democratic Party and to carry out street violence in order to thwart the Party's public activity. Milovan Djilas, who revealed the hypocrisy of the opposition with great zeal, excelled in this. For him, Milan Grol, a "major figure" of the "emigre pigsty of intrigue, treason, espionage, crime, careerism and corruption"[83] was a "conservative intellectual, German by origin, French by culture and a Greater Serb" by his politics.[84] Djilas, true enough, said that the opposition had even been given the opportunities to fight in a legal democratic manner against the existing situation[85] but he immediately went on to sound a warning to all possible supporters of the Democratic Party that they would be branded and punished as criminals if they proceeded along Milan Grol's path:

> Hidden behind the 'opposition' are the monsters of treason and crime. Peeping from behind the intellectual head of Milan Grol are Draža Mihailović (leader of the Chetniks), the Ljotić (Serbian quisling), Nedić (Serbian quisling) ideologists who are awaiting salvation

from Grol's 'democracy.' Hidden behind the 'opposition' are Pavelić's (Croatian quisling and leader of Ustashe) defeated Ustashe (Croatian separatists) and Pavelić and Maček's (leader of the Croatian Peasant Party) 'Home Guards.' Behind it stands Rupnik's (Slovenian quisling —all parenthesis are authors' notes) shameful White Guard.[86]

At the end of his accusations against Milan Grol and the democratic opposition, Djilas uttered the threat that "the people cannot stand idly by and remain indifferent to this."[87]

And indeed "the people" in the street quickly took the matter into their own hands. The best testimony to the character of this undertaking against the opposition is the following report published in *Politika* on 19 October 1945 which says that:

> yesterday morning, the 18th of this month, some groups of citizens, the majority of them young people, in different areas of Belgrade, incited, and in some places provoked, by elements engaged in introducing confusion and bringing about unrest, burnt and tore up the paper 'Demokratija'. . . . We warn the public not to be taken in by various provocations in the future because such actions can only harm the reputation of our country and disrupt the peaceful and lawful election preparations.[88]

At that moment it was not disclosed who these groups of young people were who had burned the *Demokratija*. Only later studies of archival material of that period showed that they were members of the Federation of the Communist Youth of Yugoslavia (SKOJ). Branko Petranović said:

> The meeting of the local committee (of the Communist Party— authors' note) on 22nd October 1945, noted that SKOJ had made a mistake as regards *Demokratija*. The local committee in Belgrade had come out in support of a boycott of Grol's paper but not of provoking incidents. The minutes of the local committee noted in this context that the Party must not be 'tricked' by the old forces. The members of the Popular Front had to be the guardians of law and order and the election campaign. This, however, should not be understood as a peace-loving attitude to the opposition and suspension of

the political struggle, but only a standing of arbitrariness by some 'reactionaries.'[89]

Although at the time *Demokratija* was burnt these circumstances were not known, its editorial staff condemned this act as trampling underfoot the freedom of the press.

We are for the freedom of the press. The whole country has only one weekly opposition paper and it could certainly not be said that there is no interest in it. Even so it is burnt at the stake, an honor accorded to all documents of truth from the Holy Inquisition right up to Joseph Goebbels.[90]

Milan Grol publicly expressed once again his hope in the:

victory of reason over madness, in the victory of the cause, the expression of which was burnt in 'Demokratija' last week. Papers may be burned, ideas and people persecuted, but life will proceed only in line with the laws which reality establishes in our country and the world. Not the stake but awareness of reality surmounts reality.[91]

Grol's hope was soon betrayed. *Demokratija* ceased publication after its seventh issue because the typesetters' trade union refused to print it. A more detailed official explanation of this trade union decision is to be found in J. B. Tito's conversation with representatives of the foreign and Yugoslav press on 16 November 1945, when the following question was put to him:

We have heard that the typesetters' union has refused to print the opposition paper 'Demokratija.' Does the Government think that it should suggest to the printers' union that it would be in the interests of a well-organized political life to print opposition papers insofar as they write within the framework of the law?
Answer: As far as I know, the workers have gone on strike. In our country there is the freedom to strike. The workers have gone on strike because that paper has attacked and insulted the trade unions. There was much that was illegal in that paper. The workers believed

that they should not print it. They have the right to strike and it is
not up to us to interfere in it. I do not think that the government
has any moral right to suggest to them that they must print that
paper.

Besides, this proves that the workers in our country are subjects
and not objects. They themselves can exert influence on certain
things.

There is nothing that can be changed here.[92]

Thus, *Demokratija,* as the only opposition paper, ceased publication because of the decisions of the printing workers to make use of their *inviolable* right to strike.[93] Not even the government had the moral right to
interfere in this because against the freedom of the opposition was pitted
the more authentic freedom of workers to strike as and when they saw fit
and whenever they had valid reasons for so doing.

This manner in which the only opposition paper in the country was
abolished becomes somewhat more understandable if one bears in mind
the former statements about the goodwill of the Government to guarantee
the opposition all the conditions necessary for publishing papers, including
newsprint. The opposition maintained that there was no freedom of the
press, and when the Press Law was passed, it said there was no paper,
which prompted J. B. Tito to declare: "Which country in Europe and even
in America has the obligation to ensure the opposition paper for its press?
And yet, such an opportunity is extended to the opposition in Yugoslavia."[94] Or, as Milovan Djilas immediately reiterated:

It has been said that there is no free press in Yugoslavia, but the laws
have permitted a free press even to groups outside the Front and the
Government has also placed paper at Milan Grol's disposal to publish his newspaper, which had to be called—so foreigners would get
the right idea—'Demokratija.'[95]

All the conditions ensuring *Demokratija*'s unhindered publication had thus
been provided except for the readiness of the printing workers to print it.
Much later, Dragoljub Jovanović, as a witness of that time, explained the
abolishing of *Demokratija* in this way: "*Demokratija* had a great success
as a weekly paper but it was discontinued after its seventh issue with the
explanation that the workers did not want to typeset and print it."[96]

The end of *Demokratija*'s publication represented the end of the op-position's activity outside the Popular Front. We have already said that in 1945 this opposition was relatively weak and disunited and that it was all the easier for the ruling party to recognize and tolerate it. But it seems that this kind of generosity toward a political opponent was too heavy a burden for Milovan Djilas, Moša Pijade and others to bear. Or, perhaps they themselves had very little inclination to accept and endorse such generosity because for many years before they had lived in an age of intolerance and hatred, not only toward the so-called class enemy but even toward rivals in their own party. Therefore, it was no surprise that they never kept their promise that as people in power, they would live in peace with those who did not think as they did on political matters.

A certain change in attitude toward the opposition outside the Popular Front also appeared in most official public statements. Thus, as early as 14 October 1946, J. B. Tito gave the following answer when asked what he thought of the opposition:

> My view of the position is that it does not represent a factor which could hinder in any significant way the development of Yugoslavia in the direction established in the program of the Popular Front. That it exists—I know, that it operates, often in a manner which is not legal in our country—I also know, just as I also know that this opposition will never become stronger but that it will steadily weaken. We shall adopt not other stand in respect of the opposition because its very manner of acting is enough to discredit it among the broad masses. This does not mean that we are, a priori, against the opposition, that is, against the opposition which wants to help the speedier building up of the country, the correcting of certain mistakes. I myself have often said that there are shortcomings and some mistakes. Neither I, nor any one of us, has anything against this kind of constructive opposition. An opposition which helps to put right mistakes is necessary, but not that which takes advantage of certain shortcomings in order to throw a spanner in the works of our construction and to turn the wheel of progress back.[97]

Though it was also stressed on this occasion that severe measures would not be taken against the opposition of that time, there was no longer any doubt that the *public* attitude toward the opposition had fundamentally changed: this declaration stated there was nothing against *constructive opposition,* that is, against an "opposition which wants to help the speedier and easier implementation of the Popular Front program." But this in fact does not represent a genuine opposition which criticizes from the standpoint of an *alternative* political program, but so-called comradely criticism within the framework of *one and the same* party directed at *like-minded people* in the party who, in practice, carry out a *jointly* adopted program. And even if such a "constructive opposition" uncovered certain shortcomings and mistakes, it was not allowed to question the validity of the *entire* program of the Popular Front, as this would, according to such reasoning, mean a spanner thrown into the works of our social construction. It might only contribute to setting right the shortcomings and mistakes.

It became obvious very soon, however, that substantially harsher measures would be taken, not only against the actual but also against the *potential* opposition. This was indicated by a whole series of political trials of former party leaders and their followers.[98] Thus, Miša Trifunović, former leader of the Radical Party and former minister, Milutin Stefanović, Branko Jovanović, Željko Sušić, Aleksandar-Aca Ivić, Grgur Kostić, Siniša Stanković and Konstantin Stanković were put on trail at the Serbian Supreme Court in January 1947. The main charge against them was forming a spy network with the aim of gathering military and other information and passing it on to foreign intelligence services. On this occasion, Milutin Stefanović, Željko Sušić and Branko Jovanović were sentenced to death, while the others were given prison terms with forced labor, ranging from four to eight years.

Particularly characteristics of the changed attitude toward the potential opposition was the trial of fourteen Slovene intellectuals at the end of July 1947. Those indicted were Črtomir Nagode, the leader of the 'Pravda' group which, on the basis of the agreement with Kidrič had been admitted to the Liberation Front in August 1941; Boris Furlan, professor at the University of Ljubljana, who left his native Trieste in 1930 because of fascist persecution, was sentenced to death in absentia in Italy in 1942, and joined the Yugoslav Partisans in 1944; Ljubo Sirc who escaped from an Italian camp in 1942 and joined the Partisans; Franc Snoj who was a minister in the Slovene government and a people's deputy; Leo Kavčnik,

Zoran Hrabar, Angela Vode, Metod Kumelj, Pavle Hočevar, Svetopluk Zupan, Bogdan Stare, Metod Pirc, Vid Lajovič, Franjo Sirc and Elizabeta Hribar. They were also charged with organizing espionage activity and establishing contacts with the spy center no. 101 in Austria, as well as with recruiting followers from the ranks of depraved and corrupt intellectuals. Črtomir Nagode, Boris Furlan and Ljubo Sirc were sentenced to death, while the rest were given prison sentences with forced labor, ranging from one to twenty years.

It was finally made clear *publicly* that activity outside the Popular Front was in no way permissible on the eve of the second post-war elections in 1950 when, at an election meeting at Titovo Užice, J. B. Tito stated:

> Comrades, now, before these elections, just as before the last elections, the voices have been heard of some of the remnants of the old time, who are still vegetating here and there and who have asked whether some others will also be represented at the elections? What others? Who should participate in these elections now? Can some of the parties outside the Popular Front take part in these elections? There are in the Popular Front all those who wish for a national program to be implemented, a program which has as its aim the realization of socialism. Hence, if there is the desire to implement a program, it is the program of the Popular Front. If somebody wants to implement another program, outside the Popular Front, then it is not a socialist program but a program hostile to socialism, and, naturally, we will not allow such a program at the elections. There cannot be, Comrades, two programs in our country, but only one—the program of the Popular Front, the program of building socialism. We are in the very midst of a revolutionary social transformation in our country and revolution is a serious business, revolution cannot play around with any kind of concessions and other things. Revolution is a cruel thing. Of course we wish to carry it out with the least possible sacrifices, with the least possible difficulties, but if anything should block this path of ours, it must be conquered, it must disappear.[99]

And the opposition had indeed disappeared. In vain did the editorial board of the opposition paper *Demokratija* warn that awkward individuals should also participate in discussions on general affairs:

> ... to remove awkward individuals from discussion by using brutal methods, does not serve that aim, but only momentarily and seemingly eases the position of those in power. The brutal removal of the Communist Party from the first Constituent Assembly and giving the Croatian Peasant Party grounds to abstain were not able to prevent the ideas of these political groupings from later again penetrating public life and questioning the Constitution adopted without them.[100]

In November 1945, this was a voice without an echo.

3. Opposition Inside the Popular Front

The abolition of the opposition outside the Popular Front fundamentally changed the nature of the post-war party pluralism. Though watered down and impoverished, pluralism had still not been reduced to naked party monism. This took place only after the opposition within the Popular Front had been wiped out and eliminated.

We have already said that the Popular Front began as a *party coalition* whose internal structure corresponded, at least partly, to its external coalition characteristics. This coalitionist character of the Popular Front which was a particular feature of the Slovene Liberation Front, was further strengthened and expanded when several other parties and political groups joined the Front. Thus, after the liberation of Belgrade, the following joined the Popular Liberation Front: the Yugoslav Republican Party, the Indepedent Democratic Party, the Agrarian Party, the Socialist Party, the Social Democratic Party, the 'Napred' group and, in February 1945, the People's Peasant Party. In its formal structure, the Popular Front also represented a special kind of coalition because the Statute permitted the existence of parties which retained their own political individuality. Article 3 of the Statute envisaged the existence of organized parties and groups within the framework of the Popular Front on condition that they accepted its Program and Statute and that their members should also be at the same time members of the Popular Front's committees.

Through their own representatives, these parties were represented in the corresponding bodies and commissions of the Popular Front, they issued their own proclamations and published their own papers. Thus, the Croatian Republican Peasant Party, for example, published *Slobodni dom,* and for a short time also *Hrvatski glas* as its organ in Bosnia and Hercegovina, while the Yugoslav Republican Party published *Republika.* At the First Congress of the Popular Front, all parties, groups and anti-fascist organizations gave a suitable declaration of acceptance of the basic decisions of this congress. Milovan Djilas did so on behalf of the CPY, Frane Frol of the Croatian Republican Peasant Party, Radomir Todorović for the People's Peasant Party, Milan Popović for the Agrarian Party, Vladimir Simić for the Yugoslav Republican Party, Sava Kosanović for the Independent Democratic Party, Veljko Kovaćević for the Social Democratic Party, Milivoje Marković for the 'Napred' group, Mihailo Djurović for the 'Radicals' and Vlada Zečević for the 'Democrats' (these were dissenters since both the Radicals and the Democratic Party remained outside the Popular Front—authors' note). All the better known leaders of the non-Communist parties were also elected to the federal bodies of the Popular Front.

Of particular interest is the way in which this coalitionist character of the Popular Front was interpreted in the concepts and expectations of the non-Communist parties' leaders and in the policies and views of the CPY leaders. Practically the only non-Communist party permitted in Croatia was the so-called Croatian Republican Peasant Party which, beginning with the assembly of this party's followers in the village of Taborište in Kordun on 29 April 1944, was led by people who had played a more or less secondary role in this party between the two wars. From the viewpoint of the interests of the CPY, the basic task of this revised party was to wipe out Maček's influence in Croatia, and thus a return was encouraged to the original teaching of the Radić brothers which Maček, according to the interpretation of the time, had betrayed and abandoned. What was emphasized in particular was the lack of contradictions, and later even the great closeness, between the teaching of the Radić brothers and Communism.

We old Radić followers and republicans, sincere followers of the teaching of the immortal Radić brothers, know full well what

Communism is, and we also know that we are not Communists yet we are not afraid to fight alongside the Communists for justice and honesty. Our teacher, the late Stjepan Radić of blessed memory, spoke beautifully about this when he said: 'We are not Communists, but we are not afraid to co-operate with the Communists.'[101] Today, we are in a sincere alliance with our brothers, the Communists.[102]

However, since Stjepan Radić had not entered into a unitied front with the Communists nor formed alliances or presented joint lists at elections, the inevitable question which arose was why the old Radić followers were doing this now.

There are ignorant and even dishonest people among us who simply do not understand our Popular Front. Why, they say, does not each party fight its own struggle during the elections? After the elections, it would be seen who had won them. If, by chance, one party does not win and several parties emerge similar in strength, one would know exactly how many votes each party received and how strong it was among the people and accordingly power would have to go to it. This, they say, would be democratic and would enable the old party life to be revived again, that is, it would represent a return to the old ways.[103]

In order to answer this question, some popular proverbs on accord and discord were cited: "Brothers in accord also eat meat on Friday"; "Divided brothers—a ruined house"; "When brothers' hearts agree, lead too may float, but when discord takes over, even feathers sink to the bottom." The aim of this was to imply that parties, such as they were, led to discord, while associated together in the Popular Front, they ensured accord and prosperity for the people. Therefore, that same accord which should exist in the house or in a collective is also necessary in the state. If, however, there is none because of parties and party politicking, people suffer and starve.

Let us look at life in the West European states and even in the largest of them which have not followed our example of harmony and unity. The wealthy exploit the poor and the people actually starve. . . . Thus each party and each group looks out for its own interest,

because it is in the interest of the rich, of those who exploit and op-
press the people, that they would quarrel between themselves and
tear themselves apart.[104]

Since the prosperity of the people could only be attained in the Popular
Front, in complete accord, only enemies remain outside the Front. "He
who is against the Popular Front is our enemy, which means that he is an
enemy of his own people."[105]

In addition, the question also arose as to what was the role of some of
the parties within the Popular Front. In their answer to these questions,
the Croatian Republican Peasant Party propagandists also made use of the
following picturesque comparison: "The Popular Front is like a group of
diggers who want to dig up a big field. Each digger takes one or two rows
and so all go toward the same target. When each digger has executed his
task, that is, completed the rows, the field is tilled. One of these diggers is
our party, and the rows are our people."[106] From such an idyllic picture
of the Popular Front, which reminded many of a family co-operative, it
was not far to the conviction that a leader was needed (not to use the
foreign word "avant-garde"), who would, like the head of a family co-
operative, keep all the diggers, that is, the parties, in line and in order. Or,
as *Slobodni dom* said quoting the conclusion of the Second Congress of
the Popular Front in Croatia, held on 23 and 24 January 1949, it was
necessary to explain to the people's masses the "Popular Front as the
main force which, under the leadership of the Communist Party, is building socialism in our country."[107]

We find a somewhat different interpretation of the nature of the Popular Front as a party coalition in the articles by the leaders of the Yugoslav Republican Party. This was really an attitude of loyal co-operation
within the framework of the Popular Front, but with an attempt to preserve some of the party individuality and the independence of critical
judgement and thought. The conclusions of this party on the eve of the
elections says:

> The Popular Front is not a chance creation, or a party or ruling
> government of a point in time or of an historical period. It is a his-
> torical necessity to which the people of Yugoslavia were pushed by
> the reaction long before the enemy invasion . . . . But this support

for maintaining the Popular Front does not confuse our views and
does not exclude the sensible criticism, which is raised and heard
from many quarters, of the mistakes of inexpedient work, and even
arbitrariness by certain organs of power as Minister Kardelj also
stated in the Assembly.[108]

After the elections, Jaša Prodanović assured foreign readers that the Popular Front "is not a monolithic institution but an agreement of groups and
parties."[109] At the same time he complained that the opportunity for the
Republican Party to operate outside Serbia was restricted:

> Nevertheless, it is to be regretted that the Republican Party, which
> joined the Popular Front with sincerity and loyalty, has not been
> offered the opportunity to broaden the base of its activity. Al-
> though it originated in Serbia it is not an exclusively Serbian or Serb-
> ian people's party and its political ambitions go far beyond the nar-
> row limits within which it began.[110]

In saying this he indicated that the Popular Front *was not a coalition of
equals* since one party had the opportunity of operating on the whole of
Yugoslav territory, whereas all the rest could operate only within the
framework of the restrictions which the leading party determined and
imposed on them.

  In fact, Jaša Prodanović probably realized from the very beginning that
within the Popular Front there would be no equitable co-operation and no
equal participation by parties, not only in responsibility but also in the
execution of power. However, in contrast to Dragoljub Jovanović, he was
more inclined to stress warnings of principle than to direct open challenges
at the ruling party. When he did this, it was over some specific issue or
some low-ranking leaders. Thus, he said, for instance, that the Republicans co-operated loyally in the Popular Front and that it was, therefore,
not fitting when some members (primarily Communists) of the Popular
Front in the villages, towns and districts said to Republicans: "You pull
our water cart up the hill but when you have done so you will not receive
even a drop of water. Is it necessary for the Popular Front members to
shout 'Down with the Republicans' or to utter even heavier threats? "[111]
Yet it seems that his closest collaborators had reconciled themselves to this

secondary role. Thus, according to Dragoljub Jovanović, in referring to Prodanović's assertion about the non-Communist Front members being merely the ones who drove the water cart, Vladimir Simić said: "We are the drivers of the water cart, but we will push the cart even if we do not drink a single drop of water."[112]

The irrefutable fact however remains that while Jaša Prodanović was alive the Republicans attempted not only to preserve their own party individuality but also party pluralism as such, at least in the truncated form in which it was originally embodied in the Popular Front. Some articles in the newspaper *Republika* and statements by Republicans in the Constituent Assembly bear witness to this. Thus, the Republicans came out decisively in favor not only of party pluralism but also freedom for the political opposition. In addition, they publicly stated their reasons for questioning the validity of perpetuating the power of one party. This refers to the idea, well-known and put to the test through the centuries, that power corrupts those who wield it, especially if that power is absolute. In this respect the Republicans claimed the new, people's power was no exception.

Jaša Prodanović came to this conclusion when discussing with Radovan Zogović (Communist deputy) the proposal for a constitutional provision for carrying out house searches. Prodanović pointed out that the people's power was also being corrupted because time corrupted people. This provoked Radovan Zogović into setting out his party's position on the possibilities of a change in power. He said:

> Mr. Prodanović assumes the possibility of a change in power. I believe that this power will never be replaced but merely developed. I have both the moral and the political right to believe this and I think that a discussion on the Constitution, a discussion based on the belief that this power is not stable and cannot develop or improve, would be incorrect.[113]

Although Zogović did not back up in any way his belief that the power of his party would never be replaced and did not explain how it would renew its mandate without being exposed to competition with other parties, Jaša Prodanović did explain in detail the opposing viewpoint which justified the necessity of periodical changes in power.

I take a general viewpoint and Mr. Zogović a more narrow, party stand. He says that this regime must be defended and that it must not be overthrown. . . . I take the principled stand that a regime should have principles which make it immaterial whether it is in power or not. . . . A party may begin with idealism but this changes when it remains in power a long time. No generation can guarantee that it will retain the spirit of the ideas with which it began. When in power it is difficult to remain consistent to what has been done while in opposition.[114]

At the time when Jaša Prodanović was thus justifying party pluralism and the necessity for periodical changes in power, the political life within the Popular Front was still a far cry from being entirely homogeneous and monolithic. The CPY leaders have even publicly acknowledged that different political parties were rallied together in the Popular Front. Thus, in August 1945 (several months before Prodanović statement), at the founding congress of the Popular Front Edvard Kardelj rejected the concept that political unity on the Popular Front was incompatible with the existence of different parties and political groups in that organization. In this context he particularly encouraged the participation of the peasant parties which he saw as the bulwark against the influence of conservative forces and as an important transmission belt between the vanguard democratic forces and the peasant masses.[115] J. B. Tito publicly acknowledged this fact on the eve of the elections. "People from the Popular Front go to the elections with a unified list though there are different parties in the Popular Front."[116] He had in mind basically the same concept of the multi-party coalitionist structure of the Popular Front when, in the National Assembly on 6 January 1946, he explained the structure of the new government and noted that he had taken into consideration: 1) national factors; 2) *political and party factors* and 3) the quality of the people in the government. He also said he had consulted and reached agreement with representatives of *all parties* in the Popular Front.[117] Most important, however, was the public acknowledgement that the opposition within the framework of the Popular Front is reckoned with.

As is well known, there are several parties in the Front and thus an opposition inside the Front will probably take share in parliament.

I am certain that there will be an opposition, and a fairly strong one at that, but not of the previous kind.[118]

One did not have to wait long for this prediction of the emergence of an opposition within the Popular Front to come true. Only a month later, Dragoljub Jovanović spoke out in the Constituent Assembly as an "oppositionist," while shortly afterwards the negative epithet of "reactionary" and "enemy" was given to several other deputies such as Miloš Popović, Imro Filaković, don Ante Salacan and Radomir Todorović.

Thus, following his refusal to vote for the government proposal of the law on civil servants, Miloš Popović was immediately rebuked by Miloš Carević for "thereby revealing himself in this conspiratorial business."[119] Rodoljub Čolaković publicly confirmed "that his (Popović's) answer was an integral part of that perfidious activity which is also beginning to be practiced in the Federal Chamber."[120] When, in connection with statements by Carević and Čolaković, don Ante Salacan attempted to defend freedom of speech in the Assembly and the right of a deputy to say what he thought, he was greeted with cries of "this is fascism" and "this is reaction" from the deputies' benches. After repeated heckling from the benches, he asked: "Comrade deputies, is there freedom of speech? " He was told: "No." Don Ante Salacan retorted: "If not, then thank you very much, I won't speak any more."[121]

What Popović and Salacan said prompted Mate Petrović to ask:

> who and where are their masters in the country and outside it. In specific terms, for Mr. Salacan it is Stepinac in the country and the Pope, in fact, the Black International (TR: the Catholic Church), and for the other all those who supported Draža Mihailović and his entire gang. (*Dr. Miloš Popović:* I did not have any connection with Draža Mihailović.) If you did not have actual connections you had spiritual ones. And just because of that, we must strike more firmly at the saboteurs of this exalted House, at the saboteurs of its homogeneity in passing laws.[122]

Only eight months before, Milan Grol had warned that "a reasonable man shudders at an assembly where all proposals are passed unanimously and with acclamation."[123] Now unanimity, that is, "homogeneity in passing laws," had become the prime virtue, when only enemies rejected.

Imro Filaković took the criticism of this homogeneity a step further. He criticized the fact that Communist Party members held all the important posts in the administration while the political individuality of the non-Communist parties in the Popular Front was not even manifest. "I don't want to say that the Communist Party should not have its own staff in these sections. No . . . . It has that right, but it seems strange to me that all these officials are recruited from only one party, even though we have many parties in the Popular Front."[124] There was, of course, a way for someone from the non-Communist parties to obtain a post in the administration. "At a session of the Executive Committee of our Croatian Republican Peasant Party," Imro Filaković told the deputies:

> Our president, vice-president and second secretary said that a member of the Executive Committee could also be a member of the Communist Party and thus it could happen that people are appointed who would be both and everything. But, Comrades, you see this is what I said that I did not like.[125]

With this, Filaković revealed the hidden way of "winning over" the leaders of the non-Communist parties to the cause of the ruling party. Some of them were, unknown to the public, secretly admitted to the membership of the Communist Party, and later "carried out" Communist Party assignments in their own non-Communist Party. In return they usually obtained ministerial and other high posts.

In Filaković's opinion, these posts should also have been shared out among others, which practically amounted to the demand that each party which had joined the Popular Front should retain its own individuality. Since such a demand was not bereft of risks and great troubles, Filaković was exposing himself to possible danger.

> Comrades, some of my friends have told me: 'Do not speak, because you could foolishly lose your head and nothing would be changed.' But I say this to you. I have sacrificed my life once in the national liberation movement and if need be, I will sacrifice it once again for the truth.[126]

In addition to this, in a later discussion Filaković requested that speeches

by deputies who did not agree with the attitude and decision of the majority, be published. "Since we do not have an opposition press, I demand that our speeches be published in order that the people should be able to pronounce their own judgement on them."[127]

There is no need to point out that such "heretical" demands could not pass without condemnation and excommunication. Fiercest in their condemnations were, in fact, those closest to Filaković—his party friends in the Executive Committee of the Croatian Republican Peasant Party. On 30 July 1946, they unanimously expelled Filaković from the party for sowing dissent in the party, splitting the Popular Front and fanning hatred between Croats and Serbs.[128]

The most resolute advocate of the multi-party structure of the Popular Front was Dragoljub Jovanović. He, in fact, supported party pluralism from the very beginning. He was, however, proclaimed an enemy only after the opposition outside the Popular Front had been wiped out. On 25 August 1945, immediately after Grol resignation from the government and his crossing over to the opposition, he decisively stressed the great advantages of the multi-party system.

> Parties mean criticism, criticism means discussion, and discussion means control, or a party means both discussion and control. The new people's power can also allow there to be discussion and criticism. It also agrees to control by the public.[129]

Moreover, *at that moment,* Dragoljub Jovanović also presented this conviction *on behalf of* the entire Popular Front.

> In this respect, I would like to stress before the public, and I also wish this to be heard at the plenum, that we in the Popular Front do not hold to the viewpoint of a one-party system and that they who fear dictatorship or some kind of left-wing fascism, all those who suspect Marshal Tito or any one of us of wishing to create a one-party system, can rest assured that this will not happen, not because we do not have sufficient strength to carry it out or becuase there is some pressure which says that it is not sensible to do so and this it must not be done, but only because we know our people. In their structure and mentality, our people are not right for a one-party

system. Above all, because there is a strong, long-standing tradition
in Serbia, though less in Croatia and still less in other regions. That
strong tradition means the tradition of discussion and of consulta-
tions and not of command.[130]

It is interesting that *at this point* in time (August 1945) no one *publicly*
contested Jovanović's defense of party pluralism and his explicit assertion
that our people did not like one-party systems. Does this mean that the
introduction of a one-party system was still not being considered by the
top echelons of the ruling party? Or, was the gap at that moment, between the long-range strategy, which, according to the model of the Bolshevik tradition, had as its aim the introduction of a one-party system and
current tactics, which were reflected in the tolerating of party pluralism,
so deep and insurmountable? If one bears in mind Dragoljub Jovanović's
fate after the elections for the Constituent Assembly the explanation of
the earlier disagreement is very simple. In August 1945, the ruling party
had begun its struggle against Milan Grol's opposition outside the Popular
Front. It was therefore not sensible at this time to start a conflict with a
new opponent within the Popular Front until the rival outside this front
had been wiped out and destroyed. Besides, the elections were near, and
in such circumstances Dragoljub Jovanović was better as a doubtful ally
than as a resolute opponent.

Therefore, Jovanović's praise of party pluralism on our territory was
left without a real answer. Only Dušan Kveder, a Communist deputy from
Slovenia, raised a reservation in respect of the territorial validity of Jovanović's conclusions. Kveder said:

> In our view, Dragoljub Jovanović has applied well the principle of
> historial materialism with regard to explaining the origins of politi-
> cal parties in social life, but at the same time I consider that he has
> wrongly applied the principle of historical materialism in some areas,
> and that is when he has spoken about Slovenia.[131]

The wrong application, in Kveder's opinion, was reflected in the conclusion that, in the sphere of party political life, what held good for the
whole of Yugoslavia also held good for Slovenia. However, the exception
of Slovenia consisted in the fact that it no longer needed party pluralism.

"We Slovenes in the People's Assembly believe that all of us from the Communists down to even the most right-wing elements consider that apart from the Popular Front there are no other political parties in Slovenia and that there is no need to set them up either."[132] Thus, glossing over the fact that in Slovenia the Communist Party of Slovenia continued to exist as a *separate* party, which, in contrast to the rest of the parties, had not disappeared in the Popular Front, Kveder allowed for the possibility that party pluralism might exist *outside* Slovenia. "We agree that political circumstances in other parts of the state are developing differently and that organized parties or institutions exist."[133]

The very explanation of this reservation by Kveder, which retains party monism for Slovenia and allows pluralism in other parts of Yugoslavia, lies in the fact that the Communist Party of Slovenia had succeeded even during the war in attaining what would only be attained in the rest of the federal units in 1947.[134] Since the right to an *independent* existence and organization was denied all Slovene parties with the exception of the Communist Party by the Dolomite Declaration of 1 May 1943, the Communist Party, through its spokesman Dušan Kveder, did not want to establish *again* this right of the non-Communist parties because, for reasons of temporary convenience, it *still* existed in Serbia and Croatia.

After the elections for the Constituent Assembly and the consolidation of the new power the most suitable moment arose to abandon the existing tolerance toward insubordinate fellow-travellers in the Popular Front and to implement overtly the unconcealed long-range strategy in the spirit of the adopted Bolshevik tradition. On the eve of the October Revolution, the Bolsheviks had solemnly promised that they would respect the freedom of *all* parties within the Soviet regime and that they would not suppress the rights of the minority. In his capacity as newly-elected chairman of the Petrograd Soviet, Trotsky took a solemn and pathetic oath on 23 September 1917 on which later events proved futile.

> We are all party men, and more than once we shall clash with one another. But we shall conduct the work of the Petrograd Soviet in a spirit of lawfulness and of full freedom for all parties. The hand of the Presidium will never lend itself to the suppression of a minority.[135]

This principle of freedom and tolerance was scrupulously respected and so all parties were represented in the Soviet presidium in proportion to their strength.

"Sukhanov relates that three years later, after the Bolsheviks had banned all the parties of the opposition, he reminded Trotsky of his pledge not to lend himself to the suppression of any minority. Trotsky lapsed into silence, reflected for a while, and then said wistfully: 'Those were good days.' They were indeed. The revolution was still taking seriously its own assurance that it would widen and make real the freedoms which bourgeois democracy only promised or which it granted with a niggardly hand."[136]

It seems that all the Communist parties, which had carried out the so-called Bolshevization between the two wars, were inclined to follow the path of the Russian Bolsheviks after acquiring power. Dragoljub Jovanović, who began his post-war political career as an ally of the CPY in the Popular Front, continued it as their fellow-traveller and ended up an enemy of the people experienced this at first hand. Until the elections for the Constituent Assembly, Dragoljub Jovanović had been a loyal ally. After the elections, the moment came for him to be demoted like numerous politicians of the non-Communist parties, to a mere fellow-traveller, and, when he protested, to an "enemy of the people."

That moment of truth came on 11 December 1945, in a discussion on the draft Constitution of the new Yugoslavia. Behaving as if nothing had changed after the elections, Dragoljub Jovanović began his famous oration by challenging the special, and in a certain sense, supra-constitutional, status enjoyed more and more by the CPY. Many years later he summed up that speech in the following warning: "The first Yugoslavia collapsed because there were several nations in it but only one ruled; the second will collapse if only one party should rule."[137] Nevertheless, in December 1945, this warning was much milder and amounted chiefly to the following presentation of the unresolved socio-political question:

> If the right to existence for all social forces, all political forces which wish to exist, is denied, if these forces are artifically suppressed and split, if their top echelons are destroyed or their organization made impossible—it could happen that the new Yugoslavia will perish because of such political oppression, just as the old Yugoslava perished because of nationalist oppression.[138]

Jovanović, however, put forward this prediction conditionally because at the same time he presented "a healthy . . . the only salutary formula":

We have found a way to resolve that difficulty and to avoid that
sickness by having created a politico-party federation parallel with a
national-cultural federation at another level. This is the Popular Front
It should represent the reconciliation of unity and freedom, the
freedom and unity of our peoples, just as the Federation represents
the reconciliation of the equality of the peoples and the unity of
the state.[139]

Instead of a one-party system, the salutary solution is represented by "the
Popular Front, understood as a collaboration of parties, not as a mechani-
cal coalition but as an organic collaboration."[140]

Thus Jovanović was in favor of party pluralism within the framework of
the Popular Front, which rested on *real* and *lasting* cooperation between
the parties—co-operation based on the principle of *equality*. He was, however, troubled by the question of whether that alliance would truly be
equitable and lasting. This depended chiefly on the attitude of the Communist Party as the most influential party. This was really a question of
whether the Communist Party considered the rest of the parties in the
Popular Front its allies or only temporary fellow-travellers. Jovanović's
fear was particularly provoked by Stalin's idea set out in *Borba:* "Our
party does not and cannot have allies. It can only have temporary fellow-
travellers."[141] Jovanović wondered wheither perhaps the CPY would also
set off along this path which had already led to the "constitutionalization"
of the All-Union Communist Party (of Bolsheviks) into the "vanguard of
the working people . . . and . . . the leading nucleus of all workers' organizations both at the social and the state level." (Article 126 of Stalin's
famous constitution of 1936.) In this action of the leading state party,
all other organizations become "levers" and "transmission belts" operated
by the Communist Party.

To be sure, Jovanović did not maintain that the CPY had already become the official state party by the end of 1945; he only wanted to warn
of such a possibility. "We should," said Jovanović, "also separate the party
from the state, abolish the state party, or rather, not introduce it, and
thereby liquidate any similarity to fascism."[142] In saying this, Jovanović
had in mind above all the need that, in addition to the CPY, as the *workers'*
party, the peasants too should "preserve and develop their own independent movement, not only economically, but also politically and culturally."[143] The peasants would, of course, wish for a fraternal alliance with

workers in the political, economic and cultural respect. "But, an alliance does not mean a subordinate position, it means, if not full parity, at least equality."[144] In other words, an alliance of workers and peasants, that is, of the workers' and peasants' parties, must truly be equal. In order to achieve this it is necessary to preserve the multi-party system which provides for criticism, discussion and control over all authorities, from those at the bottom right up to those at the top. "I too must be frank," concluded Jovanović. "There cannot be a one-party system in our country, or at least, not with our consent. I think that a one-party system will not be possible even with the consent of the peasantry, of the Serbian peasantry above all."[145] Jovanović also confirmed this by quoting earlier private conversations with individual leaders.

> I told Marshal Tito: 'Our country cannot be put under one cap and into one party.' As it happened, I said this just a year ago, on 12 December last year. I said: 'Our country cannot endure a one-party system. Allow other parties to develop too. They have not shown, particularly on the Serbian side, that they are against the workers' movement, but they have always wanted to co-operate with this movement as a fraternal one.'[146]

Later, when he had already been branded as a heretic, Dragoljub Jovanović further developed this criticism of the course along which, in his view, the party system of the time had been inexorably developing. He did so in particular on 17 July 1946, in a discussion about the proposed law on the Public Prosecutor's Office. Jovanović said then:

> Finally, there is one feature which is not public but which is real: the public prosecutor, this is the party, the state party, the only one, the Party written with a capital letter. One cannot have anything against the party, but on condition that it is not one party. When one says party, this means a party of something: party, that means a side, clearly cannot be only one, because this is a physical and psychological impossibility. In our country the public prosecuor is, without exception, a member of the Communist Party. The law odes not say so but it is so in practice. But the omnipotence enjoyed by the prosecutor in practice is legalized in the law. Such a

public prosecutor embodies the dictatorship of one party, it protects
the one-party system.[147]

Jovanović's support for the preservation of party pluralism and of the
individuality of the parties within the Popular Front encountered fierce
resistance from leading people in the CPY. Edvard Kardelj, Moša Pijade
and Milovan Djilas set an example in this. Moša Pijade, for example, also
proceeded from the fact that in the Soviet Union, the Communist Party
was recognized by the Constitution as the state party and as a state institution. But this, in his view, had nothing to do with the sincerity of the
Soviet leaders. "There is the dictatorship of the proletariat. That's the way
it is there."[148] The CPY was without doubt

> a force with a crucial social influence and that is how it should be.
> But to declare it a one-party system is wrong, if for no other reason,
> then at least because we should refrain from repeating, in a closed
> circle and in a sealed room, slogans which we constantly hear from
> the international reaction.[149]

Thus, according to Moša Pijade, the claim that a one-party system existed
in Yugoslavia was wrong because this was precisely what the international
reaction continuously implied. On another occasion he began his criticism
of Jovanović's speech about the co-operative movement with the words:
"We have heard the words of a well-known demagogue." Then he told how
Dragoljub Jovanović went around the country with two corn cobs, one
small and stunted, the other the size of a forearm, and how he told the
peasants that the latter had grown in a private field an the stunted one in
a field owned by the state. Besides this, he added that Jovanović ridiculed
the symbol of the alliance of workers and peasants, the hammer and sickle,
by explaining that symbol as meaning that the peasant was grabbed by the
neck, pulled with the sickle and struck on the head with the hammer.[150]
    These criticisms of Jovanović's views and declarations also contained
some ominous indications concerning his collusion with the enemies of
the people. Kardelj said "that the White Guardists, who helped the Ustashe
in Slovenia, will also rejoice when they see from Mr. Jovanović's speeches
that he defends certain party traditions as in Croatia and Slovenia."[151]
Miloš Minić mentioned in passing that Dragoljub Jovanović's speech was

identical with an article by Laza Marković, who was already in prison as an
enemy of the people.[152] It is absolutely certain that such insinuations were
very unpleasant for Dragoljub Jovanović, especially as he himself, while
still an ally of the ruling party, had also harshly condemned political opponents as reactionaries and "internal emigres." Yet it seems that the so-
called enemies outside the Popular Front had already begun to place their
hopes in him. After all, this was inevitable. In a political system which
aims at a one-party system, some of the opponents of the ruling party who
are held in check, who can no longer fight under their own flag, will always be prepared to turn to any important renegade, even if he belongs
to the ruling group and regardless of the reasons for his heresy. They are,
therefore, inclined to see their hero in anyone whom the ruling party
brands as a dangerous enemy.[153] At the beginning of 1954, this also
happened to Milovan Djilas when, from being a revered official ideologue,
he became an odious revisionist and renegade.

There is some symbolism in the fact that on 27 April 1947 it was exactly Milovan Djilas, as a future heretic, who indicated the punishment
that would befall the disobedient Dragoljub Jovanović.

> The people's masses which are moving forward, which are creating
> a new life, which crush all obstacles, these national masses, like a
> big river, like a flood, throw out mud onto their banks and push on.
> They also throw out Dragoljub Jovanović and his friends.[154]

Indeed, the Djilas metaphor had the power of an iron fist. On 15 May
1947, the Presidium of the People's Assembly of the Federal Republic
of Yugoslavia gave its approval to start criminal proceedings against
Dragoljub Jovanović, who was immediately afterwards also sentenced
to imprisonment for ten years and to the loss of political and some civil
rights for three years.[155]

Thus after the opposition outside the Popular Front was wiped out, the
most famous oppositionist inside the Popular Front too was finally put
out of action. Or, as Branko Petranović explained it:

> The definitive disappearance from the scene of Dragoljub Jovano-
> vić was marked by his being brought to trial on October 1947 for
> his connections with prominent representatives of the political

emigration and against the background of his confrontation with the policies of the CPY and his challenging its position as a democratic force.[156]

In other words, it seems that confrontation with the policies of the CPY led as a rule to prison and that this was the only place where opposition could exist. At one time the following maxim was ascribed to Bukharin: "We might have a two-party system, but one of the two parties would be in office and the other in prison."[157] That maxim had also become valid in the case of Dragoljub Jovanović who demonstrated by his own example that prison bars divide the ruling party from the opposition. But in contrast to the Soviet Union, this dividing line between the ruling party and the opposition was not, as a rule, etched in blood, as Dragoljub Jovanović's release after he had served his sentence eloquently confirms.

CHAPTER III

THE POLITICAL PARTIES' MEANS OF STRUGGLE

1. The Hegemonic Party's Methods of Struggle

The first part of this study describes the nature of the party system in Yugoslavia between 1944 and 1949. It also shows the difference in aims and values between the opposition parties and the Communist Party, or rather, it compares the liberal concept of democracy and pluralism with the standpoint of the Communist Party. The differences in the views of the Communist Party and the opposition parties become even greater if we turn our attention to the means of struggle employed by the two sides. The non-Communist political parties' traditional forms of activity were opposed by the revolutionary forms of struggle of the Communist Party, which for tactical reasons only were temporarily concealed by parliamentary rituals and phraseology. This asymmetry in the nature of the means of struggle used was accompanied, because of the character of the revolutionary aims and principles of struggle of the Communist Party, by the impossibility of its opponents using fully their parliamentary methods of debate and acquiring followers. Not only were the means of struggle of the opposing sides completely different and unequal, but not one of the opposing parties was able to use its old means of struggle: the non-Communist political parties were deprived of that without which the life and struggle of a party cannot be conceived—a party organization and a press.

Of the means used by the Communist Party in the struggle against its opponents, two were fundamental and, at first glance, different in character, though they were basically complementary. On the one hand, there was the setting-up of broad alliances comprising different political groups and members of the Communist Party holding diverging views. This structure was characteristic of the Popular Front as a general political organization. Opposed to this mode of activity of the Communist Party were the methods of direct intimidation and attacks on political opponents in the political opposition parties. The purpose of both the first and second method of activity was to neutralize and liquidate the opposition parties and party pluralism.

The attempt by Communists to link up with other democratic parties in Yugoslavia between the wars, as well as the formation of such organizations during the war (the Slovene Liberation Front), before the end of the war (the United National Liberation Front) and the formation of the Popular Front after the war, resulted primarily from the revised strategy and tactics of the Comintern since its Seventh Congress in 1935, while after the war they were also dictated for a time by current international agreements and obligations. However, in spite of all the changes with respect to other political parties, the basic attitude of the *Bolshevized* Communist parties toward their allies in the political struggle remained unchanged. This attitude to political allies can be especially well observed in Lenin's life and struggle. A great part of Lenin's political activity was devoted to co-operation with groups of different tendencies, just as a large part of what Lenin said and wrote was aimed at establishing the borders between the organizations to which he belonged and other organizations. Lenin was constantly confronted with a dilemma: inordinate advocacy for the independence of the Bolshevik Party would reduce the large-scale support on which any party has to rely for a lengthy period, whereas entering into alliances with other political parties was incompatible with revolutionary strategy. Therefore, the problem of the relationship between the Communists and other, reformist, workers' parties after 1919 is one of the most complex questions of the strategy and tactics of the workers' movement. As Philip Selznick writes, Lenin's attitude toward allies in other parties could be reduced to these allies having to be *exploited* and not *supported*.[1]

Maurice Duverger stresses that the very nature of the Bolshevism of Communist parties is opposed to compromise agreement and alliances, but that different forms of coalitions represent an efficient mode of operation for these parties—all the more so, since their complex and strong organization protects them from the contamination and disintegration to which their allies in such coalitions are exposed. Communist parties use alliances, such as the organization of a popular front, among other things, also to cover up the nature and aims of their own parties and gradually to neutralize and liquidate the parties of the alliance.[2]

With reference to the concealment of the real aims and character of an organization, in the period of their struggle for power and the consolidation of power, the *Bolshevized* Communist parties use their coalition partners, or personalities from their ranks, to show—in a society in which different ideological orientations and values predominate or are still influential, that is in a society in which these parties are to a certain degree on the fringe—that the differences between their system of values and the others are not all that radical. In surrounding itself with this "facade" of groups and individuals, such a Communist party strives, as Hannah Arendt writes, to achieve a semblance of "normality" and "respectability." What these Communist parties want to show thereby is that they are parties just like any other, that they are no less destructive than others and that they too do not reject all the traditional democratic institutions and values.[3]

To conceal the aims and character of the communist movement within the framework of organizations of the popular front type, two more things have to be achieved. A Popular Front must be presented as the creation of all the parties, groups and individuals within it and not as the creation of the Communist party. When a popular front is set up, its supra-party and general character must be emphasized. On the other hand, the equal status of all parties in the popular front must be demonstrated.

Thus, at the First and Second Congress of the Popular Front, it was stressed that the Communist Party was not imposing its own program on the Popular Front but that it was formulating the Popular Front's program and that this program was also its own program. Because of this, even the personal union between the leadership of the Communist Party and the Popular Front was concealed.[4] After 1948, the tactic of concealing the role of the Communist Party within the Popular Front was abandoned.

This role began to be referred to for the first time openly in order to refute the assertions and attitudes of the Resolution of the Cominform that the Communist Party had "faded away" in the Popular Front. The Declaration of the CPY Central Committee on this occasion stated among other things:

> But the facts, as well as the numerous statements throughout the entire war and after the war—not only by the Communists in the Front—demonstrate: firstly, that the leading force in the Front is the Communist Party; secondly, that the Communist Party is not fading away in the Front but, on the contrary, that the Party is raising the ideological and political level of the basic masses of the Popular Front and educating them in the spirit of its policy and of Marxism-Leninism; thirdly, that in practice, the Popular Front of Yugoslavia is fighting for socialism, which certainly would not be possible if diverse political groups—that bourgeois parties, kulaks, merchants, small factory owners and others, as it says in the Resolution—played any serious role in it, or if it were a coalition between the proletariat and the bourgeoisie; fourthly, that the Party has not taken over the program of the Front but, on the contrary, that the Front receives its basic directions and program from the Communist Party, which is only natural in view of the Party's leading role in it.[5]

Another aspect of this concealment of the Communist Party's role in the Popular Front was the stress laid on the fact that the Popular Front had the character of a coalition and that all the parties in it were equal. But the way in which the coalitionist character of the Popular Front was referred to at the very beginning was not sufficient to mask the aspiration to abolish these elements of the coalition as soon as possible and to transform the Front from a composite organization into a monolithic one. This is already observable in Edvard Kardelj's report at the First Congress of the Popular Front, at which he defended the attitude that it was a mistake to think that the unity of the Popular Front was incompatible with the existence of parties within it, provided that they were progressive parties working for the implementation of the joint policy of the Popular Front. On the other hand, it was also a mistake to think that it was sufficient for the parties' leaderships to unite in order that each member of those parties also became a member of the Popular Front.

His political conviction, his party affiliation, his view of the world, his religious and confessional affiliation, is the private affair of each individual. The Front, therefore, does not prevent the normal organizational life of the parties within its structure. But, what the Front demands from all of them is the will to solve these tasks. This is why we are rejecting the ordinary party coalition which does not guarantee that these tasks will really be carried out. The usual party coalition cannot mobilize the masses because it lives on compromises reached by its top echelons.[6]

It may be concluded from Kardelj's assertion that the Popular Front was not an ordinary coalition that it was a special type of coalition. After all there are different types of coalitions, that is, different types of alliances. Proceeding from the fact that the bad thing in these coalitions was that parties joining them put their own interests above the alliance, instead of the other way around, Kardelj, in speaking of the Popular Front as a coalition of a special kind, came out in favor of the program of the alliance being above the program of the parties in it and of some aspects of the parties' programs being suspended for the sake of the alliance's aspiratins. Other partners of the Communist Party in the Popular Front also supported this idea. Thus the "Electoral Proclamation of the People's Peasant Party" says:

> The Popular Front is sure of its own strength. The People's Peasant Party has confidence in its allies and associates in the Front. Our success is their success too; their victory is our victory too. *Let the Popular Front be for all* more important than their own party or personal interests.[7]

The further development of relations within the Popular Front would show that although the contents of Kardelj's exposition and of the electoral proclamation of the People's Peasant Party were the same, their purpose was not. Therefore, when he said that the Front was not an ordinary coalition, Kardelj had something completely different in mind. In line with the long-term strategic aims of the Communist Party, the Popular Front was a means of mobilizing the masses in the realization of the Party program as well as a way to conceal the real aims of the Communist Party and to bring about the gradual neutralization and liquidation of the rival parties in the Popular Front. Hence the assertion that the Popular Front was both a coalition (although not an ordinary one) and a unified organization. This ambiguity of the Popular Front was highlighted from the beginning in its organizational principles, according to which each member of a political party in the Popular Front, had also, as an individual, to be a member of the Popular Front committees.[8]

Thus, the basic aims of the Popular Front with regard to the opposition parties were mutually complementary and supportive. The concealment of the real plans of the hegemonic party in the Popular Front made possible the gradual liquidation of the other political parties and their disappearance from political life. This was best demonstrated by the fate of the Republican Party, the Croatian Republican Peasant Party and the Independent Democratic Party, which has already been referred to. All these parties gradually "faded away" in the Popular Front by accepting first their subordinate role and than their end as something inevitable. What happened to the political parties which did not agree to such a role? They split and this was more or less the work of the Communist Party which had to show that there were factions in the political opposition parties which accepted the role assigned to them in the Popular Front (the so-called "progressive core"), but that opposite them stood the hostile sections of party formations outside the Popular Front. The slogan was: "Who is against the Popular Front is our enemy, which means he is the enemy of his own people."[9] Since the hostile sections of the parties, that is, the parties outside the Popular Front, were gradually liquidated as enemies, the sections of the parties within the Popular Front sooner or later also ceased to exist.

In talking about provoking splits and discord in the opposition parties, one should recognize two aspects: either the splits occurred in parties which had not joined the Popular Front or in parties which were in it.

The legitimate status of political parties which were outside the Popular Front from the outset (the Democrats and the Radicals) was denied by pointing out from the start that dissident groups of these parties also existed in the Popular Front. At the First Congress of the Popular Front of Yugoslavia, statements on behalf of these groups were made by Mihailo Djurović (for the Radicals) and Vlada Zečević (for the Democrats).[10] By presenting itself as the most authentic representative of the Democratic

Party tradition, and by presenting actual leader of the Democrats, Milan
Grol, as a dissident, a dissident group of Democrats in the Popular Front
held a meeting in September 1945, condemning Grol's attitude and activity and electing a 10-man Action Committee, which afterwards decided
to nominate its own representatives for the Constituent Assembly on the
Popular Front's ticket and send a "Proclamation to Members of the Democratic Party."[11]

When Milan Grol submitted his resignation from the post of Vice-
Premier and when on 20 September 1945 the united opposition parties
(the Democrats, Agrarians and Radicals) called on their members not to
take part in the elections for the Constituent Assembly, the group of
Democrats in the Popular Front held several meetings in Belgrade and
elsewhere, condemning the "treacherous work" of Milan Grol and of the
group of Democratic deputies in the Provisional Assembly.[12] A conference
of the dissident group of Democrats in the Front (Front Democrats) decided that it was necessary to carry out preparations to convene a national
conference of members and followers of the Democratic Party. The participants at this conference really inteded to revive a parallel organization
of the Democratic Party whose work and activity had already been approved by the relevant authorities. The need to establish such an organization was relevant only to the extent that, and as long as, the impression
was gained that the existing Democratic Party of Milan Grol would be able
to influence more significantly the mood and attitudes of public opinion
in Serbia, that is, attract a greater number of those dissatisfied with the
new regime. The Democratic Party had the greatest influence among the
opposition parties in Serbia as a result of the activity of the group of
Democratic deputies in the Assembly, and articles in the party paper
Demokratija. Though restricted and fettered, the rise in the Democratic
Party's influence was also manifested in the great interest shown by the
public in the Party paper throughout the period it was published.

As the political scene in Croatia was practically dominated by one
political party (the Croatian Republican Peasant Party), the attention of
the Communist Party was concentrated on it. Though the system in Serbia
was fragmented, one party, the Democratic Party, nevertheless, was pre-
eminent with its influence, and thus it was not unusual that *Borba,* the
then organ of the CPY, gave exceptional prominence during the pre-election
struggle for the Constituent Assembly to reports from the conferences of
the Front Democrats at which the legal Democratic Party was attacked.

At the conference of the Front Democrats, a resolution was also adopted which critically reviewed the activity of a part of the Democratic Party leadership, beginning with the Party's last congress on 19 March 1939. The resolution noted that the last congress of the Democratic Party had elected a Main Committee and an Executive Committee to represent the Party in all actions. The Main Committee, however, had not met, either before or during the war. The Front Democrats had approved Milan Grol's arrival from London and his entry into the Provisional Government, but they were disappointed that, without the Party's authorization, he had appointed as Party's representatives in the Assembly people, the majority of whom did not enjoy the confidence of the Party. One should recall right away that all the representatives of the parties, with which the Anti-Fascist Council of the National Liberation of Yugoslavia had been enlarged, were appointed in this way, as well as the fact that this method of expanding the Assembly suited, above all, the Communist Party which was able to have an insight into the profile and reliability of the new deputies, as well as influence their election. The composition of the committee for expanding the Anti-Fascist Council of the National Liberation of Yugoslavia pointed to this conclusion. Lastly, one should not ignore the fact that at the time when the Party's representatives were co-opted to the Assembly, the Front Democrats did not publicly object to the Democratic Party's deputies.

At the aforementioned conference of the Front Democrats, an Action Committee was also elected, which was empowered to convene the elected representatives of the district committees of the Democratic Party and to do everything possible in order that the grouping within the Popular Front should put up candidates. All members of the Democratic Party throughout the country were also asked to hold conferences in all districts and to appoint at least two delegates from each district for the national conference. A provisional committee of members of the Democratic Party in the Front for Belgrade was also elected.

Worthy of attention is the statement made about the situation in the Democratic Party to *Borba* by Miloš Carević who, besides Vlada Zečević, was one of the most active representatives of the Front Democrats.[13] Carević maintained that Milan Grol had no right to submit an application on behalf of the Democratic Party seeking permission for the work of the Party to be resumed because a Party congress had not been held since

1939. Naturally, for the new regime it was an incomparably lesser evil if some members of the pre-war Party's administration determined who would represent the Party in the Assembly, and if they submitted on behalf of the Party applications seeking the resumption of the Party's work, than if Party Congresses should be convened; in other words, that the Party organization be re-established in their entirety. The existing authorities did exactly the opposite: they tried to prevent the restoration of party organizations in their former shape, and should this restoration take place, tried to ensure it was of limited scope. Carević, who knew all this, disputed, however, Grol's right to submit an application to the Ministry of Internal Affairs on behalf of the Party for approval of the Party's activity. It is also interesting that Carević presented this procedural objection of his after the resumption of Democratic Party activity had been approved by the relevant authority. To make the matter even more paradoxical, the decision approving the work of the Democratic Party was also signed by Vlada Zečević, the leading representative of the Front Democrats, in his capacity as Minister of Internal Affairs. With his statement Carević indirectly questioned the legality of a decision of a relevant authority as well as the conduct of a leading representative of his own political grouping in the Front. Naturally, Carević did all this after *Demokratija* had called on the Party followers, as well as other opposition parties, not to take part in the elections, regardless of the fact that the work of the Democratic Party had already been approved.

In a statement which he gave to *Borba,* Carević also gave a "sociological analysis" of the group of signatories of the application seeking the resumption of the Democratic Party's activity. First of all he pointed out the regional affiliation of the signatories. According to him, all the 165 signatories, with one exception, were from Belgrade. Of the 165 signatories, 19 had been deprived of the right to vote. As far as the professional structure of the signatories was concerned, according to Carević, it raised even greater suspicion. There were no workers and peasants and it was dominated by the intelligentsia and, judging by the number of those who had been deprived of the right to vote, mainly by "dishonest" intelligentsia at that. The professional structure of the signatories looked like this: one-quarter was made up of pensioners, one-quarter of officials (mostly former ones), while for every three workers and three peasants there were 16 lawyers, 22 people without a profession, two landlords, one priest and

one pharmacist. The rest were shopkeepers and cafe owners. Carević said
nothing about the profile of the Front Democrats, among whom there
were also priests and lawyers, though probably more reliable and, therefore,
more "honest." His objection to the professions of the signatories was all
the more strange since the Democratic Party was neither a workers' nor
a peasant party.

Though he did not intend this, Carević's objections, nevertheless, sug-
gested something else. Firstly, they showed that it was not possible for
party organizations to be restored outside the center where their administration lay (Belgrade), in other words, that the administrations and leaderships of parties existed in the main without party organizations. On the
other hand, the signing of such an application in Belgrade, where the political life was exposed to public scrutiny, posed less of a risk to the signatories than would have been the case in the interior. The professional
structure of the signatories of the Democratic Party's application also
bears witness to the conditions in which Party life took place: the signa-
tores did not have any connection with state service (they were individuals
who were self-employed, pensioners or former officials), that is, those for
whom party activity could not have had any consequence for their em-
ployment in state service.

But splits were not provoked only in parties outside the Popular Front
but also in the parties in the Front which wanted to preserve a certain
degree of party independence. Thus, the resignation of the Agrarian
Party from the Popular Front (or rather, a section of the party) in an attempt to preserve the Party's independence, resulted in a parallel party
formation within the Popular Front. The statement on the resignation
of the Agrarian Party from the Popular Front was made at the beginning
of November 1945 by Mita Stanisavljević, one of the Party's Vice-Presi-
dents and President of the Agrarian Deputies' Club. According to Stani-
savijević, the decision was a result of part of the Party leadership making
it impossible for its main organs to meet, because the Popular Front had
refused to give the Agrarian Party separate agrarian lists at the elections,
and because some Party members had become candidates without the
approval of the Party organs. The statement claimed that the Agrarian
Party had joined the Front believing it to be a composite organization
consisting of individual political parties, but since the work and organization of the Front aimed at creating from it a one-party organization and

since the Front's economic policy (and especially the co-operatives' policy) was not in harmony with the interests of the broad popular, and particularly, peasant strata, the Party had decided to implement its own program outside the Popular Front.[14] Before this split in the Agrarians' rank was made known, another Vice-President of the Party, Marko Vujačić, issued a statement that no Agrarian Party of any kind existed outside the Popular Front.[15]

Thus, we have dealt with the struggle which the Communist Party was waging against the other parties in the Popular Front, a struggle which was neither head-on, nor open, but covert. The other means of the Communist Party's struggle against the opposition parties and against those sections which had not reconciled themselves to their new position, were different forms of intimidation, defamation and attacks on political opponents. The intimidation of opposition parties and their members was carried out in two ways: on the one hand, through declarations by representatives of the ruling party and articles in the Front's press, and on the other hand, the work of the Front's activists in the field. Since the immediate consequences of the threats to members of the opposition parties were felt more in the field, and since it was easier to attack the anonymous activists of the Front than the leading personalities of the Communist Party, the opposition parties favored the first mentioned forms of intimidation. The hegemonic party, of course, did not directly instigate all the incidents at ground level but contributed to them by fiercely attacking the opposition parties verbally.

Examples of attacks on the non-Communist parties in the press, in speeches and in other ways, are numerous. Reading about such settling of accounts with political opponents, it is difficult not to recall Lenin's explanation of the way in which he conducted polemics with his opponents, the Mensheviks:

> I purposely chose that tone calculated to evoke in the hearer hatred, disgust, and contempt for the people who carry on such tactics. That tone, that formulation is not designed to convince, but to break the ranks, not to correct a mistake of the opponent but to annihilate him, to wipe him off the face of the earth. Indeed that approach evokes the worst thoughts and suspicions against the opponent.[16]

Such assessments of the opposition parties, permeated with such a tone, presented in the speeches of leading personalities of the Communist Party and circulated through a great number of papers, are but a step away from attacks on those who distributed the legal papers of the opposition parties, from the burning of opposition newspapers, and from physical attacks on some leaders of the parties of the opposition.

The articles by Jaša Prodanović, the leader of a loyal party in the Popular Front, also bear witness to the different aspects of intimidation of members of the opposition parties, including those who were in the Popular Front. This all the more so, since they appeared in a party paper which was published unhindered for a full 13 years, and whose publisher (Vladimir Simić) was President of the Federal Chamber of Assembly and Vice-President of the Federal Assembly while the paper *Republika* was published. Jaša Prodanović's articles referred to here were more literary than political, more conciliatory and moderately reproachful in their tone:

> In the transformation of our country, not everything runs smoothly, without shocks, without mistakes and errors, without impermissible pressure from below, without harmful fervor and exaggeration. Common sense has still not succeeded in moderating the inflamed passions of the masses; the desire for revenge is still manifest here and there; a righteous man still suffers occasionally while the guilty, who has wormed his way into the ranks of the idealistic fighters by some ruse, becomes arrogant. This ferment cannot and should not last long if one wants the best for the country and the people. Inflamed passions should be cooled, temperaments tamed, iritation lessened, one should not act out of spite or in order to do a good turn to someone but according to justice and the law; there should be neither sweetness nor anger. Unjustified threats should fade away and justifiable fear disappear.[17]

In his article, "Between the Hammer and the Anvil," Prodanović writes about attacks on the Republicans from the *right* (because of collaboration in the Popular Front), but also from the *left.* According to Prodanović, those attacks from the left did not come from the leaders of the allies the Popular Front (from the Communists), but "down below, among the people, in villages and towns, regions and districts, where the situation is anything but tolerable." In stressing that this kind of situation appeared after all revolutions, Prodanović pointed out that among the Republicans' opponents there were few genuine participants in the liberation movement, and on the other hand, that the situation in the country was nevertheless improving, that mistakes were being put right, that the courts were handing down milder sentences, that pardons were more frequent, cruelties in the application of the law lessened, convicted people were being treated more humanely and that the thirst for vengeance was disappearing.[18]

All these forms of intimidation, threats and defamation of political opponents have been described without reference to the legal framework in which the entire post-revolutionary political and party life developed. What is the *role of law* in such situations? Are the law and the judiciary in a position to introduce elements of personal security and stability after the revolutionary struggle? Lastly, what is the attitude of the revolutionary forces toward the law and the courts? On the subject of the Communist movement in revolutionary events, Lukács, in his syntagma on *lack of prejudice toward the law,* gives a good explanation of the *Bolshevized* communist parties' model attitude toward the law in the period when the power that has been gained is not yet consolidated and political opponents and people not holding Party views are still active.[19] This principle of lack of prejudice toward the law basically means opposition to liberal principles like those of the *rule of law and the independence of the judiciary.*

According to the traditional liberal and democratic concept, one assumes that when courts are working normally all parties in disputes are equal, even when the parties in a dispute are the state and the citizen, and that the court decides on the grounds of the parties' demands in a dispute with a suitable interpretation of the law. In the original Bolshevik concept, the basic task of the judiciary should be the liquidation of political opponents and enemies, and not the resolution of disputes which have arisen by applying the law. According to the traditional liberal concept, of all the powers, the judicial power is the "weakest" because it is least able to threaten the freedom of the citizen. Montesquieu wrote of judicial power that it is invisible and actually not a power at all, and he called judges "mouths which pronounce the words of the law" and "creatures without a soul." In contrast to this concept of the judiciary as an independent and weak power stood the concept and practice of the courts in post-revolutionary Yugoslavia as a *dependent and militant power,* a concept of the court as a "castle from which the people would truly settle accounts with their enemies."[20]

This concept of law and of the judiciary was criticized by the papers of the opposition parties. In so doing they not only pointed to the threats to the independence of the judiciary in practice, but also to constitutional principles and legal provisions (concerning the selection and dismissal of judges) which called into question the sacrosanct principle of the independence of judicial power.[21] In the first issue of *Republika,* Jaša Prodanović wrote how the great ideal of the independence of the courts had not been maintained in the 19th and 20th centuries, when, through their ministers, rulers told judges how they should try political offenders and when they threatened judges who turned a deaf ear to such commands. The Serbian kings, or rather the kings unworthy of this title, not only removed disobedient judges but also abolished the constitution and laws which guaranteed the independence of the courts and the judges' security of tenure. Passing on to contemporary circumstances, Prodanović wrote:

So it was, but it should not have been, that judges were appointed *from above.* This must not and should not be the case when judges are chosen by the people. The freedom of the judges to conduct a trial must also be protected. Pressure should not be exerted on them *from below.* Mob rule should not be above the court. Irresponsible groups from the popular masses should not be allowed to attack a judge's conscience with shouts and exclamations. When the people choose judges, it is assumed that they will select the most capable, the most just, the most honest and the most conscientious. And when they have chosen them, let them live in peace to study the facts carefully and scrupulously, to listen to the accused and their defense counsel, and to witnesses, for and against. Freed from the influence of the irresponsible masses, judges must leave behind on the threshold of the courtroom any personal and party hatred and become nothing else but the sole impartial representative of justice and the law. And if they make a mistake, let it not be from malice, because of an unjustified prejudice or under pressure from the irresponsible masses. There are higher courts, and even a supreme court, which will correct mistakes.[22]

In drawing attention to the wisdom and sincerity of Prodanović's article, Milivoje Č. Marković, Vice-President of the Social Democratic Party and a member of the leadership of the "Napred" group, drew attention to the fact that many worthy judges were out of work, that is, in jobs which did not suit their qualifications, whereas judges' positions were filled by people who lacked appropriate qualifications.

> This is the result of the citizens' judgement based on the criterion of political affiliation or reliability. A very bad criterion. If a good judiciary is wanted the only standards are: conscientiousness, specialist training and ability for the job.[23]

2. Forms of Activity of the Opposition Parties

When reference has been made to the great difference in the means used by the Communist Party and the opposition parties in the post-war party system, it has also been stressed that the latter were, in fact, prevented from using their traditional, parliamentary ways of struggle. The crucial point here is that, as a rule, these parties were not permitted to revive their organization and to publish their own press, which is a necessary condition of party pluralism.

The fact that the party organizations could not be restored in the new conditions led to the non-communist parties existing more as a formality than a reality, their existence being chiefly *fictitious*. This is why Dragoljub Jovanović said:

> I am in favor of a Popular Front but of a Popular Front which will really be what it implies, and which will not be a toy, or a facade, or a smokescreen for one single party. I have full respect for that party, I am full of admiration for the sacrifices which its people have made, not only during the past four years of the armed struggle, but also during the whole of the past quarter of the century . . . . But, though I respect the Communist Party, not only ours but also throughout the entire world, I cannot reconcile myself to the idea that it alone has the right to exist. We, others, also have a fictitious existence, but that is like the life of flowers in a vase, like the life of a plant which has not roots, which is not allowed to start growing and to develop in a normal way.[24]

Thus, the old political parties retained their pre-war names and adopted programs and statutes by which they adapted themselves to the new reality; they had their leaders and organs, but not a developed party machine or party organization, with a network of local party committees. In renewing their work after the war, the parties were left without members, who had deserted them in the changing post-revolutionary conditions. They could not address the section of the membership which remained steadfast because the necessary means (money, the press, the unhindered possibility of party agitation and others) were not longer at their disposal. One contemporary historian succinctly described the existing situation when he said:

> The Popular Front had filled the entire political spectrum and there was no place in it to organize opposition forces or to present programs which were different from those adopted by the People's Front or at variance with the policies of the CPY.[25]

Only one party, the Croatian Republican Peasant Party, was able to restore some kind of network of district committees, because the Communist Party tried in this way to provoke a differentiation and to separate the largest possible number of its members from the former leadership. In the first years of its publication, the Party paper, *Slobodni dom,* contained information about internal party life (the restoration and founding of district party organizations on Croatian territory), whereas after the Second Congress of the Popular Front of Yugoslavia, on 26 September 1947, the branches in the districts were no longer mentioned in *Slobodni dom,* and the earlier column "From the Croatian Republican Peasant Party" was also discontinued. Subsequently, the paper carried reports about consultative meetings of party followers in some cities as well as about plenary sessions of the Party's representatives. In reply to a question from a foreign journalist, Franjo Gaži, the President of the Executive Committee of the Croatian Republican Peasant Party said in 1948 that in every district in Croatia where Croatian people lived, there was a district organization of the Party with its own presidium and committee, while the Party's Executive Committee, headed by a 70-member Presidium was in Zagreb.[26] It is evident from *Hrvatski glas,* the paper of the Croatian Republican Peasant Party Committee for Bosnia and Herzegovina, that the founding of the Party's district organization had started in Bosnia and Hercegovina. In contrast to this party, no other party succeeded in restoring its own party organization to the same extent; in its paper, the Republican Party did not even have a column or news relating to internal party life.

Not only were the old parties as such curbed, put out of action and reduced largely to their leaderships, but their activity too was widely restricted. Among the federal units, the parties existed in a developed form only on the territory of Serbia and Croatia. The very fact that political parties were barely able to exist in some regions of the new state while they were incapable of pursuing any activity in other areas, indicated that their life could not be a long one.

The absence of party pluralism was also officially explained in some of the federal units. By the nature of things the most interesting situation was in that federal unit where, even during the war, political parties waived their existence within the framework of a front organization (the Liberation Front of Slovenia) in favor of the leading role of the Communist Party of Slovenia. At the First Congress of the Popular Front of Yugoslavia, Josip Vidmar claimed that the First Congress of the Liberation Front of Slovenia had shown

> that in Slovenia there is no place for any other party, or for any other political organization, because there is only one all-people's movement in Slovenia and that is the Liberation Front of Slovenia. The invaluable merit for all this goes to the most progressive party that has ever existed in Slovenia, and that is the CPY. What it has achieved with its tireless education of us non-communists and with its tireless enlightenment of the masses in Slovenia, and which has been so clearly demonstrated at the First Congress in Ljubljana, is that the people have moved toward complete unity and will never again want any other kind of party in the future, but only the unified will of the people.[27]

A concomitant feature of the inability of the political parties to restore their organization was the absence of a party press. None of the remaining political parties, with two exceptions, was in a position to promote its views through the press or answer criticisms levelled at it. Of the two weeklies which were published over a relatively long period (*Republika* until

1956 and *Slobodni dom* until 1963), only the first demonstrated a certain degree of independence, whereas the second was the paper of a party which from the very beginning, served as a transmission belt of the Communist Party. In addition to *Slobodni dom,* the Croatian Republican Peasant Party Committee for Bosnia and Hercegovina published one more paper, *Hrvatski glas,* which was short-lived (12 issues); the cessation of its publication coincided with the abandoning of attempts also to restore this party organizations in Bosnia and Hercegovina.

The aforementioned weeklies were the organs of parties in the Popular Front. Only two of the parties outside the Front began publishing their own papers. Thus, *Narodni glas* emerged as the "organ of Croatian Peasant Politics," its publisher was Radić's widow Marija, and its editor-in-chief, Ivan Bernardić. The paper should have been independent but pursued a parallel course with *Slobodni dom,* the official organ of the Croatian Republican Peasant Party. Due to some of the contributions the first and only issue of the paper, which in fact had two impressions, was—banned.[28] The other party weekly which left a deep trace, in spite of only seven issues being printed and the last banned, was the paper of the Democratic Party, *Demokratija,* whose editor-in-chief was Milan Grol.

Besides these two papers not conected with the Popular Front, the paper *Novosti* began publication three times a week in Belgrade (only three issues appeared). In contrast to *Demokratija,* which was a party paper, *Novosti,* according to its own announcement, began publication as an independent newspaper, citing the fact that only one semi-official and independent newspaper, *Politika,* was published in Serbia, which meant that the independent press was in only one pair of hands, in other words, it was monopolized. Since monopolies were an "expression of unhealthy circumstances and had more harmful than useful consequences," *Novosti* appeared to fill a void in the Serbian press. For clarity's sake, it should be noted that a daily with the same title was published from 1923 to 1929 as an independent newspaper, whose proprietor was Jovan M. Jovanović, leader of the Agrarian Party. This connection with the Agrarian Party was also felt in the post-war *Novosti,* because the first issue recalled its background and because it also contained the statement by the Vice-President of the Agrarain Party about the resignation of this party from the Popular Front.[29] In addition, the editor-in-chief of the paper (Dušan Baranin) was also one of the Agrarian Party secretaries.

During their publication, the papers of parties outside the Popular Front, but also those in it, were confronted with a series of difficulties, one of which was crucial. The printing shops and paper production were nationalized after the war and were thus placed at the disposal of only one party, the ruling one, and its general political organization—the Popular Front. In addition to this basic but adequate method, there were other ways of fighting against the opposition parties and their papers: the refusal of the paper vendors' union to distribute them, demands by those who distributed the papers in the interior for fewer copies (though, judging by the readers' appeals to the editorial boards, the demand for the papers was increasing), the refusal of the typesetters' union to print opposition papers, physical attacks on paper vendors, and in one instance, even the burning of a paper. Papers which were published for a longer period (*Republika* and *Slobodni dom*) and which were subsidized also ceased to appear because of material and financial difficulties.[30]

Denied from the outset the possibility of fighting through its own press and organization, the main arena for the opposition's political struggle was parliament and parliamentary bodies. If one bears in mind that the majority of the opposition parties did not have their own press and that the ruling party held the monopoly of the information media, and that it was able to present or not, as it saw fit, the course of parliamentary debates and the arguments of the opposition, then it becomes clear that this area of opposition activity was also of limited value and scope. Nevertheless, seen from the present day perspective, when the events of which we are writing have become largely a matter of history, the post-war parliamentary debates represent one of the best sources of information concerning the character of the debates of that time about democracy and pluralism between the non-communist parties, which chiefly advocated the idea of political liberalism, and the ruling party, which defended the orthodox, Bolshevik concept, adapting it to its current tactics. As the parliamentary milieu made possible the most open presentation of these two concepts, the differences between them became the most evident there. This was all the more so because a number of the participants in the Assembly debates, conscious of the significane of the occasion, did not bow to passing tactical considerations; rather, as Dragoljub Jovanović once said, they spoke "not only for today, but a little for history and for the future as well."[31]

The most important debates were conducted in the Provisional Assembly, at its Presidium and in the Legislative Committee. The work of the Provisional Assembly and of its bodies, did not even last two full months. Yet all the most important political laws were passed in that short space of time. In addition to members of the bourgeois parties expounding their own views and critical objections regarding the proposal of individual laws, an opposition bloc ("an opposition outside the Front") also surfaced in the Assembly during this period. It consisted of 13 Democratic Party deputies who were joined from time to time by several representatives from other parties. Occasionally the opposition's proposals and attitudes had objections raised against them which could hardly have been described as imbued with the spirit of intolerance, but this group of deputies was able to present and explain its views.

Following the establishment of the Contituent Assembly, in the work of the Federal Assembly until the middle of 1947 the role of the opposition was undertaken by several deputies chiefly of the Peasant parties, among whom the most committed was Dragoljub Jovanović. From the time the Constituent Assembly had been convened, or rather from its transformation into a regular assembly, speeches by several opposition deputies (opposition within the Front) were often accompanied by attacks, threats and demands that they withdraw from the Assembly, as well as advice from the chairman that it was best for these deputies to submit to the unanimous will of the Assembly and to give up speaking.

The deteriorating conditions for action of the opposition parties and opposition activities of individual personalities from the ranks of these parties after the elections for the Constituent Assembly and the passing of the Constitution, can best be traced in the fate of Dragoljub Jovanović, who, in 1946 and 1947, was the central figure around whom a number of deputies from the peasant parties (the People's Peasant Party, the Croatian Republican Peasant Party and the Agrarian Party) had rallied. In July 1946, Dragoljub Jovanović, who was General Secretary of the People's Peasant Party, was stripped of his mandate as deputy of the People's Assembly of Serbia. By August 1946 the decision was taken at the Law Faculty in Belgrade to remove Jovanović, as honorary professor, from the University in Belgrade "because of unscientific and anti-people's statements in his lectures." He was expelled from his own party in October 1946, stripped of his mandate as deputy of the Federal Assembly in April

1947 and indicted before the Supreme Court of Serbia in October 1947. The measures taken against Dragoljub Jovanović represent mainly a re-action to his statements in the Assembly and to various other forms of public activity which are standard practice in systems of party pluralism.

Jovanović was stripped of his mandate as deputy of the People's Assembly of Serbia on 26 July 1946 on account of his "anti-people's atti-tude," as the explanation of the Mandates Committee stated. The Com-mittee's report charged Dragoljub Jovanović with a number of things.[32] Firstly, that he had slandered the Soviet Union by saying that it was interfering in the internal affairs of our country and helping one party. On the other hand, by declaring that a single party was in power in Yugo-slavia, he denied that the people were executing the power and he wanted to cast doubt on the character of this power before the rest of the world. These assessments of Jovanović's attitude related to his statements in the Constituent Committee. Lastly, the report of the Mandates Com-mittee of the People's Assembly of Serbia in connection with stripping Dragoljub Jovanović of his mandate as deputy, stressed that in his speech in the Federal Assembly on the proposed Law on Co-operatives (July 1946), he had attacked the highest state bodies, or more precisely, the Federal Assembly by claiming that with such a proposal "the Assembly had stabbed the peasants in the back."

When Dragoljub Jovanović was deprived of his mandate, Jaša Prodano-vić, who like Jovanović was also a deputy of both the Serbian and Federal Assembly, said that "he did not agree with the manner in which the pro-posal had been submitted and he declared that he would vote with his friends against it." Prodanović explained in greater detail his disagreement with the way Jovanović was deprived of his mandate in an article in *Republika.*[33] As in similar previous delicate circumstances, Prodanović again recalled the fact that in fateful and important moments a sensible politician was required to make concessions but not to abandon his basic principles as well, to haggle on questions of public morals and to approve of actions contrary to the Constitution and the law. Recalling his struggle in Yugoslavia between the two wars against various unconstitutional actions, from the expulsion of the correctly elected deputies of the muni-cipal communist administration in Belgrade and the denial of mandates suffered by Communist deputies after the unsuccessful assassination at-tempt on King Alexander, he stressed that today he could likewise not act differently, that he could not behave in one way when he was in opposition and in another way when he was in government. The proposal to strip Dragoljub Jovanović of his mandate was, according to Prodanović, contrary to Article 7 of the Constitution, according to which the people's representatives were responsible to their electorate, while the law would lay down in which cases, in what conditions and in what manner, the electorate could recall their representatives even before the expiry of the period for which they had been elected. At the time when Jovanović's mandate was taken away on the basis of the Standing Order of the Assembly of Serbia, which, to make matters worse, was passed before the Federal Constitution came into effect. Prodanović also pointed out that Dragoljub Jovanović's case could not have been covered by any of the provisions of the Serbian Assembly's Standing Order because the Order provided for a deputy losing his mandate only in the event of his death, if he was unjustifiably or constantly absent from Assembly sessions, if he was convicted of a dishonorable act and if by his conduct in the Assembly and outside it he damaged the reputation of a people's deputy. Finally, Jaša Prodanović was of the opinion that the proposal of the Mandates Committee had been put before the Assembly in such a way as to make it impossible for the deputies to consider everything and make a decision.

In August 1946, the Main Committee and the First Extraordinary Congress of the People's Peasant Party expelled Dragoljub Jovanović, the General Secretary and Radomir Todorović, President of the Party, from its ranks.[34] At the Congress, which was attended by 545 delegates, it was stressed that Dragoljub Jovanović had also sabotaged the struggle against the occupying forces during the war and that he had been in collusion with the people's enemies. It was also claimed that together with those of his ilk he had continued this work after the war as well, at first perfidiously and covertly, and then, from December 1945 in the discussion about the draft Constitution, overtly. Ninko Petrović, the then Secretary of the Executive Committee of the People's Peasant Party, particularly objected to Jovanović criticizing the Soviet Union's policy toward Yugoslavia, emphasizing that Jovanović's "shameless attack on the Soviet Union —on Mother Russia, on that which is held most dear and most sacred by very man of ours, has provoked scorn and disgust in every patriot."

By making such an appraisal of Dragoljub Jovanović's activity during the war, the delegates at the People's Peasant Party Congress virtually invalidated the earlier declarations of the leading CPY officials who had spoken with sympathy about the participation by Jovanović and his Party in the political life of the new Yugoslavia. In an extensive editorial in *Borba* at the end of February 1945, one of the leading Communists' officials, Milentije Popović had hailed the decision of the Main Committee of the People's Peasant Party to joint the United Popular Liberation Front of Serbia,[35] while at the first Congress of the Popular Front of Yugoslavia, Edvard Kardelj, in stressing that the Popular Front was not a homogeneous organization, had particularly emphasized the role of the peasant parties, "which have expelled the reactionary leaderships from their midst and placed themselves side by side with the working class and all progressive forces in the struggle for democracy and national freedom."[36] At this Congress, Jovanović, like Kardelj, also submitted a report, and thus he too represented the progressive and accepted elements in the peasant parties. This confidence in Jovanović was further underlined by the fact that he with Communist Moša Pijade was entrusted with preparing the draft of the election proclamation of the Popular Front, with speaking at a number of election meetings throughout Serbia, with giving statements to the foreign press about the forthcoming elections, and so on. At that time, Dragoljub Jovanović's conduct during the war was well known to his future opponents in his own Party and in the Communist Party, which is evident from the negotiations conducted with him concerning the admission of the People's Peasant Party to the Front. To put it another way, Dragoljub Jovanović's behavior before, during and after the war had been accepted without any criticism as long as he abstained from criticizing the Communist Party, that is, as long as he supported its policies.

Dragoljub Jovanović explained his subsequent criticism and opposition to the Popular Front, and his previous abstention from criticism by the temporary nature of all Popular Front formations. Jovanović maintained that the Popular Front was "a need" and "a necessity," and not an "eternal category." Popular fronts were only a "temporary combination," whereas parties outlived the Front. That is why Jovanović said that "if you want to have strength in the Front you must have strength in the party." At a meeting of People's Peasant Party followers in May 1946, Jovanović said:

It is a common phenomenon in the world for Front organizations to be dissolved in all countries. The Front is something which exists in war-time. As soon as the war ends, the Front also ends. As soon as peace comes, the Front should also be disbanded. The danger from fascism is past. Fascism has been defeated and now each man should go to his own side. The Front is no longer necessary, it has performed its role.[37]

In the summing-up speech at his trial, Jovanović explained his opposition activity by saying that the new socio-political order had been consolidated and that it could now derive benefit from constructive criticism but suffer damage from obsequious flattery:

When I saw that we had gained the republic and that we had placed this community on a firm footing, I thought that now we might criticize a little, that we might find fault a little and improve things a little, because the child was big enough to take a few knocks.[38]

Another question, and it could be the subject of a separate critical analysis, is whether some of Dragoljub Jovanović's critical objections, about the excessive bureaucratization and centralization of social and political life, about excessive statism, some of his objections in the field of agrarain policy and the concept of co-operatives, as well as his assessments of foreign policy (with regard to the Soviet Union), were later accepted by the Communist Party, and if so, to what extent.

Dragoljub Jovanović was charged in particular with attempting to rally a group of dissatisfied deputies from the peasant parties and attempting to form a Peasant Bloc. In the course of the attacks on Dragoljub Jovanović and during his trial the reason why rallying dissidents from several permitted parties should not be allowed was never given. At Jovanović's trial this matter took on another dimension because the other accused, Franjo Gaži, who, along with Jovanović was supposed to have been in the leadership of the Peasant Bloc, maintained that the idea of the Peasant Bloc had originated with two "foreign agents," Stephen Clissold and Hugh Seton-Watson, with whom he was in collusion.[39]

Dragoljub Jovanović's ideas about the Peasant Bloc basically originated from the ideas about the relationship between the working class and the peasantry, between the peasant and workers' parties, which he put forward in 1940 at the time when the People's Peasant Party was formed. Apart from some minor tactical concessions, Jovanović did not essentially disown these ideas and the leadership of the Communist Party was unable to criticize him for deviating from the conditions under which he joined the Popular Front. In his pamphlet on socialism and the peasantry, published in 1941 to serve as a kind of rationale of the program of the newly-founded People's Peasant Party, Jovanović advocated the concept that like the bourgeoisie and the working class before, the peasantry in Yugoslavia was also today demanding its own separate movement, but in contrast to the basic orientation of the Agrarian Party, that movement had to be left-wing and socialist. The peasants, according to Jovanović:

> want to co-operate with the urban workers, but as their equals and not as their tool. The best guarantee of equality is a separately organized movement which runs parallel with the workers' movement and, like it, aspires toward socialism.[40]

Although the peasantry did not refuse a priori co-operation with progressive people and groups of the bourgeoisie, it believed that its true and natural allies were the workers. While it could co-operate with bourgeois parties from time to time, the peasantry considered the workers' parties to be its lasting allies:

> Agrarian socialists do not accept that the cities or the urban workers have a monopoly over the revolutionary spirit, nor do they cede their leading role in great events to the advantage of anybody. They do not seek a monopoly or a leading role for themselves at any price. The locomotive of the future, they believe, cannot run along a single track: neither along the peasant track alone nor the workers'. Two tracks are necessary, the peasants' and the workers'. On a bend events could make almost the whole weight of the locomotive fall on the peasant track. When such a case occurred in Bulgaria, the peasants were left on their own, without the workers' help. The opposite happened in Russia. The peasants extended the workers loyal and fraternal help.[41]

Even before the war, Dragoljub Jovanović had been pointing out Lenin's contribution to the interpretation of the peasant question. In contrast to some bourgeois right-wing politicians (members of the Yugoslav Radical Community) who after the war underwent a conversion overnight and emerged as members of the new ruling party, Jovanović was in fact closer to some ideas of "Marxism-Leninism" before the war. He stressed that Lenin's merit consisted in having introduced the peasants, in addition to workers, into the revolutionary struggle. Jovanović wrote, Lenin

> did not abandon the Marxist dogma about the revolutionary spirit of the proletariat, but he rid himself of the social democratic scorn for peasants. When one recalls the conditions in Russia, the situation of Russian *muzhiks,* their lack of culture and their religious narrow-mindedness, one can understand that Lenin had to give some kind of leadership to these peasants, just as he placed at the head of the working class a firmly organized, strictly disciplined party as its vanguard.[42]

Let us, however, return to the conditions in which the opposition parties operated. A group of opposition deputies (first Front and later *extra*-Front opposition) had acted in several ways in the Assembly. It criticized the program and policies of the hegemonic organization and attempted to oppose it with its own program and measures. This was unacceptable to the hegemonic party because in its view, the permitted party pluralism should have been manifested in support for the Popular Front program, backed by the hegemonic party, instead of challenging it. In the liberal concept, an attack by one party on the program of another is a natural and legitimate state of affairs in systems with an opposition. At the beginning of the second half of the last century when an institutionalized opposition was emerging in Great Britain the slogan was still valid that the task of the opposition was more to criticize the government's program than to present its own positive program—to oppose everything and to propose nothing. By the way in which the activity of the opposition deputies in the Assembly was appraised in our country, one would gain the impression that, as far as the hegemonic party was concerned, the sole task of the opposition was to support all the proposals of the government, which, by the way, a number of opposition parties' deputies did do with much zeal. In his speech on Belgrade Radio on 12 September 1945, J. B. Tito stressed that there were certain mistakes in the work of the Popular Front which were insignificant in relation to what had been done, and that the leaders of the Popular Front did not hush up these mistakes. In contrast to the Popular Front, the opposition could hardly wait for such mistakes to arise in order to use them for their own dark aims. These dark aims were the struggle against the program of the Popular Front. To put it more precisely, the objection to the *extra*-Front opposition was that in the Assembly "they have not taken a positive attitude to any of the questions on which they have essentially had no criticism to make," while at the same time they had constantly pointed out mistakes in the work of the people's authorities, mistakes in the work of the Popular Front, they had criticized its program and had constantly demanded "some freedom from fear, some democracy of their type, which is no democracy at all, and some rights for those who do not deserve to have them."[43] Criticizing the Democratic Party program, Vladislav Ribnikar wrote in a similar vein in *Politika;* in his view, the Democratic Party program was not calculated to attract adherents but to rally opponents of the Front.[44]

In criticizing some decisions of the legislative proposals of the majority, opposition deputies resorted to yet another method of struggle during the work of the Provisional Assembly. On several occasions they submitted their own proposals which, bearing in mind the balance of forces in the Assembly, were not able to bear any immediate fruit. However, the submission of such proposals was not aimed only at putting the opposition viewpoint against the government's program and policies, but also at showing up the discrepancy between "election laws and electoral reality."[45] Thus, Dragić Joksimović, a Democratic Party deputy, proposed several laws to the Assembly. In advancing his reasons for his proposal of a law concerning freedom against fear, Joksimović referred to the Tito-Šubašić Agreement of 1 November 1944, which bound the new government to issue a declaration which would emphasize and guarantee freedom from fear. In the declaration this freedom was not even mentioned nor had a law been proposed which would settle this question, and thus Joksimović proposed the adoption of such a law, being guided in his own words, by reports from the interior of the country indicating that this law represented a "pressing and basic need." The proposed law described as a criminal act any action by organs of people's power, army and institutions of Democratic Federal Yugoslavia, which by its nature intimidates people or contains a threat to citizens so that they either do or do not do something against their will,

while a more serious form of this offence was to carry out such an act from the day when elections were called to the day when they were held. The proposal, which was very brief, also laid down the court procedure and sanctions for this criminal act.[46]

Finally, the last method left to opposition parties deprived of party organization and party press, and consequently faced with an impossible position in the elections for the Constituent Assembly, was *abstention.* In their report on 20 September 1945, the united opposition parties (Democrats, Radicals and Agrarians) decided not to put up their own electoral list. The Socialist and Social Democratic parties, as well as opposition groups in Zagreb and Ljubljana, also took up this stand.[47]

The opposition parties justified their decision to abstain by their unequal position in relation to the hegemonic party, an inequality which according to them was manifested in several ways.

Firstly, they pointed to the arbitrary manner in which a number of people had been deprived of their electoral rights and to pressures exerted during the elections. The actual number of those struck off the electoral register was small and did not exceed 3.5% in any of the federal units, and in most of them it was considerably lower. More important than the number of those taken off the electoral register was the manner and atmosphere in which some people lost their right to vote, and in this an element of pressure was also exerted on those who had not been deprived of their electoral rights. Speaking about too many people being struck off the electoral register in some areas, an observer of the period explained this as a relic of the war and the result of inexperience in the machinery and of its revolutionary purism. He also says that in some areas a large number of individuals were deprived of their right to vote at the beginning of the election campaign but that this right was later restored to them: in some villages in Podravina and Slavonia the percentage of those struck off the register at the beginning of the election campaign reached 30-40%.[48]

The second objection of the opposition parties related to the fact that elections were carried out by the organs of people's power which had been

chosen in an irregular manner and at different times, and who naturally
had not been elected in the same way in which elections for the Constituent Assembly had to be carried out—on the basis of a contest between
several political parties. Moreover, the existing organs of people's power
were under the control of a single party. Having this very point in mind
when explaining the grounds for his draft laws on elections of people's
power organs, Dragić Jaksimović, a Democratic Party deputy in the Provisional People's Assembly, stressed that "after sixteen years of irregular
political life, the political revival of our country should begin from below,
i.e. first there should be elections for local people's committees, for district people's committees and for regional people's committees, and only
then should the election of deputies for the Constituent Assembly take
place."[49]

Thirdly, in the opinion of the opposition parties the electoral system
of nominating candidates and distributing seats was very complicated and
gave all the advantages of proportional representation to the federal lists,
while on the other hand, by making it difficult to prepare such lists, it
ensured the actual monopoly of the Communist Party which had at its
disposal the whole state machinery to prepare the lists. Due to this, the
opposition parties pointed to the similarity between the national lists
of the electoral practice in pre-war Yugoslavia from 1931 to 1941, and
the federal list for the election of deputies for the Constituent Assembly.[50]
Those who disputed the pertinence of the opposition's criticisms rightly
pointed out that these two electoral systems were not identical,[51] but
the fact remained that, as in the pre-war period, the opposition parties
were faced with major difficulties if they planned to put forward a list
for the whole country. Though according to the electoral law of 1945,
nominations were not made only on the basis of the federal list (there
were also independent district lists and district lists within the framework
of the federal list), and though the federal list did not, as before the war,
have to have one candidate for each electoral district but only half of the
total number of district lists was required for the federal list, the circumstances in which the elections were conducted, the circumstances in which
there was no possibility of an organized restoration of parties, such conditions for the opposition parties were difficult and insurmountable. This
was all the more the case since all the provinces, the future federal units,
were inaccessible to the opposition parties.

Abstention which represented the old method of struggle by the democratic political parties in pre-war Yugoslavia, took two forms—the refusal of political parties to participate in the work of the Assembly because of the circumstances under which the elections had taken place, and the refusal of parties to participate in elections, as was the case in the elections of 1931 when there was only one list for the whole country.

After the decision on abstention, attacks on the opposition parties in the press and in electoral speeches became even more severe and in addition yet another name for the opposition began to circulate—*reaction*. From then on the opposition was referred to as reaction (in the cities and in the speeches by Milovan Djilas, Moša Pijade and others). Dragoljub Jovanović also joined in these attacks but in a different manner. In contrast to Djilas[52] and others who equated the opposition with the forces of reaction, Jovanović stressed the difference between these two concepts, attempting to prepare the ground for future opposition activity by his own party in the Popular Front. Dragoljub Jovanović wrote that in comparison to former strong socialist opposition in Serbia before the First World War, headed by Kaclerović, Lapčević, Tucović and Popović, the opposition of his time was weak, old and lacking in self-confidence, and thus only abstention was appropriate.

> Opposition is a matter of great import. No-one knows that better than those who have spent their whole life struggling for a new world. But there can be no opposition without faith, without confidence in one's own ideas, without readiness to suffer and to die. The people who are today playing at being the opposition do not have a single one of those qualities. . . . What we have before us is not an *opposition* which brings something new but *reaction*, a winter which is wresting itself from the grip of young spring. Opposition drives the wheel of history; reaction stops it. Opposition is borne by young people; reaction come from the old, it appeals to those worse than itself and it serves its born enemies.[53]

After this statement by the opposition leader, the law on the election of people's deputies for the Constituent Assembly was supplemented before the actual elections. The supplement provided for the introduction of a ballot box which was not marked with the name of a candidate or the electoral list ("the box without a list"), in order that all those who did not wish to vote for any district candidate on any list, that is, who did not wish to vote for any of the official national lists, were able to put their ballot all into this box. The proposal to introduce a box without a list was interpreted by the parties in the Popular Front in two ways.

We shall deal first with the interpretation by Jaša Prodanović, who, in fact, proposed the introduction of a box without a list, by proceeding from the need to preserve the secret vote in circumstances when only one group was contesting the election and when the opposition was calling for abstention. Prodanović's opinion was shared by several more deputies of the opposition parties. Prodanović was guided in his proposal by the electoral law of Serbia, dating from 1890, or more precisely by one of its amendments of 14 June 1910. This law provided for a box without a list in the event of there being only one list put forward for a district. Should this list receive an equal or less number of votes then the box without a list, the elections were repeated and if there was only one list again at the repeated elections, the relevant court even without the elections being held, gave the mandate to candidates from the registered list and announced their election. In a nutshell, the point of departure was the assumption that the existence of only one list might be the result of some oversight or mistake, and in the event of there being no change in this respect at the repeated elections, candidates from the registered list were given the mandate though the elections were not actually held, because once again the law proceeded from the assumption that there were no elections where there was only one list.[55]

The provision for a box without a list in the electoral law of Serbia corresponded to the traditional liberal concept that there were no elections when there was only one candidate ("a one-horse race"). Jaša Prodanović, however, advocated the box without a list with one deviation from its original concept: in his view, the box without a list should make the secrecy of voting possible.

Interpretations, however, by Communist Party representatives in the Government and in the Assembly, starting with Edvard Kardelj, who as Minister for the Contituent Assembly, formally submitted this proposed supplement to the law to the Presidium of the Provisional Assembly, were different. According to Moša Pijade, the box without a list should have prevented the opposition from claiming the votes of those who, for objective reasons, did not take part in the elections, that is, to prevent:

all manuevers by the opposition which would also count as its supporters people on their deathbeds, the sick or people temporarily
absent from their homes, and all those who, for whatever reasons
would not vote. In this way we shall have a clear-cut situation because the opposition will not be able to count as its own supporters
all those who did not vote, but only on those who dropped their
ballot ball into that box.[56]

The opposition also responded to the introduction of the box without
a list by calling on its followers not to vote in the elections, while "individuals who are not in a position to act otherwise, can use the box without
a list."[57]

Commenting on the supplement to the electoral law, *Politika* went a
step further than the official interpretation, which held that they who
abstained were objectively prevented from voting, and it drew the conclusion, with regard to the provision of the box without a list, *that those
who did not vote in fact also voted for the list of the Popular Front:*

From a strictly formal and legal point of view, the people who do
not go to the polls do, in fact, vote because they have made it possible in advance for the candidates for whom the majority voted to
be elected. Their abstention from voting implies consent to the
election. From this viewpoint there is no need to insist that each
voter should use his right to vote.[58]

Finally, one should also recall that some of the official assessments of
the box without a list and of the voters who used it, made the elections
superfluous in the traditional sense. Thus, for instance, in replying to
questions put to him by the editors of *Slovenski poročevalec* and *Ljud-
ska pravica*, Boris Kidrič explained the nature of the box without a list
in this way:

The person who casts his ballot ball in the third box is against the
democratic and national achievements of the liberation struggle, he
is against the equality of the Yugoslav peoples, he is against the
agrarian reform, against people's democracy, against the Republic
and so on, in a nutshell, he is in favor of the old Yugoslav system of

national oppression, foreign interference in our sovereign and state affairs, unscrupulous social exploitation, fascist dictatorships and royal tyranny.[59]

All the differences between the traditional liberal concept of democracy, advocated in Yugoslavia after the war not only by the bourgeois parties but also by the present peasant and workers' parties, and the opposing Bolshevik concept have led to a different understanding of the meaning and purpose of elections. From the Bolshevik viewpoint, elections are a fiction; instead of enlightening consciousness they confuse it. By appropriate education the Communist Party should stimulate and strengthen the revolutionary conviction of the masses, and no elections of any kind can be a substitute for this kind of party activity. The true meaning of elections in the post-revolutionary period lies in their unanimity.

The elections, however, did not have this character in all localities. The results of the elections above all bear witness to differences in the way the system of party pluralism had taken root in individual federal units. In all federal units the turn-out at the elections was between 92 and 98% of the electorate, but in Serbia it was around 77%. Figures also show that the largest number of votes cast in the box without a list was in localities which were economically, politically and culturally more developed and in which the parliamentary tradition had deeper roots. In addition to Serbia, these areas were Vojvodina, Slovenia and Croatia (see Table 2).

If the percentage of those who voted for the Popular Front lists is calculated in relation to the total number of voters, and not in relation to the number of votes cast, as was done in accordance with the supplements to the electoral law on the introduction of the box without a list, then that percentage in Serbia was 68.28% (Federal Chamber) and 66.96% (Chamber of Nationalities), while in Slovenia and Vojvodina, it was below 80% (see Table 3). In some constituencies in Serbia, the total number of those who voted for the Popular Front in relation to the total number of voters was between 50 and 60%, while in individual electoral districts it was less than 50%. Lastly, one should also bear in mind the fact that there were candidates of more parties on the Popular Front list and thus people (mostly communists) were often elected who had received less than 50% of the votes of those who had gone to the polls.[60]

TABLE 2

Results of the Elections for the Constituent Assembly

Federal unit or autonomous province	Federal Chamber			Chamber of Nationalities		
	votes cast	for PF* list	for BWL*	votes cast	for PF* list	for BWL*
	(percentage)			(percentage)		
Serbia	77.16	88.59	11.41	76.70	87.31	12.69
Vojvodina	92.20	85.40	14.60	92.12	80.65	19.35
Kosovo and Metohija	97.68	96.78	3.22	97.31	95.36	10.75
Croatia	91.77	91.52	8.48	91.66	89.25	10.75
Slovenia	95.29	83.25	16.75	95.29	82.23	17.77
Bosnia and Hercegovina	92.53	95.21	4.79	92.04	94.17	5.83
Macedonia	96.82	95.85	4.15	96.75	95.87	4.13
Montenegro	96.13	97.93	2.07	96.17	97.35	2.65

(*PF = Popular Front; *BWL = Box without a list)

Lastly, it should also be placed on record that all those who regarded the meaning of elections as an expression of unanimity in post-war Yugoslavia were speaking as faithful champions of a revolutionary viewpoint of the nature of elections, which Lukács explained as follows:

> What is at the basis of the entire technique of elections, even when it is not conscious, is the desire to attract followers, which bears within itself the danger of separating the convictions from the action, thereby arousing a tendency toward petty-bourgeois views and opportunism. The educational purpose of the Communist Party, its influence on the groups of the proletariat who are unclear and wavering,

TABLE 3

**Number of Votes Cast for the List of the Popular Front in Relation
to the Total Number of Voters**

Federal unit or autonomous province	Federal Chamber	Chamber of Nationalities
Serbia	68.28	66.96
Vojvodina	78.73	77.98
Kosovo and Metohija	94.53	92.79
Croatia	83.99	81.80
Slovenia	79.32	78.35
Bosnia and Hercegovina	88.09	86.67
Macedonia	92.80	92.75
Montenegro	94.14	93.61

can only be truly fruitful if through the clear teaching of revolutionary activity, it strengthens the revolutionary convictions of those groups. In line with its bourgeois nature, any election campaign travels in a totally opposite direction which can be truly overcome only in exceptionally rare cases.[61]

With this, the tensions between the liberal and Bolshevik ideas and movements in Yugoslavia reached their peak. The circle was closed. It was a meeting of two worlds, a meeting between people who were unable to understand each other and who could not convince each other of the superiority of their views. Only the later political development of Yugoslavia would gradually show that in the political thought of liberalism there is a democratic core, the validity of wich is universal and the rejection of which represents a threat to freedom.

CHAPTER IV

IMPORTANT CONTROVERSIES IN CONFLICTS BETWEEN THE COMMUNIST PARTY AND THE OPPOSITION PARTIES

In 1945 and 1946 the subject of the dispute between the individual parties was not only the party and political system, which amounted to the question of power, but also a number of other issues, from intra-national relations, the recognition of individual nations (for example, Montenegrin nation), the constituting of individual federal units and their territorial limits (the question of Sandžak) to the law on the electoral lists and the electoral system for the distribution of deputies' seats. In this section we shall examine the disputes in the Assembly concerning the position and role of the judiciary, basic freedoms and rights and the rule of law, as well as the protection of the inviolability of the person in the field of criminal law.

1. Independence of the Judiciary

One of the best indicators of the real nature of a given political system is the way in which justice is dispensed and the institutional position which the judiciary occupies. From the very beginning of new Yugoslavia, this was a subject of far-reaching controversy which affected the very essense of the judiciary—the question of its independence and impartiality.

In fact, these questions had been raised even during the war but they were openly discussed only when the battles for the liberation ended. The draft law on the rights of citizens in military courts, submitted to the Presidium of the DFJ Provisional People's Assembly on 9 September 1945 by the deputy Dragić M. Joksimović, eloquently testifed to this. The aim of this proposal was to make it possible for convicted persons, their lawyers and closest relatives to see the documents listing the charges and receive the relevant copy of the verdict by military courts. In the proposer's opinion, the law had to guarantee this right of the convicted person, since they had been deprived of it. Dragić Joksimović said:

> It is well-known that the position of the accused persons before military courts has been very difficult: the trial held in camera, the indictment only read during the proceedings, access forbidden to lawyers, the verdicts not handed out, no right of appeal—in a nutshell, the right of defence has been restricted and limited. Acting in accordance with the regulations of the law on granting amnesty or pardon, the convicted persons, either personally or through their relatives, have asked for copies of verdicts in order to facilitate the wording of the appeal for amnesty or pardon, but they have been regularly denied this request.[1]

It should be said immediately that military courts handled cases not only during the war but also afterwards. It is surprising, therefore, that their proceedings were so compressed and without the customary guarantees of the rights of the accused to the professional help of a defense counsel in court. Even less understandable is the fact that the cases legally conducted in military courts were kept secret from the parties concerned and their relatives and that a special law was needed in order to make court documents freely accessible.

In fact, these objections were not only levelled at the military courts but also at the regular courts. Thus, when the draft law on the election of people's deputies to the Constituent Assembly was discussed in the Assembly, Tripko Žugić pointed out that the courts, right up to the top, as well as all the other authorities, were politically exclusive.[2] Immediately an interesting discussion developed concerning the nature of the new post-war judiciary and the ends it should serve. This took place at the time when the law on the organization of the people's courts was passed (DFJ Služ-beni List, 67/45). A particularly contentious question was whether judges should have suitable legal training, that is, whether they should be gradu-ates of a law faculty. This law had envisaged that, as well as being asses-sors (members of the jury), laymen without any professional training could also be permanent judges (Article 17). This should, it seems, even have been the rule rather than an exception. Miloš Žanko, Frane Frol, Miloš Minić, Vladimir Simić and Edvard Kardelj spoke on behalf of the Assembly majority in favor of such a ruling.

Miloš Žanko assured the deputies "that the proposal for qualified judges would come into conflict with the general principles of the new people's power."[3]

> To limit the calling of judges to lawyers would in our conditions mean turning that social public function into a professional calling and excluding from the judiciary precisely those fundamental moral qualifications and qualities which a people's judge ought to have.[4]

In electing judges, therefore, priority should be given to moral and not professional qualifications. In this, laymen, as men of the people, had priority over lawyers, who were, of course, not excluded, "but in our view," Žanko said, "it would not be right were they to have the mono-poly in the judge's profession."[5]

The real meaning of these *moral* qualifications, which candidates for judges should have, was best explained by Miloš Minić. He revealed right away that what was at stake was not moral, but *political* suitability, by which he meant *loyalty* to the current policy of the ruling party. "The demand for judges to be lawyers," Minić said, "originates from the con-cept of taking the line of least resistance, of employing judges, who can better understand the law, instead of taking the other line which is much more correct, that of ensuring a loyal cadre of people for our people's courts."[6] According to Miloš Minić, lawyers could, of course, be judges but only on condition that they be "infinitely loyal." Therefore, in choos-ing between uneducated but loyal laymen and trained lawyers who were not loyal, the former had to be given absolute priority. Minić said:

> All of us would like our judges to have legal training, to know legal science, but if we do not have enough trained lawyers who are at

the same time infinitely loyal to the people and the achievements
of the national liberation struggle, then it is better that, because they
do not fulfill all the necessary conditions, laymen be elected to our
courts where there are no professionals. . . .[7]

Of particular interest are the real reasons which Miloš Minić had in
mind when he questioned the loyalty of most lawyers and their suitability
as judges. In his words:

> . . . were the attitude to be taken that only lawyers should be elect-
> ed to be permanent judges then, by consistently applying this atti-
> tude, the old judicial machinery would be kept alive—the only dif-
> ference being that the old judges would be shuffled around. The
> old judicial system would be kept alive which, as we all know full
> well, was, with very few exceptions, corrupt, spineless, separated
> from the people, totally subordinate to the influence of the rulers.[8]

If these words were to be taken literally, it would seem that Miloš Minić
was in favor of the true *independence* of judges in relation to *whoever* was
in power, including the new post-war rulers. However, this is only the first
superficial and basically erroneous impression. Because only the day before, Miloš Minić had reproached the lawyers, above all the judges in Belgrade, for still not accepting the achievements of the new people's power.

> The majority of our lawyers, inasmuch as they are not reactionary
> elements, and there are also some of those, without doubt represent
> a conservative element. . . . The Belgrade courts, which almost
> without exception are staffed by lawyers, and often by judges of
> long-standing, are too lenient toward the enemies of the people of
> all hues. At a time when our peoples are making great efforts to
> repair what the occupying forces together with the traitors have
> destroyed, the Belgrade courts are not sufficiently alert in the strug-
> gle against speculators who are great enemies of the people. The
> sentences pronounced by the courts on them are so mild as to vir-
> tually encourage speculators, in fact they do not prevent and root
> out this evil. . . . People guilty of such serious crimes are sentenced
> by our courts only to several months or a year in prison.[9]

Thus Miloš Minić understood the independence of the judiciary differently. According to him, judges should be independent only with regard to the old pre-war rulers, and inasmuch as they were not always so, then it could be said of them that they were spineless and under the influence of the rulers. Yet, insofar as these same judges under the *new* authorities continued to adjudicate according to their own conscience and their own appraisal of the gravity of an offense, and on the basis of this appraisal pronounced sentences which *others* considered too mild, then, in Miloš Minić's view, this was not a sign of their independence but of their conservatism.

In contrast to such statements by representatives of the Assembly majority, the representatives of the minority resolutely defended the independence of the judiciary and its role in ensuring personal security and the protection of human freedoms and rights. Tripko Žugić said:

> Woe betide the country where the judiciary is not up to par. You can have a bad police and a harsh regime in a country, but if you have courts which are up to par, then you also have security of life, honor and property. If you do not have courts—you have nothing.[10]

And this could happen if courts lacked both moral and professional qualifications. "If we have a court entirely staffed by laymen, which not only cannot apply rules and legal provisions but cannot grasp the meaning of legislative provisions either then we know where this leads to."[11]

In a similar vein, Ilija Stojanović also stressed that thorough professional knowledge on the part of judges was a necessary condition for the correct discharge of judicial duties.

> Our view has been that the foundation of any state system is a well-organized judiciary, or as the old proverb has it: 'Justice is what makes the country and the cities tick.' To judge is not easy. To judge is difficult. There is no doubt that a judge must also have strong moral qualification, but he must also have a certain solid knowledge of things, precisely in view of the gravity of the questions.[12]

In addition, Ilija Stojanović disputed Žanko's claim that by introducing professional training as a necessary condition for selecting a judge, lawyers would have a monopoly in trials, since with the application of the principle of collective opinion in court proceedings the judges' bench, in addition to the permanent judge, was also made up of two lay assessors who took an equal part in the trial.

> Furthermore, it was said a little while ago, that it is not right for the legal profession, for lawyers, to have a monopoly in court proceedings because they cannot have it anyway. If we understand correctly that the three-man collegium is made up of three judges who will participate with equal right in the court proceedings, then in order that this be so the assessor himself cannot be an ordinary citizen but must be a real judge, that is, someone who will assist the judges. One could not, therefore, speak about a monopoly when it is known that one of the people would be a qualified lawyer, and the other two from the people, also elected by the people just as the one who is a qualified lawyer.[13]

This dispute between the majority and minority in the Assembly in practical terms amounted to the question of whether permanent judges should have professional legal training, or whether the duty of the permanent judge could also be discharged by untrained but politically suitable and loyal laymen. This is a very old dispute which had been thoroughly discussed and resolved several times. Should we, let us say, give preference to the idea and practice of the rule of law, which restricts the arbitrariness of authorities, then we have to accept the premise which calls for appropriate knowledge of the law and training in judgment in individual cases. This was stated by Sir Edward Coke, Chief Justice of the Court of Common Pleas in England, when he disputed the right of the king to pass judgement himself in any case. On that occasion, James I, on the advice of Bancroft, the Archbishop of Canterbury, stressed his right also to pass judgement in any case since he considered the judges to be only his plenipotentiaries whose powers he could revoke at any time. When Coke pointed out that only courts could pass judgement according to the law and custom of the country, the king said that he thought that the law was founded upon reason and that he and others had reason as well as the judges. Coke, however, replied that causes which concern the life, or inheritance, or goods or fortunes of his subjects are not to be decided by *natural reason,* which all men possessed, but by *artificial reason,* and judgement of law, which law is an act requiring long study and experience. Hence, reason is required to solve individual legal disputes, but not the natural reason of any man; rather the acquired perfection of reason which is developed by long study, examination and experience. Moreover, not even the king is above the law, above that reason brought to perfection, as Henry de Bracton said, the king is not under the man but under God and law (". . . Rex non debet esse sub homine, sed sub Deo at lege.")[14] It was precisely this fruitful idea that found in the law the means to restrict the arbitrariness of political power.

In 1945, a great majority of the deputies in the Provisional People's Assembly were not inclined to accept the conviction that this kind of "acquired perfection of reason" was necessary to adjudicate in individual cases, but maintained that ordinary reason without any kind of legal knowledge and experience was sufficient for the profession of a judge. Vladimir Simić went even further when he assured the deputies that he believed: ". . . in the people when it is a question of trial and of sentencing, when the people judge freely, not basing the verdicts on written law."[15] In a similar manner, Frane Frol rejected objections that permanent lay judges could not cope when resolving complex civil lawsuits. Frol said:

> Were we to go back to the old complicated regulations which manifested all the contradictions of yesterday, then that viewpoint could also be justified to a certain degree, because those contradictions and that complexity intentionally served the interests of the minority which had passed such regulations. But today, when the laws in force are fully comprehensible, both in their ideas and style, to the broad popular masses, those objections are unfounded. If people's justice is wanted—and that is the only real justice—then the just man who understands the aspirations of the people will apply it, and it is of no crucial importance whether he is an expert or not.[16]

Setting such criteria for the election of permanent judges and limiting the period for which they were elected to three or five years, led in practice to the loss of their independence. This subordinate position of the judiciary was justified, among other things, by the need to introduce unity of power. Thus Frane Frol explained that one could not set aside the judicial function as a separate power because ". . . the people's power is united and indivisible and is always vested in the people, and thus the judicial function too is always tied to the source of universal power, to the people."[17] This was the view which was also applied in a similar manner in Soviet Russia after the October Revolution. A peculiarity of the post-revolutionary system in Russia was also, among other things, the fact that any value of judicial independence was hastily rejected in the name of the supremacy of this system over the "mistaken" theory of the separation of power.

The question which arises is why it was necessary to abolish the independence of the judiciary when it is well known that this independence does not mean arbitrariness as well since the judges, when meting out justice, are tied to the law as the *general* norm. In our opinion, this was done because the aim was for the courts to be guided first and foremost by the political expediency of the time, which, because of the changing and unpredictable nature of the current policy, could not allow identical procedure in more or less identical cases. Thus, the political expediency of the time, which was constantly subject to unpredictable twists and turns was contrary to the principle of the rule of law and equality.

Matters are different in a legal system where courts adjudicate only according to the law and administrative or party organs cannot issue them binding guidelines. In such a system, judges are bound only by the law and any subjective expediency is reduced to the minimum and often even excluded altogether. Yet, this is exactly what the architects of the Soviet legal and political system wanted to avoid. From the regular courts which passed judgement according to the principle of independence, they set out to make court martials, which do act according to "court procedure" and pass "verdicts," but which at the same time are guided by the political expediency of the time. Any possibility of preserving the inviolability of human rights and freedoms is thereby permanently lost because an independent judiciary is the last line of defense for human security and freedom. Or, as Montesquieu pointed out: "If judicial power is added to executive power, the judge could demonstrate the violence of a tyrant."[18]

Perhaps one should stress once again in this context the nature of judicial independence. What it really means is independence from any orders or special instructions from any senior official and even from the legislator himself should the latter use his legislative authority to issue instructions on how individual cases should be adjudicated, or in any other way restrict or prevent judges adjudicating according to their conscience. Or, as young Marx so aptly observed:

> A judge has no superior above him except the law. But he is bound in each individual case of the application of the law to interpret it in the way in which he has understood it after conscientious examination. An independent judge does not belong either to me or to you.[19]

In other words, judicial independence is possible if judges are bound only by the law as *general, impersonal* and *principled* norms. This is also the safest guarantee of the inviolability of basic human freedoms and rights which are protected by such laws.

Thus, the judiciary can be an antidote to the abuse of executive power and a valid means of protecting equality before the law and individual freedoms and rights only if it is *independent.* The architects of the post-revolutionary legal system in the Soviet Union and other East European countries, however, rejected this time-tested value and reduce the judiciary to the tool of the current policy. In so doing they have incorporated the possibility of the abuse of the judicial function and the unlimited violation of basic human rights into the judicial system. This was an irremediable evil because it was contained in the antidote itself. Marx's warning that a judge must be *independent* when applying the law to individual cases, that is, that he is bound to "interpret the law in the way in which *he understands* it after conscientious examination," was not paid attention. In 1945, Miloš Minić and people who thought like him disputed the validity and justification of *this kind* of judicial independence, and they were thus able to denounce the Belgrade judges for alleged leniency toward accused enemies, though it was obvious that these judges formed their judgements according to their own and not somebody else's conscience. Marx had also pointed out that "an independent judge does not belong either to me or to you," that is, to either side of the dispute, either to the prosecutor or to the accused. It seems that in 1945, Miloš Minić believed that the judge did, nevertheless, belong to someone, that is, that he belonged to the same side as the public prosecutor.

In fact, from the very beginning the institution of the public prosecutor, with its sweeping powers and influential role, called into question the independence and impartiality of the judiciary. In a system upholding the rule of law with reliable guarantees of trials to ensure human security and freedom, the public prosecutor is only one of the two sides in a disptue, having no special privileges or extensive extra-judicial powers. According to Dragoljub Jovanović, the public prosecutor in the Yugoslav post-war system was an all-powerful oran of the judiciary. He warned:

> In our present judicial system, the prosecutor is something much more than a party in the dispute, he is the all-powerful organ, especially in today's courts, with their untrained and unprofessional judges who are under the influence of educated people. The public prosecutor has special power which neither the Constitution, nor, I think, this law, wants to endow him with.
>
> The public prosecutor today is omnipresent and omniscient. He is a politician and a businessman, a writer and an artist, a doctor and a veterinary surgeon. He knows everything, he understands everything and he can do anything he wants. This law goes a step further and puts the public prosecutor into people's committees as well. He also joins the executive committee as an equal member, true enough in an advisory capacity, but not only is he present but he also takes part in disscussions, and we know what the voice of such a powerful man as the public prosecutor means. In places low and high, especially low, he is dreaded and feared. Many people represent power, but in the eyes of the people he is the real power bearing all the features which the people attribute to that function.[20]

The supremacy of the public prosecutor over the court was also enhanced "because the investigation of charges has been taken away from the court and handed over to the public prosecutor."[21] In Dragoljub Jovanović's words, this was, true enough, a step forward from the former practice when the investigating power was the police. But genuine progress in guaranteeing legal security would be attained only when the entire investigation process was handed over the authority of the courts. In addition, Dragoljub Jovanović resolutely objected to "the public prosecutor without exception being a member of the Communist Party," thereby "incarnating the dictatorship of one party."[22]

A further explanation of this exceptional role of the post-war public prosecutor can be found in Miloš Minić's answer to Jovanović's objections. Whereas Dragoljub Jovanović saw a similarity between the group of citizens which helped the public prosecutor[23] and the Roman institution of *delator* (*delator*—informer, denouncer) who "informed the authorities of what one did and thought, where one went and how one behaved,"[24] Miloš Minić saw "this only as an even deeper democratization of the whole machinery of our people's power, and not what Mr. Jovanović would like to describe it as."[25]

Miloš Minić also reproached Dragoljub Jovanović for lagging behind progressive legal science by demanding that criminal investigation should be within the jurisdiction of the court.

> Mr. Jovanović was extremely sincere when he said that the system of investigation as laid down by this law bothered him most. For, before the war, the investigating judges were members of the court. Now the investigator is the organ of the public prosecutor's office. Mr. Jovanović does not see this as a mark of progress. Our courts today are not burdened with a function like investigation which has no connection at all with trial. This is the function of the executive power. We have made a step forward by freeing our judiciary from a function of the executive power, from investigation, enquiry and examination, and we have transformed our courts into what they should be, that is, into courts which should adjudicate, which always have two parties before them, which hear one side and the other, and which then, coolly and objectively, reach their decision. With this, we have really made a step forward. Mr. Jovanović's legal theory is a little old-fashioned.[26]

In 1945, Miloš Minić, of course, was not in a position to know that this *progress* in legal science would later be abandoned and that, after the rejection of the Soviet model and influence, the criminal investigation would be handed over to the jurisdiction of the judiciary and special investigating judges. When this did happen Miloš Minić did not find it necessary to withdraw his earlier accusations against Dragoljub Jovanović's "old-fashioned" legal theory. Thus, it was demonstrated that in his dispute with Miloš Minić, Dragoljub Jovanović was right, but, unfortunately for him, not at the right time. But, if in 1946, Dragoljub Jovanović was more far-sighted in his appraisal of what progress in legal science and practice truly represented, Miloš Minić made a better prediction of Dragoljub Jovanović's immediate personal fate when he told him:

> What is at stake are not legal questions but purely political questions. He (Dragoljub Jovanović—authors' comment) says: 'the prosecutor's office is an organ of the Communist Party. An investigator is an organ of the prosecutor's office. All this is in the hands of one party. An investigator can arrest a man and the prosecutor can bring him to court; in the courts are untrained citizens, the prosecutor is all-powerful and it can happen to anyone, and perhaps Mr. Jovanović is afraid for himself, that one day someone might start proceedings against him, that the matter is investigated, that he is brought to court, and in the court are untrained people while the prosecutor is all-powerful, and perhaps one could end up in prison—if the party whose organ the prosecutor is felt like it. You see how much malice and distrust of our people's power there is when you link up all these attitudes.[27]

It was shown, however, that this fear of Dragoljub Jovanović's was justified: in May 1947, he was arrested on the order of the public prosecutor's office and sentenced to nine years in prison, perhaps in just the very same way which Miloš Minić had so reliably foreseen a year before.

The omnipresence and omnipotence of the public prosecutor's office was, however, not the only factor restricting the authority and independence of judiciary in the first post-war years. There were also other state and political organs, and particularly the internal security organs. We also find confirmation of this in the rare critical statements by individual people's deputies. In the discussion on the proposed federal budget, Imro Filaković gave the following examples of arbitrary arrest:

> Though the compulsory purchase was necessary the practice of purchasing surplus produce in individual villages was such as to alienate the people from the people's power . . . . Of the many examples, this is one of the milder ones: Antun Matković from the village of Šljivoševac in the district of Donji Miholjac surrendered all of his surplus

produce yet he was brought before a people's court. The court acquitted him but the internal administration department in Donji Miholjac kept him in prison for another 16 days and put him under pressure to join the Popular Front.

There are very hard-working people in the villages who are in jail because of the compulsory purchase of surplus produce. If one takes into account that some of the purchasing commissions ordered that chickens be cooked for them, which represents a violation of private property, then it could be said that the practice of compulsory purchase was, in very many places, at the very least, crude. The villages of Šag, Bizovac and Sveti Djuradj are an example.[28]

This example of arbitrary arrest confirms that at the time when compulsory purchase was carried out, there was no consistent application of the legal institution of *habeas corpus,* which, as a means against arbitrary deprivation of freedom, sets out the obligation of the police to bring an arrested person *immediately* before a court, and to free him *immediately* if that is the ruling of the court. Moreover, in addition to this violation of the legal principles guaranteeing human security and freedom, the right of immunity from legal proceedings of elected people's deputies was not respected in this period either. Imro Filaković warned the National Assembly about this when he said:

In my district, three district councillors and three presidents of the local committee were imprisoned. Some of them were imprisoned for political reasons though this was mentioned only on one occasion at the trials. All these cases of imprisonment are contrary to the law because all of these committee members are protected by immunity but as far as I know only in one instance was the release from jail requested by the executive committee.[29]

If, on the other hand, the police brought an arrested person immediately before the court this was not a sufficient guarantee that the trial would be impartial and honest and this was also confirmed by Radomir Todorović's account in the National Assembly of how the district court in Stara Pazova had arrested a peasant on 21 March 1947 and the very next day, 22 March, sentenced him to five years imprisonment.[30] Perhaps this also led Imro Filaković to conclude that the control commissions and public prosecutor's offices lightly resorted to coercion for political purposes:

> These two institutions are akin. Let us take the example of a campaign. The control commission operates side by side with the campaign. It explains, corrects, advises, helps and sometimes also calls on the help of the public prosecutor's office. Toward the end of the campaign or on its completion, the public prosecutor's office rounds up the wrongdoers and hands them over to the court. In my opinion, the control commissions are too weak and all the public prosecutor's offices too strong. Accordingly, it turns out that we are hardly led but much prosecuted. When one takes into consideration that all the public prosecutors and all the inspectors of the control commissions are recruited from one party then this makes matters even worse.[31]

Due to this subordination of the judiciary and the prosecutor's office to political needs of the time, there were no firm guarantees of human security and freedom in the first post-war years. Moreover, according to the official concept of the time it was not the task of the judiciary to ensure the inviolability of basic human rights and the equality of all citizens before the law, but, in the words of Jakov Blažević, it had to be "the tower from which the people would truly settle accounts with all their enemies."[32] The post-war judiciary made a truly zealous contribution to achieving this aim.

2. Basic Freedoms and Rights

The real substance and practicability of basic freedoms and rights represent the most reliable criterion of the moral integrity of any given political system. This undoubtedly applies also to socialist societies where the emancipating character of the revolution through which they were established is particularly emphasized. Human rights and freedoms represent the minimum of conditions without which people cannot develop and progress as autonomous and independent moral beings. The reliable guarantee of and consistent respect for basic human rights is therefore the *conditio sine qua non* of a good society, such as a socialist society, according to the concept of its founding fathers, should also be.

For the human rights to be really feasible, the uncontrolled expansion of the limits of power to the detriment of guaranteed freedom should be prevented. To achieve this, it is first of all necessary to determine through the constitution the clear boundaries of power and establish an *inviolable* sphere of individual freedoms and rights which the power must not touch, and then provide the appropriate institutional guarantees which will make these boundaries of power relatively firm and reliable. They are primarily the independence of the judiciary, real electibility, public accountability and a periodic change of rulers, freedom of public opinion, a free and independent press and corresponding party pluralism.

Thus, the basic rights and freedoms must represent a counterbalance to the entire political expediency and the essence of legal constraints, that is the limitation of state power. It seems, however, that immediately after the war, an essentially different concept of human and civil rights was officially accepted. It presumed that any clear border between power and these rights should be eradicated. Perhaps this concept was best expressed by Jovan Djordjević who, in December 1945, spoke as a government representative at the sessions of the constituent committees of the Federal Chamber and of the Chamber of Nationalities. According to him, civil rights were certain legal means *placed* (authors' italics) at the disposal of our citizens." This was a basic innovation in relation to the original liberal idea which holds that civil and human liberties are not rights which the state power *presents* to its subjects but that they represent the essential aims and limits of that power. In addition to this, instead of the original idea about the difference between and opposing nature of civil rights and state power, Jovan Djordjević advocated the official concept of their being mutually intertwined and unified. Djordjević continued:

> Fourthly and lastly, it is necessary to emphasize here that civil rights, which are usually defined by all constitutions as some special means of restricting and neutralizing power, as a counterbalance to the concept of the activity and growing strength of power—this concept, then, the constitutional right, known throughout the whole of the bourgeois democratic world, did not play a leading role at the time when the civil rights were determined. Why? Our state is not based on the famous conflict between citizens and power. Civil rights, therefore, do not represent usurpation of power or limitation of

power, but civil rights in our country are formulated in harmony, in the *unity of power and citizen* (authors' italics). This is made possible because in our country, state power is in essence people's power. And insofar as our power is stronger, broader, more powerful and more democratic, so too are civil rights broader, more democratic and stronger.[33]

This idea of the unity of civil rights and the existing power was the result of an uncritical and, in many respects, naive belief that the new power and its exponents would be *essentially* different from all erstwhile rulers. While all earlier rulers were inclined to abuse power and constantly expand its boundaries to the detriment of guaranteed freedom, immediately after the war individuals emerged who maintained, and perhaps even believed, that the new leaders would be devoid of these dangerous inclinations. Radovan Zogović also professed to that belief when, in December 1945, he assured the deputies of the Constituent Assembly that in this matter the new people's power could not be compared in any way with the old, reactionary power, and that the fear therefore, that the new people's power too would be inclined to restrict and trample on constitutional liberties and rights was not justified. Zogović said:

> Although I fully understand the positive component contained in Mr. Prodanović's fear that the Constitution perhaps will not always be carried out correctly, I think that in voicing that fear there are some illogical elements. Our Constitution legalizes the situation which already exists. It lays down and provides the prospects for the development of the people's power which as a popular, elected representative power emerged in the national liberation struggle. Any comparison between the old and today's power is therefore, illogical, just as the fear that the people, which is that power, would alienate this power and turn it against itself is also illogical.[34]

In 1945, this naive belief in the incorruptibility of the new state leaders did not, however, represent what was generally believed. This is especially confirmed by Jaša Prodanović's amendments to the proposed draft constitution and his observations on the nature of every people's power, including the new one. In the discussion on this draft, he pointed out that

laws could be "good, liberal and well formulated but there have nevertheless been abuses. In Serbia, too, we have felt and experienced this. One
and the same law is different when a good power applies it and when a
bad power circumvents it."[35] In this respect, the authorities in new Yugoslav are not exception either. Jaša Prodanović said:

> I am afraid that the same thing might happen in new Yugoslavia as
> in the old. In old Yugoslavia the Constitution was promulgated and
> then by the laws the constitutional freedoms were a little curtailed,
> circumscribed and emasculated. Afterwards came the interpretation,
> and that interpretation also restricted the laws still further. The Con-
> stitution provided a certain number of rights. The legal interpreta-
> tion reduced those rights a little; this was skillfully camouflaged, and
> then came ministerial decrees and lastly their execution which made
> the legal provisions even more severe, so that by the time you had
> gone from the first constitutional provision to the execution there
> was hardly any liberty left at all. An interesting case has occurred
> in our new Yugoslavia. The interpretation of the law on electoral
> lists does not correspond to the provisions of the law and thus an
> innocent man can lose his right to vote if the law is applied in this
> way.[36]

In contrast to the numerous champions of the new leaders, Jaša Prodanović was aware that the nature of the power had not been changed
through the mere change in leaders, that is, the tendency was still there
to degenerate into arbitrariness and despotism. He therefore vigorously
advocated the introduction of firm and reliable guarantees which would
restrain power and reduce it to bounds set by the Constitution. The first
condition which had to be fulfilled, therefore, was that the constitutional
provisions on human and civil rights should be precisely and unambiguously
defined. For Jaša Prodanović had observed that particular dangers lay
within those constitutional definitions of civil rights which described those
rights as inviolable, except in cases established by law, which really meant
a *carte blanche* for the legislator to restrict and even trample on them at
his will. Prodanović continued:

I think that our most important concern is that when a good constitution is worked out, when its provisions are precisely defined,
when they are clear and not ambiguous, the laws too must properly
derive from that constitution, they can only be made less rather than
more stringent, and any further work must correspond to what has
been laid down by the Constitution.[37]

When the draft constitution was discussed he therefore advocated that
individual civil rights should be *absolute* so that they should not be restricted in any way, and that, in addition, certain prohibitions should be
written into the Constitution which would prevent any power from en-
croaching on the inviolable sphere of guaranteed freedom.

Jaša Prodanović demonstrated the practical scope of his concept by
quoting the example of freedom of the press, association, assembly, public
meetings and manifestations and the right of the sanctity of the home.
First of all, he questioned Article 27 of the draft Constitution which
stated: "Citizens are guaranteed freedom of the press, speech, association,
assembly, public meetings and manifestations." His judgement was: "This
provision, as entered here, is not clear enough because it is open to erroneous interpretation, and one day a law could be passed which would
restrict this freedom and destroy it."[38] The deficiency of this provision
was reflected primarily in the fact that it did not *expressly* ban journalists
and publishers from taking advance payments, practice of censorship and
of giving prior permits for political associations and indoor meetings. Jaša
Prodanović, therefore, proposed the following amendment:

Advance payment cannot be authorized for publishing newspapers,
magazines and other printed material, nor can censorship.
Official approval need not be sought for political associations.
Indoor meetings may be held without the authorities being present.

With these explicit constitutional bans, Jaša Prodanović attempted to
tie the hands of the authorities *in advance,* in order that subsequent laws,
in the form of an exception to the general rule, would not introduce de-
posits and censorship, through the back door and practically abolish freedom of *political* associations, assemblies and public gatherings. Edvard
Kardelj, then Minister for the Constituent Assembly, rejected this amendment by saying that this matter should be settled later by law. "It is my

view," Kardelj said, "that we should leave this Article as it is and resolve the matter later by law."[39] This was because, in his view ". . . democratic rights are not something absolutely valid for all times," but, depending on given circumstances, they can be expanded or restricted, *given* or taken away.

> We have already passed laws on association, assemblies and the press. Those laws are essentially democratic and correspond to Article 27, and yet they contain certain restructions which we shall be able to remove later. But I believe that they correspond to the present situation and that it would be a mistake were we to *give* (authors' italics) greater liberties because the law on freedom would be turned into a law for those who destroy freedom.[40]

As opposed to Kardelj, Jaša Prodanović did not consider the Constitution to be the instrument of the current policy by which, according to need, civil liberties and rights would be either expanded or restricted. For him, the Constitution retained its original meaning from the time of the struggle against Prince Miloš's absolutism, and hence its purpose was to block and dam absolutism and arbitrariness by the exponents of state power. This concept of the Constitution was particularly evident in Prodanović's attempt to ensure as far as possible the sanctity of the home with the appropriate constitutional prohibitions. He therefore proposed an amendment to the draft Constitution which laid down that searches could not be carried out at night. When Leon Gerškovic, a government representative, rejected this proposal by explaining that "to include such a provision in the constitution means to leave the night free for enemies to work,"[41] Jaša Prodanović expounded the well-known idea of the corruption of any, even the so-called, people's power. "It is a good thing that this is people's power, but even people's power becomes corrupt. Time corrupts people. Supremacy, and particularly power makes the people a bit softer."[42] In Jaša Prodanović's works, there are not exceptions to this.

> No generation can be guaranteed to remain true to the spirit of the ideas with which it had begun, still less so other generations. When in power it is difficult to remain true to what was done when in opposition.[43]

The fundamental purpose of the Constitution is, therefore, to prevent the worst consequences to which the corruption of those in power inevitably leads. Prodanović continued:

> There are greater evils but a constitution is made in order to prevent acts of tyranny by individual authorities. A power might be good and have a good constitution but if another power emerges, another regime which is no good, it will commit illegal acts and acts of tyranny and it will disgrace itself before the whole of Europe, before the whole world. It is not all the same whether you have a good or a bad constitution. If you have a good constitution, then those who destroy it are opponents of the state. If there is no such constitution, then bad governments can do what they want. It is better that there should be a strong barrier and that someone who wants to do something bad trips over it.[44]

As regards the sanctity of the home and the attempt to violate it, that barrier was represented by the constitutional ban on house searches taking place at night. It scarcely needs to be said that this proposal by Prodanović was also rejected.

In fact, immediately after the war ended, and particularly when the first FNRJ Constitution was passed, classic human rights were subjected to raison d'état and the political expediency of the time. The best example of such an attitude of the politicians of the time is the fate of the right to strike, which workers' organizations had fought hard for as an inviolable *constitutional* right in the 19th and 20th century. In November 1945, it seemed that the right to strike really was an inviolable right which no one, not even the Government itself, could touch. At the time, the Premier, as we have already noted, unambiguously declared: "There is freedom to strike in our country. Workers have gone on strike . . . . They have the right to strike and it is not up to us to interfere."[45] In January 1946, however, when this right should have been incorporated in the first Constitution of new Yugoslavia, its validity was disputed. Gligorije Mandić, Nikola Jakšić and Milovan Djilas particularly excelled in this.

For Gligorije Mandić the proposal to incorporate the right to strike in the first Contitution was essentially reactionary and directed against the people:

The day before yesterday, Comrade Djilas read to us a comment that some people, I don't know whether this refers to individuals or a group, are proposing that the freedom to strike be incorporated in the Constitution. They justify this by saying that the freedom to strike has always been a powerful weapon of the working class. I believe and I think that you understand that whoever is proposing this has nothing in common either with the working class or the working people, and at the very least that he has not read the Constitution. This is a people's state, a state of the workers and peasants, a state of the working people, and the strike is a powerful weapon of the working class in a state which is not a people's state. Today, when our draft Constitution guarantees full liberties both to the working class, its organizations and the whole of the working people, such a proposal is reactionary and anti-people's through and through.[46]

Thus, according to Gligorije Mandić, the right to strike had all of a sudden become reactionary though at the time when the first Constitution of new Yugoslavia was being passed, the majority of enterprises were still in private hands because industry and commerce had not yet been nationalized.

Even more serious accusations against the then champions of the right to strike were made by Nikola Jakšić. In his words, they were the deposed enemies of the people who were resorting to the most diverse means of struggle against the new people's power.

They who have considered the strike to be their bitter enemy and who shuddered whenever they hear this word, like it today and consider it suitable because through it they could weaken the positions of our Government. It is no surprise, therefore, that the demand for the right to strike to be incorporated in our Constitution is made not by workers but chiefly by the time-tested enemies of the working class, by the enemies of the people's power. Popular discussion of this draft has demonstrated the craftiness of these enemies who are attempting slyly, or if this fails, directly, to make such demands. If in our circumstances the strike becomes the means of the reaction in its struggle against the people's power, and that means against the working class and all the people, against their welfare, then it is reactionary.[47]

It seems, however, that the legalization of the right to strike was not proposed only by the opponents of the new power but also by individual champions of the new system who had not forgotten that the right to strike was a fundamental means of struggle of the working class even in circumstances when the state had taken over the role of the private employer. In Milovan Djilas's words, Col. Petar Brajović, later a general and People's Hero, proposed "that the question of the freedom to strike be included in Article 20 of our Constitution."[48] Naturally, Djilas did not classify him as an enemy but he nevertheless did not accept his proposals. Djilas said:

> I think that such a formulation of the question of the freedom to strike in our Constitution would not be correct. A strike in institutions which are people's property, and, therefore, also the property of the working class, would not, in fact, correspond to the interests of the working class; it would be contrary to the interests of the working class.[49]

The right to strike, however, was not the only right which the new authorities did not want to legalize and guarantee. A similar fate befell Dragić Joksimović's proposal that freedom from fear should be guaranteed by a special law. In connection with this, he quoted the Agreement between the National Committee for the Liberation of Yugoslavia and the Royal government of 1 November 1944 ('DFJ Official Gazette, 9 March 1945), ordering the new Government to issue a declaration which would particularly emphasize and guarantee freedom from fear.[50] Dragić Joksimović warned:

> Contrary to this Agreement, freedom from fear was not only not emphasized and guaranteed in the Government's declaration of 9 March that year, but it was not even mentioned. At the third session of AVNOJ, that is the Provisional National Assembly, which started work on 7 August and finished on 26 August the same year, not a single new law was proposed which would regulate this important legal aspect. Reports from the interior of the country convince me, however, that to pass a law on freedom from fear is an urgent and basic necessity.[51]

This was sufficient reason for Dragić Joksimović that a special law should be passed on the basis of which any action by the organs of the people's power, the army and institutions of the DFJ, the nature of which was to intimade the people or threaten citizens to do something against their will or not, would be punished as a criminal offence against freedom from fear.

A resolute opponent of this proposal was Moša Pijade. He did acknowledge that the text of the Tito-Šubašić Agreement "contains that *phrase* (authors' italics) about freedom from fear."[52] Yet it seems that he did not want to acknowledge that this was above all freedom *from* tyranny and from abuse by those in power. He even believed that to *guarantee* this freedom was not necessary at all. Because, according to him: "No upright citizen with a clear conscience has had until now, nor has now, nor will have in the future, any reason to fear anything whatsoever."[53] Moša Pijade, however, did not go into the question of who decided whether an individual was an *upright* citizen and on what basis that decision was made. Though he did not give an explicit answer to this question, a tacit reply was contained in his attack on Dragić Joksimović about the latter having written the proposed law:

> with the obvious intention of portraying the situation in our country as if the vast majority of the people were intimidated, living in constant fear of actions by the authorities, the civil, military, judicial authorities, etc. This would be the same as saying that there is no legality in this country at all and that every citizen could at every step be exposed to lawlessness, terror, deprivation of his rights, persecution, etc.[54]

In other words, since his view of the new order was different from that of Moša Pijade, Dragić Joksimović's opinion could not be correct and well-intentioned. A correct opinion could only be held by those in power and they in the nature of things, did not need freedom from fear. Or, as Moša Pijade put it: "*We* (authors' italics) do not need freedom from fear . . ."[55] They on the other hand, who think differently could not be given such freedom because they are not well-intentioned.

One of the first political laws passed at the end of the war was the Press Law ('DFJ Official Gazette," No. 65/45) of 24 August 1945. It should

have ensured the freedom of the press as one of the fundamental conditions of democratic political life and equitable contest for votes in the
forthcoming elections for the Constituent Assembly. But even while it
was being passed serious doubts were expressed whether freedom of the
press would, in fact, be realized.

A frequent argument used by the communists between the two wars
in questioning the existence of a free press, was the claim that the material
resources for the publishing of newspapers were in the hands of a few rich
individuals. Now the erstwhile critics of the so-called bourgeois press were
confronted with the same arguments. The representatives of the Democratic Party warned on behalf of the Assembly minority that the proposed
press law was

> a purely formal law whose Article 1 manifests the freedom of the
> press. However, the freedom of the press, like the freedom of opin-
> ion and freedom of political activity does not depend only on a few
> pro-visions of a formal character, but also on material and political
> facts. The material conditions of the press (newsprint and printing
> works) are owned by the authorities which are politically exclusive.
> It is not a coincidence that among hundreds of papers published to-
> day under the directive and control of the Popular Front, there is
> not a single one which would represent an independent opinion out-
> side the Front.[56]

Edvard Kardelj attempted to explain the nature of this monopoly of
the material resources for the publication of papers. In his words, the fact
that these resources were in the hands of the state power in no way called
into question the freedom of the press, because, as opposed to previous
authorities, the present power had come from the people. Having equated
in this way "the people" with "the people's power" Kardelj could easily
conclude that "that fact"—"the fact that the material resources are in the
hands of the people, which means in the hands of people's power"—"is
actually the guarantee that our peoples will have a free press, not only on
paper but also in reality."[57] The question however, arose as to whether
only people who thought the same as the ruling power would manage the
resources for publishing papers or whether those who thought differently
would also be able to use them. The question was answered by Mitra

Mitrović-Djilas, who accepted fully Kardelj's explanation that:

> the freedom of the press is guaranteed . . . because the means of the
> press are not in the hands of enemies, because the people are not de-
> prived of these means but because they have taken them over to a
> large degree from their enemies and keep control of them; they are
> in the hands of the people's power.[58]

In her words, our press "can write freely and unhindered on matters close
to people's hearts."[59] But, such freedom of the press was not accessible to
all. "Surely we shall not," Mitra Mitrović-Djilas warned, "give newsprint to
those who want to sow discord amongst the people while our children, for
example, in Bosnia and Herzegovina, have no primers."[60] Those, on the
other hand, who sought the freedom of the press for everybody have forgotten that certain people had been deprived of the right to write and
publish. "The minority, furthermore, says that our power is politically
exclusive and that there is not a single paper today which would represent
some independent views outside the Popular Front. This is indeed not a
coincidence,"[61] —warned Mitra Mitrović-Djilas. Only this way could the
press become "a true means and organ for the cultural education and political enlightenment of our people."[62]

Since it was nevertheless expected that opponents would use the freedom of the press even though they did not possess the requisite material
means, new legal restrictions on this freedom were introduced. This was
done in Article 11 of the first Press Law of 24 August 1945, which, among
other things, banned the dissemination of printed matter containing false
and alarmist news threatening state and national interests, and insults or
slander directed at the DFJ Supreme Federal and regional representative
bodies. When this law was being passed, the Assembly minority pointed
out that these prohibitions contained undefined and loose terms which
made it possible for these laws to be interpreted and applied in practice in
an extremely arbitrary manner. Dragić Joksimović said that on the basis
of the expressions used in these provisions which were "arbitrary, elastic
and inadequately defined," it was possible "to ban the dissemination and
sale of nine-tenths of all printed material."[63] "And when one takes into
account what the explanation of the law considers to be incriminating and
what it considers to be an achievement then the question which arises is:

what can the press talk about and discuss if even principled changes and reforms can be incriminated."[64] Or, as Edvard Kardelj explained:

> For a long time, so to say from the time the work on the political laws which have been and are being passed, started, one main counter-argument has been put forward by the minority and Mr. Grol. They are afraid of arbitrariness and excessive latitude in the formulations of these laws and they think that these formulations make for various abuses by people's power.[65]

Such a judgement, however, was completely without foundation, Kardelj maintained, because, in his view, it was not undefined concepts which were at stake: rather, the whole affair "with regard to the minority and Mr. Grol amounts to a lack of confidence in our people's authorities."[66]

A further possibility for the arbitrary restriction of guaranteed freedom was the procedure for pronouncing a ban on the dissemination and sale of printed material. According to Article 13 of the first post-war Press Law, such a ban was ruled by a district court on the advice of the public prosecutor. Such a regulation would not have provoked great suspicion had the following exception not been provided for in Paragraph 2 of the Article:

> In particularly urgent and justified cases, the public prosecutor may impose a temporary ban in a written explanatory ruling on the circulation and sale of a paper or periodical. In that event, he will simultaneously pass his decision on the ban to the editorial board and the relevant district court and order the people's militia to confiscate the printed copies and, if necessary, seal the printing press plates, etc.

It was feared that this *exception* would become the customary rule, that is, that *every* case of banning the dissemination of printed material would be "urgent" and "justified." Dragić Joksimović, therefore, voiced the conviction "that one cannot speak about the freedom of the press if the public prosecutor is given such a prominent right to intervene in every case with regard to banning papers and periodicals."[67] This warning was not accepted and in subsequent laws this exception became the general rule, so that the public prosecutor was always the one to impose a *temporary* ban, the final ruling on which was made by the district court.

With these methods, the new power established total control over the press and the entire publishing activity. It only remained for similar control to be established over the foreign press to the extent to which the nature of the internal policy at the time dictated it. This was done with Article 15 of the aforementioned Press Law. It seemed to establish free imports and circulation in the DFJ of newspapers, books and other written material printed abroad with the priviso that only Yugoslav and foreign enterprises and institutions with special authorization from the Federal Ministry of Information had the right to disseminate the foreign press. This was really a system of prior approval which, true enough, did not affect the object but the subject of the dissemination of the press. It applied, however, only to papers and books in foreign languages. Excepted from this rule were the imports and dissemination in the country of papers, books and other material printed abroad in the languages of our peoples or intended for our people, as they were permitted on the prior approval of the Federal Ministry of Information. This was preventive censorship of all material printed in the languages of the people of Yugoslavia. Most importantly, the legislator gave the Ministry of Information *absolute* freedom to issue authorization or refuse approval as it saw fit. In Dragić Joksimović's words:

> These and similar regulations gravely restrict the principle of freedom of the press, because they give the Ministry of Information the sovereign right to act as it sees fit, while limiting to the highest degree the use of foreign printed material by the citizens of our state.[68]

Thus, immediately after the war, the freedom of the press was fettered by numerous and in many respects arbitrary restrictions. With the passing of the first Constitution on 31 January 1946, it seemed that the freedom of the press would indeed become sacrosanct since it was guaranteed without any *constitutional* restrictions except for generally prohibiting the use of civil rights for a *forcible* change of the existing constitutional order. Furthermore, this prohibition did not in practice concern the freedom of the press since the written word itself could never be violence as such. But, the Constitution was one thing, the laws another. The new law on the ratification and changes in the Press Law ('FNRJ Official Gazette,' 56/46) not only ratified all the earlier restrictions on the freedom of the press, which the first Constitution had not even incorporated, but also introduced a new restriction. On the basis of Article 11, Section 4 of the new law, a ban on the dissemination of printed material could be imposed if it "calls for or incites to changing or violating the constitutional order for anti-democratic ends." This was not a call for a *violent* change in the constitutional order, which was also banned by the first Press Law (Article 11, Section 3), but for a *non-violent* change for anti-democratic ends. Since this definition of the ends was extremely vague, the body imposing the ban was practically given a free hand to interpret the actual meaning of these ends in a given instance *according to its own lights.*

The ultimate range of restricting the guaranteed freedom of the press was reached in 1947 with the law on the publication and dissemination of young people's and children's literature and press ('FNRJ Službeni List' 29/47). It introduced the system of prior permits for the publication of papers and books intended for children. According to this law, young people's and children's books and other literature could be published by state and other publishing houses, associations and individuals only with the prior approval of the Ministry of Education of the People's Republic on whose territory the book, periodical, drawing or similar material was printed. In fact this was not preventive censorship but a system of *exclusive* publishing rights which the Ministry of Education granted to especially selected and trusted publishers. All other individuals or associations who did not merit this exceptional confidence of the state authorities, were not able to publish even works which had otherwise been printed and circulated without hindrance.

The extremely vague definition of what represented press for young people and children represented the most effective means for complete control of the press. Dragoljub Jovanović in particular pointed this out when speaking in the Assembly debate on the proposal of this law. He said: "Minister Djilas, who has proposed the law, says himself that the nature of a work will not be determined by a writer declaring it to be intended for young people, but by its content."[69] Such a definition of the literature for young people could be applied virtually to any literary work. In this context Dragoljub Jovanović quoted Anatole France who said that children never read what was specifically written from them and they had thus claimed as their own the greatest works of world literature whose authors had never even thought of writing specifically for the young.[70]

In Dragoljub Jovanović's view, this law practically introduced preventive censorship for the greatest part of printed material.

Dragoljub Jovanović also insisted that such preventive censorship was superfluous since there was nothing and nobody outside the control of the authorities. He said:

> In the same vein this is superfluous today in this country where all the newsprint is owned by the State, were almost all of the printing works are owned by the State, or where trade unionists are disciplined in such a way as to prevent the printing of anything which this system does not like. The threat and fear from writers is particularly superfluous. Since time immemorial, authors and Pharisees have never been a threat to a single regime.[71]

Lastly, even if something should slip through the fine mesh of control, there would still be the watchful eyes of individual literary "commissars." "We in Serbia have Radovan Zogović and Čedomir Minderović, and each republic has people who watch over the literature and who will not pass anything which would be unfavorable to the regime."[72] Therefore, Dragoljub Jovanović concluded, such a law was plainly superfluous. It would only be necessary if the free sale of newsprint were allowed and if all the rest of the press not intended for the young was free. As long as this is not allowed, the prior censorship of young people's press and literature serves no purpose. Nevertheless, four years had to elapse before the then "guardians" of children and young people realized this. On 30 December 1950, this law was finally repealed ('FNRJ Official Gazette,' 3/51) with nothing fundamental having been changed in the efficiency of state control over the press and publishing activity.

3. Criminal Legislation

Criminal law was one of the branches of the law which had already undergone great changes by the end of the war. These changes, true enough, did not encompass the whole of criminal law but primarily the field of so-called political and economic crime.This was also the sphere of great and irreconcilable conflicts between the Communist Party and opposition parties.

The dispute centered on the protection of that part of criminal legislation which defined the so-called *political* criminal acts as criminal. The view of the deputies of the authorities of that time, had been that criminal legislation should protect above all the newly-established power and this in a way as to prevent any change in that power. Any change would have meant a return to the old. Or as Milovan Djilas said, in defense of the new power:

> In Yugoslavia there is only the possibility for this power alone or for a return to the old power. We want this power. . . no other but only this power and this kind of power. . . . [73]

Representatives of the then Assembly minority were against such a concept of the basic purpose of the law on political criminal acts because it would abolish the possibility of reforming the existing power; as Milan Grol said at the end of August 1945, it was still not truly a people's power.

> Where people's power is truly what this word means, that is, a power elected by the people and legitimately established, it is clear that to violate it is the same as committing an offense against the homeland. But this thesis cannot be applied if the people's power has still not been established in this way and if the people's power is not the people's but the regime's. These are two different terms and meanings. In such a case, criticism of such a power cannot be considered an offense and the question is who commits a greater offense against the state and homeland: the one who seeks reforms or the one who bans and refused them? [74]

What the Assembly minority had in mind was not only the retention of the existing power in the form in which it had originated from the war, but also its further reforms which could result in a periodical change of the exponents of this power as well. Therefore, the concept of homeland, as a legitimate form of criminal and legal protection, has to be strictly distinguished from the concept of power and the regime. If this difference was confused, then, in Grol's words, political opponents could easily be equated with enemies and traitors to the homeland.

In the times of the reaction the concept of the homeland was exploited and equated with the concept of the regime. But even in the
dark days, the regime hesitated to classify political opponents as
traitors and enemies of the country and the homeland. One should
guard against this especially today when many thousands of un-
fortunate and unwitting offenders can be easily classed in that
category of the most reprehensible offenders who are accused of
and disgraced by serious charges and whom no-one will pity or
defend.[75]

The immediate reason for this debate between the majority and minority
in the Provisional National Assembly at the end of August was the draft
law on criminal acts against the people and the state. Since the minority
were inclined to describe this law as a second edition of the pre-war 1920
law on the protection of the state, on whose basis nationalist separatists
and communists were prosecuted, the representatives of the majority attempted to deny any similarity between the two laws. "Some want to present this draft law," Moša Pijade said, "in the same light as that infamous
pre-war law on the protection of the state. I think that there is nothing
more erroneous than to be taken in by such deceptions."[76] Moša Pijade
did point out that any criminal law, including this one on criminal acts
against the people and the state had "*in the first place* (authors' italics)
to protect the state interests,"[77] which by the same token could probably
also be said of the notorious 1920 law on the protection of the state. The
difference lay, however, in the character of the old and new power. In
Šime Balen's words:

> There can be no comparison of any kind with the old law on the
> protection of the state which was passed to defend a small clique,
> primarily the King's clique, and which was not only directed against
> the proletariat but also, if you so wish, against the entire state. As
> opposed to that, this law wants to defend the people's achievements
> from that clique which never defended Yugoslavia.[78]

In a similar vein Jože Vilfan maintained that the law on the protection of
the state of old Yugoslavia was an "emergency measure, a law of terror,
which the minority used in order to keep themselves in power by force,"

whereas the new law on criminal acts against the people and the state was a "regular criminal provision of the kind any state has in its general criminal code."[79]

The Assembly minority's second serious objection to this draft law on criminal acts against the people and the state concerned its political exclusivity. Particularly disturbing was the fact that this law was being passed on the eve of the elections which, in Dragić Joksimović's view, could be understood as "a pressure and a threat"[80] with which to influence the election results. In addition the view also emerged among the public at home and in the foreign press that this law was not aimed only at offeders but also at political opponents. The Assembly majority considered this to be nothing else but a malicious rumor. Moša Pijade: "It is most unobjective as well as biased to say that this law has such a tendency, that it wants to hit out at the political opponents of the groups which pass it."[81] Šime Balen also presented a similar assertion when he said: "It is not directed against political opponents, and it is evident both from the work of our session, from the work of the Provisional Assembly and from the work with the grass roots that they have the possibility to come out against the majority."[82] Thus, in August 1945, Šime Balen assured doubting Thomases that *political* opponents would continue to enjoy the opportunity of *publicly* speaking against the ruling majority. Yet, only two years after the systematic application of the law on criminal acts against the people and the state, the voice of political opponents was no longer heard in the Yugoslav public.

The question which naturally arises is how did it come about that criminal legislation was not only used to punish actual wrongdoers and criminals but also to silence, wipe out and even persecute political opponents. This was achieved above all by *the broad and extremely loose formulations* of what constituted a criminal act and which gave the prosecuting organs the opportunity to treat as a criminal act any action or lack of action by any individual whose continued liberty would be *politically unsuitable.* This was not, however, a peculiarity of the post-war Yugoslav development but only a pale imitation of the Bolshevik practice of settling accounts with political opponents. In his letter to the Commissar of Justice, Dimitri Ivanovich Kursky, on 17 May 1922, Lenin demonstrated how terror against political opponents could be given a suitable legal form. To this end he proposed the introduction of a new criminal offense of propaganda which had to be given *"the broadest possible formulations* (authors' italics) in law, because only the revolutionary conscience will determine the greater or lesser application in practice."[83] Lenin knew full well that this criminal act had to be defined in law in an extremely loose manner, in order that almost any action could be brought within its scope by subsequent free interpretation according to the so-called revolutionary conscience. To achieve this *blanket discretionary norms* containind undefined and loose terms are usually used and thus the body interpreting and applying such norms has carte blanche to establish in a given situation the finer points of their meaning and content. In fact it was Lenin himself who in his draft of the supplementary paragraph to the Criminal Code, gave an example of such *broad and loose formulations.* [84]

We also encounter this extremely loose definition of criminal acts in the first criminal laws passed by the new authorities after the liberation of Belgrade and of the whole country. There were, primarily, the decision[85] of the Anti-fascist Assembly of the National Liberation of Serbia about the court for the trial of crimes and offences against Serbian national honor. The first decision establishing the court was passed on 11 November 1944 ('Official Herald of Serbia," 1/45). It only set up the court and laid down the sentences which it could pass while providing no definition at all of individual criminal acts which would be prosecuted and punished according to this decision. It stated only that these were crimes and offences "which cannot be classified as high treason or as assisting the occupying forces in committing war crimes," and that the Anti-fascist Assembly of the National Liberation of Serbia would later pass "the necessary legislative decisions which would define in greater detail the offences which the court for the trial of crimes and offences against Serbian national honor would try, as well as the structure and procedure of the court." The court, however, did not wait for legislative decisions containing a detailed definition of individual criminal acts to be passed, but immediately initiated the trials of some individuals. Thus, on 24 January 1945, Žarko Stupar, former lecturer at the Faculty of Law, in Belgrade, was sentenced to four years forced labor and to the loss of Serbian national honor for eight years.[86] On 3 February 1945, the well-known actress Živana-Žanka Stokić was sentenced to the loss of Serbian national honor for eight years:

because during the occupation as a member of the Belgrade National Theater she participated in the 'Veseljaci' ('Merry People') and 'Centrala za Humor' ('The Center of Wit') Theatres which were under the gracious patronage of the German occupying forces, and especially because she took an active part in the programs of Belgrade radio, which was under the direct control of the Germans, and thus in its daily broadcast 'Šareno Popodne' ('Colorful Afternoon'). In so doing she culturally and artistically collaborated with the occupying forces and traitors at home by placing her artistic talents and her great renown as an actress at their service.[87]

A whole series of similar trials followed and it was not until 9 April 1945 that the decision on the court for the trial of crimes and offences against Serbian national honor defining individual criminal acts was passed. This meant that all the people charged before that date were sentenced for actions which had not by then been established as punishable *by law,* and that in each individual case the court itself performed the role of legislator.

The new ruling on the court for the trial of crimes and offenses against Serbian national honor, passed on 9 April 1945 ('Službeni Glasnik Srbije,' 3/45), finally legalized the definition of what constituted a crime against Serbian national honor, but it too was extremely general and loose. According to Article 1 of the decision

crimes and offenses against Serbian national honor . . . are considered to be those acts which harm *or could harm* (authors' italics) the prestige and honor of the Serbian people and its sustaining strength, insofar as they do not belong to the category of high treason and assisting the occupying forces in committing war crimes.

For the sake of greater precision, some forms of these criminal acts were listed (Article 2), including those which made great arbitrariness in their practical application to individual cases possible. Thus, according to this ruling, it was a crime or offense to "maintain close and friendly relations in any way with members of the occupying army," or for "people in responsible positions in the state administration to have failed to make the necessary efforts to prevent the shameful defeat and capitulation of Yugoslavia in 1941." When, after numerous trials, the purpose of this special court was fulfilled, a decision was passed on 27 June 1945 abolishing it ("Official Herald of Serbia," 18/45).

The law on criminal acts against the people and the state provoked the greatest inter-party disputes. While it was being passed, the representatives of the Assembly minority sounded a serious warning about it containing extremely loose definitions of incrimination. Dragić Joksimović stressed that "the gravest aspect" of this law was "the arbitrary definition of what is incriminating," as it was left to the arbitrary interpretation of a power which was politically exclusive.[88] Joksimović said:

> It also accuses agitation against the achievements of the national liberation struggle and against the people's authorities, which means that the very discussion of these loosely defined terms and any agitation for reforms in general is also incriminating.[89]

Milan Grol described as a great danger resulting from this law

> the broad and loose character of what constitutes a crime and which is subject to arbitrary interpretations, particularly at a time of intolerance, at a time of exclusivity and mutual distrust.[90]

However, this was not the most explicit example of loose definitions of what constitutes a crime in criminal legislation. The laws on the eradication of impermissible speculation and economic sabotage and on the ban on provoking national, racial and religious hatred and discord, merit much greater attention in this respect. According to the law on the eradication of impermissible speculation and economic sabotage ('DFJ Official Gazette,' 26/45), the following actions were also punished as impermissible speculation: "any contract between the producer, wholesaler and retailer aimed at increasing prices, or at maintaining high prices and preventing their reduction"; "multiple reselling and the introduction of unnecessary middlemen in the sale of essential supply goods which could result in goods becoming more expensive"; "purchasing essential supply goods in marketplaces (outdoor markets) or on their way to market-places (outdoor markets) from producers or other people for the purpose of reselling them"; "discouraging producers or other persons from producing such goods or offering them for sale" (Article 1, Sections 8-11). Punished as sabotage

were, among other things, "closing down economic and transport enterprises, suspending or restricting work in them without justification," and
"contracts between producer and middleman aimed at reducing production or suspending work in economic and transport enterprises or on agri-
cultural farms" (Article 2, Sections 6 and 7). All these different forms of
the criminal act of speculation and sabotage were defined in such a broad
and loose manner that many customary business activities which monitored
the conditions on the market could be classified as a criminal act, which
in particularly serious cases was also punishable by death. This is all the
more strange since today these acts are not punishable as a rule or are considered only minor offenses punishable by a fine. Matters do, however,
become more understandable if one bears in mind that in 1945 when this
law was passed, economic activity was for the most part in private hands
and the authorities of the time were inclined to use criminal repression
instead of the customary fiscal, monetary and other measures, as a means
of conducting current economic policy.

Besides these broad and extremely loose formulations of what constituted individual criminal acts the application of analogy in criminal law
represented an additional opportunity of silencing and persecuting political opponents. This was a method which violated the basic principle of
modern criminal law—the principle of legality. This principle is expressed
by the maxim *nullum crimen, nulla poena sine lege* (there is no crime or
punishment without law) and its basic meaning is expressed by the provision: "Nobody can be punished for an act which, before it was committed, has not been established by law as a criminal act and for which
the law has not prescribed how the person who commits it will be punished." To make the application of this principle of legality possible, it
is necessary for the criminal act in all its aspects to be described accurately
and in detail by law and the penalty for the criminal act determined.

The post-war Yugoslav legislators, however, did not respect the value
and necessity of the principle of legality whose application to criminal law
restricts the arbitrariness of the executive, and especially of the police, and
safeguards the sacrosanct sphere of individual security and liberty. They,
in fact, did not want to tie the hands of the prosecuting organs *in advance,*
but attempted also to make possible illegal punishment of those acts which
the legislator *did not explicitly* designate and describe as criminal acts. To
that end, they introduced analogy into criminal law, which could not pass
without objections.

The first such example was the law on the eradication of impermissible speculation and economic sabotage ('DFJ Službeni List," 26/45). It described the criminal acts of speculation and sabotage by following up the extremely general and loose definition of the essence of these acts with, *for the sake of examples,* twelve cases of impermissible speculation (Article 1, Paragraph 2). Sections 13 and 17 laid down that "other cases similar to the aforementioned ones" would also be punished. The real intention of the legislator, on account of which the possibility of analogy was introduced, was best explained by Andrija Hebrang when, rejecting the proposal put forward by Frane Frol that this possibility be omitted, he said: "I am against Comrade Frol's proposal because we must also allow our authorities wide opportunities to prosecute speculation in those cases which we have not precisely provided for in law."[91] In other words, the prosecution organs should be given a free hand to establish in each individual case whether one action or another was a criminal act which in fact meant that in any given individual instance they took on the role of legislator.

Of particular interest is the explanation of and justification for the introduction of analogy into criminal laws given in November 1947 during the Assembly discussion on the proposal of the general section of the Criminal Code. According to Vojin Carić's testimony:

> This is the analogy—the *analogia legis* and not the *analogia iuris*—which provoked most of the objections during the public discussion conducted in the press about the draft as it was published and which nevertheless is indeed also the basis of this legislative draft.[92]

This referred to the following provision which was also adopted without any amendments:

> Criminal responsibility exists for that socially dangerous act which, though not explicitly defined by the law, corresponds by the similarity of its aspects to the criminal act which is specifically defined by the law. In such a case the basis of responsibility and the extent to which it is punishable are established according to the provisions for that criminal act for whose aspects criminal responsibility has been established (Article 5, Paragraph 3–'FNRJ Official Gazette,' 106/47).

In explaining this provision on behalf of the Legislative Committee of the
Chamber of Nationalities, Josip Hrnčević demonstrated why the principle
of *nullum crimen sine lege,* a principle of the old science of criminal law,
had not been taken literally.

> The principle of 'nullum crimen sine lege' in our criminal legislation
> does not represent the adoption of a formal definition of a criminal
> act but a measure for consolidating our new democratic legality.[93]

What was at issue was the rejection of the old formal definition of a criminal act and the acceptance of the so-called material definition. Or, as Mihailo Grbić explained:

> Instead of the formalist principle of criminal law concerning the no-
> tion of a criminal act, the draft is founded on the materialist concept.
> . . . Allowing analogy in this way within precisely defined and legally
> limited frameworks, which corresponds to the materialist concept of
> a criminal act, a great contribution will be made to the consolidation
> of legality and the liquidation of arbitrariness, which has been pos-
> sible in judicial practice so far.[94]

The best explanation of the real reasons why analogy was introduced
into the new Criminal Code was given by Vojin Carić. According to him,
this was done primarily becuase the legislator was not in a position to fore-
see new punishable acts arising from basic changes in the current policy.
Such a case emerges,

> if, as a consequence of changed socio-political circumstances, the
> need arises to proclaim as guilty and punish someone who is socially
> dangerous because he obstructs the implementation of new aims
> dictated by the changed socio-political circumstances.[95]

This really meant the complete subordination of legal prosecution to the
needs of *momentary* political expediency. Perhaps the best example of
implementing those "new aims dictated by changed socio-political circumstances" is the break with Stalin. Until the summer of 1948, the

glorification of Stalin as the brilliant leader and teacher of the world proletariat was not only permitted but was even advantageous: it was a way in which political careers were made. From the summer of 1948 to praise Stalin was not only sacrilege but also one of the greatest crimes against the people and the state. It was an act which led to a long term of penal servitude.

CHAPTER V

ABANDONING THE IDEA OF PARTY PLURALISM

1. All Traces of Party Pluralism Disappear

With the opposition within and without the Popular Front liquidated, the complete uniformity and homogeneity of political life was more or less attained. It only remained to wipe out the last visible traces of the former party pluralism for the new generations, brought up in a monolithic society, to think that post-war pluralism had in fact never really existed.

We have already said that the CPY had a resolute long-range strategy aimed at abolishing pluralism and introducing a one-party system. Yet, for reasons of temporary tactics and expediency, prominent Party leaders made periodic statements for the public at large, acknowledging *in words* that a multi-party system was both permissible and even legitimate. These reasons, on the whole, became superfluous after the elections to the Constituent Assembly and the Yugoslav public was gradually prepared for any traces of party pluralism to be removed. The first portent of this fundamental change appeared in mid-1946 when J. B. Tito warned that the re-introduction of the multi-party system could have dangerous consequences for the unity and happiness of the people:

In my speech at Cetinje, at the celebration of the Day of Uprising
in Montenegro, I said that there were people who thought that our
unity was no longer necessary; that, since we had ended fighting on
the battlefield, we could throw in the towel. They say that the time
of peace has come when we should begin politicking again in the old
way, when various parties would again each pull in their own direction, when we would argue among ourselves, as before in the old
Yugoslavia, at the expense of the people—one is for this program,
another for that, and so on. Ten programs, and not one of benefit
to the people! No, comrades! The people have made their own program and are implementing it through our united Popular Front.[1]

In this statement we encounter for the first time the claim that different political parties were by no means necessary. The reason given why
this diversity should be abandoned was "the unity of all the peoples of
Yugoslavia, the unity of all the nationalities, but especially the unity within each people."[2] This unity, however, was not possible if there were several programs—"one is for this program, another for that . . . . Ten programs, and not one of benefit to the people." In other words, the unity of
all peoples and nationalities and of each people in particular was possible
only if there was *one* program, and if this program was implemented by
a single organization—"our united Popular Front."

We find another indication of this basic change in the *public* attitude
to party pluralism in October 1946, in J. B. Tito's answer to the question
of what he thought about the opposition. He pointed out:

It does not mean that we are *a priori* against an opposition which
wants to assist in the speedier and easier implementation of the
Popular Front program, in the speedier rebuilding of the country
and in correcting certain mistakes. I myself have often said that
there are shortcomings and some mistakes. Neither I, nor anyone of
us, have anything against this kind of constructive opposition. An
opposition which helps to correct mistakes is necessary, but not the
kind which takes advantage of certain shortcomings to put a spoke
in the wheel of our development and turn it backwards.[3]

Though on this occasion too a public undertaking was given that the opposition would not be persecuted, there was no longer any doubt that an opposition, in the true sense of the word, would not be tolerated. This reply to American journalists stated that there were no objections to a *constructive* opposition, that is, only that "opposition which wants to assist in the speedier and easier implementation of the Popular Front program." This is not really a genuine opposition which criticizes from the standpoint of an alternative political program but a so-called comradely criticism within the framewrok of one and the same party, addressed to the like-minded party members who are implementing a jointly adopted program. Even if such a "constructive opposition" should detect certain shortcomings and mistakes, it must not question the validity of the Popular Front program as a whole as this would mean, according to this interpretation, putting a spoke in the wheel of our social development. It could only contribute to correcting mistakes.

One did not have to wait long, however, for the CPY leadership to declare itself unambiguously against the existence of all parties and any opposition as independent political organizations, be they within the Popular Front or outside it. This was done in September 1947, at the Second Congress of the Yugoslav Popular Front. The Congress decided that

> the Popular Front had developed into and become a permanent all-people's political organization with a permanent program, an organization different from all previous political parties and party blocs. It represents a new form of political life, indispensable to our new social order in implementing the unified economic program. Our Popular Front today represents the political unity of workers, peasants, the people's intelligentsia and all working people, and it includes the Communist Party, which has the leading role in it.[4]

The rejection of the legitimacy of party pluralism, which existed at least to a certain extent at the time when the Popular Front was set up, is particularly evident in the new interpretation of the way in which the Popular Front had been founded. Instead of the coalition-like and multi-party character of the Popular Front, at least in some parts of the country, emphasis was laid on the special way in which our Popular Front began, not from above with agreements between different political parties, but from below, from the popular masses, regardless of previous party political affiliation or social position, and under the leadership of the Communist Party . . . . [5]

This emphasized that the Popular Front had not started as a coalition of *equal* participating parties, as several of the most prominent CPY leaders had resolutely maintained in 1944 and 1945, but as a mass movement which had only one leader and which, consequently, should be the only one in existence.

This conclusion, which had led to any traces of the earlier party pluralism disappearing completely was also clearly implicit in the report by the President of the Popular Front of Yugoslavia. He resolutely asserted that *all* the bourgeois parties had lost their prestige and trust and that they should therefore no longer exist:

This shows that all of the pre-war bourgeois parties have been discredited and have lost the right to speak on behalf of the people today. They have shown that they are incapable of running the country; that in the new social order their existence is not justified and that it has become superfluous.[6]

Yet this alone could be the reason for these bourgeois parties being in opposition, because loss of prestige and of the ability to lead in a multi-party system is, as a rule, paid for with loss of votes in elections. After all, as soon as there are several parties with different programs, it is obvious that not all of them could speak on the people's behalf but only the party which wins the elections.

In addition to these political and moral reasons, the abolition of party *competition* in the exercise of power was also justified by higher theoretical reasons. To this end the assumption was put forward that the construction of socialism demanded not only ideological but also political unity, which had to be monolithic in all things. Or, as the President of the Popular Front put it:

The new social order in our country also requires a new form of political life. Numerous political parties with their heterogeneous concepts in our country would represent the greatest hindrance to the speedy and lasting development of our country.

Not only the political but also the economic structure of our country excludes the possibility of the existence of numerous political parties with old programs and old concepts.

A single economic program also demands political unity. Imagine the following scenario: the war has ended, a start has to be made on rebuilding the country, all the people have to be mobilized to carry out numerous and important tasks, and we have diverse parties, led by various people like Grol, Maček, Šubašić, Lazica Marković, Gavrilović, etc. One says: We should not build this bridge first but that other one. Another will say: Why should more help be given for instance, to Bosnia, Lika or Montenegro, instead of some other republic? And all of them together would probably say: Why throw away billions to restore destroyed villages? We should wait until we have recovered a bit or received reparations. . . . We can be sure that such parties would spread these and similar ideas among the people. This would paralyze our strength, it would frustrate everything which brings our country closer to growth and prosperity.[7]

Thus, at a time of great want and general poverty, the President of the Popular Front warned about there being no *prosperity* and *growth* if many heterogeneous parties were to remain. This practically amounted to a choice between party pluralism and economic backwardness and poverty on the one hand, and a monolithic one-party system and economic growth and prosperity on the other. This is what today the so-called modernization theories which deal with questions of accelerated economic development of very backward Third World countries usually recommend. These countries have, as a rule, no democratic traditions, which did, however, exist on the Yugoslav territory, particularly in Serbia, from 1903 to 1914. It should also be pointed out that absolute, monolithic political unity is not a prerequisite for implementing a single economic program but only an appropriate majority in the parliament which passes it. It also means that while such a single economic program is prepared and voted on, different parties can make various proposals, for example, as to where a bridge should be built or who should be given greater assistance. But in the long run, after voting, only one proposal becomes the state plan and program which is carried out in practice. Putting forward various proposals cannot therefore be an obstacle to the gradual progress toward growth and prosperity.

The greatest inconsistency in these attitudes and conclusions of the Second Congress of the Popular Front lay in the fact that they were directed against all parties except one—the CPY—and that they were not directed against the party system *as such* (which could be either multi-party or one-party) and in favor of some kind of *non-party* democracy, but only against party *competition* which would threaten the leading role of the only one remaining party. In other words, with the exception of the CPY, all parties, insofar as they had not already been wiped out as opposition parties, were required to merge with the Popular Front and lose their own political identity. The merits of the only leading party were emphasized in order to justify this exception:

> The CPY was the initiator and organizer of the Popular Front of Yugoslavia even before the war. It gave the Front all its great experience in organizing and leading a struggle. It gave the Front its cadres, tempered in the struggle, who have served and are serving today as an example—by excelling in fighting in the liberation war, by excelling in rebuilding the country. Becuase of those very characteristics the Communist Party also has the leading role in the Popular Front today. The broad masses have continued to entrust that role to it.[8]

In order that there be no doubt whatsoever about this leading role of the CPY, both in the war and the post-war reconstruction, he warned:

> When the new state was set up, the Communist Party became the leader in the entire field of social development: in building the people's power, that is—in the organization of the state, in building the country, in economic and cultural life and so forth. It performs that role as an integral part of the Popular Front because it is the Front's leading party.[9]

In light of the subsequent conflict with the Communist Party of the Soviet Union, what was of particular interest was the question: "Does the

CPY have some other program outside the Popular Front? No—answered J. B. Tito. The Communist Party has no other program. The program of the Popular Front is also its program."[10] Thus the CPY alone retained its own separate party organization but accepted in turn the Popular Front program in the adoption of which other political parties, which had in the meantime lost their own organizational independence, had also participated.

This was, however, only the first step toward the complete disappearance of the last remnants of the former party pluralism. The next decisive step was taken at the Fifth CPY Congress in July 1948. On that occasion, besides leading to other unfavorable consequences, the Resolution of the Communist Information Bureau (Cominform) on the situation in the CPY also contributed to a rapid ideological homogenization of the Popular Front. Attacks by Stalin and the Cominform on the CPY brought into particularly sharp focus the question of relations between the Communist Party and the Popular Front. The "critics" of the CPY severely reproached it for dissolving itself, as a vanguard, Bolshevik organization, in the Popular Front, that "non-party mass of all classes and strata" and of all kinds of "bourgeois" parties. The CPY was accused of accepting the idea that it could not and should not have its own separate program but that it should content itself with the program of the Popular Front. This only went to show, in the words of these "critics," that CPY leaders were Menshevik liquidators who had revised the Bolshevik concept of the party, thereby preparing the liquidation of their own party as "the party of the working class."[11] J. B. Tito was also personally reproached for having declared at one point in his speech at the Second Congress of the Popular Front that the Front's program was also the program of the Communist Party.[12]

These objections could not go without answers or explanations. The CPY leadership countered by saying that this was a case of misunderstanding the relations between the Party and the Front in Yugoslavia, the essence of the Front and the implementation of the leading role of the working class in it. In their reasoning, ". . . the Party is not taking on the program of the Front, on the contrary, the Front receives its basic direction and program from the Communist Party, which is natural considering its leading role in it."[13] This means that the earlier declaration at the Second Congress of the Popular Front—that the Communist Party had no other program but that of the Popular Front—could not be taken in its literal but in its hidden sense, which the ill-intentioned "critics" did not want to recognize. In fact, this hidden, esoteric meaning was subsequently confirmed at the Fifth Congress with the passing of a *separate* CPY Program.

There is no doubt, however, that the reproach about the CPY being watered down in that "non-party mass of all classes and strata" contributed to a decisive and faster change in the earlier pluralistic character of the Popular Front. One of the first people to give a relevant ideological rationale to this change in the current policy was Edvard Kardelj. In his report at the Fifth Congress of the CPY he unambiguously declared:

> The Party has always fought, both openly and publicly, for the leading role of the working class and the Communist Party in the national liberation uprising. Our Party has never concealed this policy, but, on the contrary, it has been telling the working masses that the leading role of the working class and the Communist Party is the chief condition for the victory of the national liberation uprising, because, apart from the CPY, there is no other force which could unite the peoples of Yugoslavia and the working masses in that struggle.[14]

Thus Kardelj contradicted the earlier positions of the CPY. While the liberation struggle against the occupying forces was still going on and while allies and fellow fighters were still needed, the CPY leaders had stressed, with regard to the relations between the coalition parties in the Popular Front, that "to speak about greater or lesser influence of one party or another would be unjustified" and that in the Front "diktat by any side is out of the question."[15] But when the guns fell silent and when the question of power arose, Kardelj no longer agreed to the absence of diktat and to the same influence and equality of the coalition parties in the Popular Front, but ascribed the leading role to the CPY and denied organizational and political independence to the other parties.

The actual ideological explanation of the need and historical necessity for such an irreplaceable leading party was very simple.

> The leading role in the Popular Front belongs to the Communist Party because it reflects the aspiration and role of the most progressive social class and because it is guided by the ideology and science of that class—the science of Marxism-Leninism.[16]

This is in fact, that same reasoning which the Bolsheviks used to justify their own sacrosanct leading role. Following this, all that was necessary was to emphasize the internal monolithic state of this leading party and thus come very close to that well-known model of monolithic unity which was established according to the following plan: one view of the world (Marxism-Leninism)—one political program (the program of the ruling party)—one political party (the Bolshevik party)—one great and infallible leader and teacher.

This *overt* and *public* proclamation of the CPY's leading role in the Popular Front also quickly led to their mutual relations being determined in a different way. This was done at the Third Congress of the Popular Front in April 1949. The Cominform's claim that the Popular Front was a "temporary coalition of bourgeois parties" and that the CPY was "drowning" in such a front, was once again rejected. Since Stalin and the Cominform had severely criticized the CPY for not having its own separate program and having accepted the Popular Front program, a converse move was made.[17] At the Fifth Congress, the CPY passed its own separate program which the Popular Front accepted as its own. The Third Congress of the Popular Front said:

> The program of the CPY fully expresses the aims and aspirations of the Popular Front of Yugoslavia, and on this basis, it calls upon all organizations and members of the Popular Front to work comprehensively for the implementation of this program as their own.[18]

Article 2 of the newly adopted Statute of the Popular Front clearly laid donw that "a member of the Popular Front of Yugoslavia cannot be a member of a political organization whose program is contrary to the CPY program . . . ."[19] All the former political opposition parties were thereby completely reduced to fellow-travellers of the CPY. As collective members of the Popular Front, they were obliged to accept the CPY program as their own, though they had not been able to participate at all in its drafting. In addition, Article 1 of the Popular Front Statute *explicitly* stated for the first time that the CPY was the "leading force" of this all-people's political organization. The hegemonic role of the CPY was thus also formally prescribed.

Following such statements by the most responsible leaders of the CPY and the relevant decisions in the Popular Front Statute, any kind of independent existence for the individual opposition parties, and even the very act of mentioning their names in public, became untenable. The majority of the former parties were quickly broken up and for all practical purposes put out of action, and their leaderships dispersed. In time even public references to their names ceased. Some parties simply went underground and, thanks to that, still maintained some semblance of existence for a relatively long time. This refers in particular to the Republican Party and the Croatian Republican Peasant Party which left the deepest traces in post-war political history.

Since the Republican Party was, on the whole, bereft of a wider membership and a large number of its regional branches, the main indicator of its gradual extinction was the *Republika,* owned and published by Vladimir Simić. Though the paper was subsidized by the Popular Front,[20] its publication ran into numerous difficulties such as the refusal by some newsagents to sell it, that as, an artificial decrease of its sale. From time to time the paper published reports quoting specific examples of interference with its sale and distribution. Staša Milijanović, for instance, attributed these actions to:

> local Popular Front mistakes committed by people in currying favor and gaining merits, by people addicted to the habits of the chronically sick state and political organism of the old Yugoslavia, where criticism, even the most loyal one, was not tolerated, and self-criticism unheard of.[21]

Since these arbitrary actions increasingly threatened to acquire a systematic form, Staša Milijanović decided that one should not keep quiet any longer and that the Popular Front members who obstructed the paper's circulation should be told that *Republika* was the organ of a legally permitted party, that that party was organically contained within the Popular Front and that what the paper wrote came under the law on the press.

In 1947 and 1948 the editorial board of *Republika* increasingly complained about newsagents who cancelled orders or who did not return unsold copies. At the same time, the nature of the published articles gradually changed. Except for several editorials by Jaša Prodanović, there were no more complaints about the irregularities and excesses in revolutionary times. The articles were written in a new exhortative and Popular Front manner: they eulogized the Front, Yugoslavia, the Soviet Union and the "calloused hands of Marshal Tito" (Aleksa Tomić's speech at the First Congress of the Popular Front of Serbia).

Thanks to such a change in the manner and content of the writing, *Republika* significantly lengthened its publishing life, though it still bore the notorious reputation of an "opposition" paper which rallied mainly malcontents among its readers and associates.[22] Dragoljub Jovanović confirmed this when writing in his memoirs of the days spent in Mitrovica jail:

> When they again allowed political prisoners to read the press, after four and a half years of 'starvation' in this respect, Radovan Marković, the State Security Administration (UDB) man in the prison and the prisoners' 'guardian angel,' openly declared that we could not receive *Republika* because it was an opposition paper. This was on 22 October 1952.[23]

In 1956, the last year of its publication, *Republika* still had this reputation. Most of the contributions on its pages were still by republicans and other non-Communist writers and its title still stated that *Republika* was the paper of the Yugoslav Republican Democratic Party. What continued to distinguish this paper from other dailies and weeklies were articles on culture and political history of the Serbs and other Yugoslav peoples. One was also reminded of the paper's republican origin and the Party's past on appropriate occasions such as the death of prominent republicans. The obituary of Svetislav M. Berić, a lawyer from Bogatić, stated that while still a student he had joined the Republican Party, and that he had worked as a law clerk with Boža Manojlović, a republican, who had died in the Banjica camp. It was further stated that Berić had broadened his social and political views "by being in the company of one of the most prominent theoreticians of the Republican Party, the late Dr. Mihailo Ilić, former university professor, who was shot by the occupying forces."[24]

Two and a half months after his obituary of a respected republican, the time also came for *Republika*'s death notice. The penultimate issue of *Republika* appeared on 4 September and the last issue, after a long break, on 16 October 1956, with a frontpage editorial entitled: "Notice of the Editorial Board to friends, subscribers and readers of 'Republika'." The editorial said that it would depend on the paper's friends, associates and readers whehter the cessation of its publication would be temporary or permanent. The editorial board explained that material difficulties were the sole reason for the paper temporarily ceasing publication and expressed the hope that, with the readers' help these difficulties would be surmounted. It went on to say that the editorial board had done everything in its power to improve the situation (including increasing the number of pages from eight to ten and introducing entertainment columns, and that the circulation had begun to increase. However, from April 1956, *Politika* had also begun to be published on Tuesdays, that is, on the day on which, almost as of right, *Republika* had been published for ten years, and its circulation began to decline.

Taking its final leave of associates and readers, the editorial board dealt with what it was leaving behind.

> As a political paper the organ of the Yugoslav Republican Democratic party, which joined the Popular Front during the war and made its contribution to the proclamation of a republican form of government, *Republika* has deliberately and distinctly followed and participated in every phase of the general development of the country and its peoples . . . .[25]

In the words of the editorial board, in that activity the paper had been free. The editorial board further listed everything that had been published in the paper, beginning with the chronicle of international events to the numerous contributions on the national, political and cultural history of all our peoples. It also stated that most of *Republika*'s published information concerned the facts about the work and activity of the Yugoslav Republican Democratic Party in the past.

> Besides the historiographic value of these authentic facts, they in themselves and with their moral-political and social content, provide the best answer to the question about the only possible attitude of the people of this movement to contemporary events, as well as about the form and content of their paper, *Republika,* such as it was and, such as, regardless of its not being published at present, it continues to be.[26]

The last political party which with its paper and name was a reminder of the post-war period of socialist development having started with party pluralism, thus disappeared from the political scene of Serbia and Belgrade.

A considerably more superficial and fainter though longer trail was left by the Croatian Republican Peasant Party (HRSS). This was perhaps the only party which was permitted (the word should be understood in its literal sense) to extend at least to a modest extent, its local and district committees. The power of the time tacitly allowed this in the hope that Vlatko Maček's influence in Croatian villages would thereby be eliminated. Or, as Branko Petranović put it:

> The Party retained some of these organizations in order to paralyze the activity of the deposed classes and to eradicate the influence by some of the older politicians and by the spirit of Maček's ideas. . . . In 1947, the CPY Central Committee was not in favor of liquidating the HRSS. The Party leadership proceeded from the assumption that the CPY organization should work more or less within the HRSS organizations, maintaining through it the unity of the democratic masses in the village. The existence of the HRSS countered the actions of the Maček followers to restore the HRSS.[27]

Due to the gracious attitude of the CPY in 1945 and 1946 the HRSS leadership began to establish rural and district committees in every region with a Croatian population. In January 1946, the Executive Committee of the Party drew up instructions for elections in local and district organizations of the HRSS, which ordered the Party's representatives in every village and initiative committees of district organizations to conduct elections in their areas for the committees of the HRSS local organizations.[28] Work was then begun to establish these organizations and committees and this was regularly reported in *Slobodni dom* in the column entitled "From the Croatian Republican Peasant Party." Moreover, HRSS local and district organizations were not only established in Croatia but also in Bosnia and Hercegovina and in Bačka.[29] *Hrvatski glas,* published by the HRSS Committee for Bosnia and Hercegovina, especially bears witness to this.[30] The resolution of the First National Conference of the HRSS, held in Sarajevo draws the conclusion: "The revival of party life and the election of HRSS committees for Bosnia and Hercegovina will have a beneficial

effect on the efforts and work of all the peoples of the country, and particularly on the Croat's correct political orientation."[31] There was also a
warning that all attempts to form new factions among the Croatian people
were both superfluous and harmful, since any split in Croat ranks would
weaken the Popular Front. This, in fact, was a warning to malcontents
who thought of founding a new political party.

At the same time, the reasons also became clearer for the gracious attitude of the CPY to such an increase in the basic and district organizations
of the HRSS. The CPY did not display the same attitude toward similar
attempts by peasant and other bourgeois parties in Serbia. In contrast, for
example, to the leadership of the Yugoslav Republican Democratic Party,
particularly in Jaša Prodanović's lifetime, the HRSS leadership, established
in the village of Taborište in Kordun on 29 April 1944, had accepted from
the very start the role of transmission belt of the CPY, having thus waived
the party's separate status and identity. This was not the role of an equal
adviser but of a disciplined fellow-traveller who follows his leader unques-
tioningly in everything. The CPY gave preference to this kind of fellow-
traveller over the rest of the opposition parties. What contributed to this
in particular was the fact that the HRSS did not, in fact, have a separate
political program but had accepted the Popular Front program from the
outset. It was Mile Glavaš who with the following words warned a small
group

> of our covert enemies who want the HRSS to serve them as a barri-
> cade behind which they will work contrary to the general line of the
> Popular Front. . . it is necessary first of all to bear in mind (and this
> should never be forgotten) that the HRSS is an integral part of the
> Popular Front and that its activity cannot and should not deviate
> from the course of the Popular Front. All the more so, and, if you
> like, because the Popular Front is in full accord with the program of
> the HRSS, and with the teaching of the Radić Brothers.[32]

It was even asserted that the post-war social and political order was a consistent and complete realization of the Radić brothers' teaching.

But very quickly even this accommodating collaborator became superfluous. After the Second Congress of the Popular Front in September
1947, the CPY withdrew its support for the continuing existence of the

local and district branches of the HRSS. The entire HRSS party organization was reduced to the Executive Committee in Zagreb and its newspaper *Slobodni dom*. According to Branko Petranović, this was a result
of the new CPY attitude to party pluralism: "By abandoning the further
development of the HRSS, the Party retained the organization's top
echelons through which manifest support for the policies of the Popular
Front was expressed."[33] The first sign of this change was observed on the
pages of *Slobodni dom*. After the Second Congress of the Popular Front,
reports on the activity of HRSS area branches no longer appeared. Even
the column entitled "From the Croatian Republican Peasant Party" was
abolished and this eloquently confirmed that in the organizational sense,
the Party was on the whole reduced to the Executive Committee in Zagreb. In April 1948, Franjo Gaži did declare that "in each district of the
People's Republic of Croatia, where Croats live there is a district organization of the Croatian Republican Party."[34] But this was one of those
statements intended for foreign consumption.

The last traditional characteristics of the former Croatian Peasant Party
from the time of the Radić brothers also started to disappear. As opposed
to the Communists, the members of this Party were not indifferent to
Christianity but were, as a rule, devout believers. After the liberation, the
HRSS also tried to retain this feature. This was reflected, for example, in
solemn editorials in *Slobodni dom* at Christman and Easter, in citing regularly the motto "Faith in God and Peasant Concord" and in the publication of an annual calendar—*The Republican Christmas Book*—which,
among other things, fulfilled the function of a Catholic calendar. Even new
customs were initiated in the traditional Catholic spirit. Paying respects
to J. B. Tito did not begin with the celebration of his birthday but of his
name-day which fell on 19 March, the day of St. Joseph, the Immaculate
Virgin Marty's bethrothed.[35] With the subsequent policy of atheization
this traditional form was rejected. At first, the formal celebration of J. B.
Tito's name-day was abandoned, and only his birthday was celebrated.
Later, the observance of other marks of respect for Christian rites was
also done away with. Radić's motto "Faith in God and Peasant Concord"
appeared for the last time in the title of *Slobodni dom* on 26 November
1948, while 26 March was the last time that an editorial on the occasion
of Easter was published. After that, *Slobodni dom* differed not a whit
from the papers of the CPY and the Popular Front.

In 1950 it was publicly acknowledged that the HRSS was left without regional branches and an organized membership. This was disclosed at the regional consultative conference of HRSS followers, held on the eve of the plenary meeting of the Executive Committee which had not met since 1946.[36] At the plenary meeting on 11 October 1950, held "for the purpose of revitalizing the Executive Committee and choosing a new Presidium,"[37] Ante Vrkljan explained why a separate party organization had been abandoned. According to him:

> while the restoration of the broad network of HRSS organizations in 1945 and 1946 and at the beginning of 1947, had a positive effect on the revival of political life in the village on the one hand, it led, on the other, to weaknesses, because there was infiltration by village speculators, Maček's followers, clericalists and even some Ustashe. This organizational form was, therefore, abandoned with an ever increasing number of the Antun and Stjepan Radić followers joining the district, city and basic organizations of the Popular Front. The work of the members of the Executive Committe has since then proceeded exclusively within the framework of the Popular Front.[38]

In other words, the HRSS had had to give up its branches in the villages and district organizations because enemies had begun to infiltrate them. This was also the price the HRSS had to pay in order to preserve the "indestructible alliance with its working class brothers, organized in the Communist Party."[39] The very nature of this alliance within the framework of the Popular Front was best expressed by the following instructions: "The entire work of the Popular Front should continue to be directed as an increasingly consistent and full implementation of the Communist Party's political line."[40]

Thus the HRSS was reduced to only the Executive Committee in Zagreb and *Slobodni dom* as its organ, both of which, in Branko Petranović's words, "expressed and implemented manifest support for the Popular Front policy." The reason for this relatively rapid disbandment of the HRSS was the change in the CPY attitude toward individual political organizations. The CPY decided that various cultural and educational organizations like *Seljačka Sloga* (Peasant Concord), *Napredak* (Progress), *Prosvjeta* (Enlightenment) and *Preporod* (Rebirth), were a more appropirate means for attracting the peasant masses, penetrating the villages and eradicating the influence of the bourgeois parties. To that end, Branko Petranović says: "after 1945, the Communist Party of Croatia championed *Seljačka Sloga* more than the HRSS committees, though these existed right up until 1948."[41] This, in fact, was also the reason why *Slobodni dom* ceased too write about the local and district HRSS organizations and described instead only the activity of the *Seljačka Sloga* cultural and educational organizations which was spreading rapidly. In 1954, there were 502 branches of *Seljačka Sloga* with 35,000 members in Croatia,[42] and the following year, 553 branches with 41,000 members.[43]

The last act in the gradual disappearance of the HRSS was reflected in the eradication of the Party's very name. By the mid-1950s, the name of the Party only appeared in the heading of *Slobodni dom.* Several months used to go by without the name of HRSS being mentioned on the pages of *Slobodni dom.* It was only mentioned, as a rule, in very rare circumstances, for example, on the death of some prominent Party member[44] or on the anniversary of the inaugural meeting in Taborište near Slunj.[45] Finally, the name HRSS itself also disappeared. In the last issue of *Slobodni dom,* of 26 December 1963, the editorial board informed its readers and associates that the paper was ceasing publication "for material and financial reasons." The board omitted, however, to mention the name of its publisher—the HRSS and a reader at that time could not have had any inkling that this stereotyped explanation of financial difficulties concealed the eradication of a scarcely visible trace of the former party pluralism.

The fact that the last vestige of party pluralism was eliminated after so many years will certainly surprise the reader today. To explain this it would be necessary to look at the minutes of the closed meetings of the then leading bodies of the CPY since it was on their attitude that the fate of the opposition parties depended. Since such an inspection is impossible, a proper explanation cannot yet be given. The vestiges of former party pluralism were probably so faint and harmless that they could not cause any considerable trouble. Besides, the politicians of that time, inclined to pragmatism as they were, were not bothered by a certain discord between the claim that the multi-party system had long since been superceded and the fact that a paper continued to appear which, at least on paper, was published by a non-communist party. This made it possible, for example, to accuse Milovan Djilas at the end of the 1950s of intending to *reintroduce* a multi-party system while at the same time, *Slobodni dom* continued to be published by the HRSS until the end of 1963.

Yet, besides these negligible illogicalities, the basic question of the nature of the party system had been resolved as far back as the end of 1947. The final elimination of the external semblances of the former pluralism was speeded up with the objections raised by the Cominform about the CPY "being diluted" in the Popular Front. As early as 1948 the Popular Front therefore, lost not only its pluralistic but also its political character because its basic activity was reduced to organizing public works.

> The tendency to transform the Popular Front into an organization to rally labor and organize labor drives increasingly gained the upper hand. Execpt for some areas, there were no political conferences, entertainment for young people, or physical culture rallies. The Popular Front organizations increasingly acquired the appearance of purely labor organizations. Actions prepared without political work reduced the Popular Front to an organization for mobilizing manpower. CPY measures were implemented by organs of people's power or directly by Party cells and committees.[46]

Thus, the Popular Front was reduced to a mere "transmission belt" to perform current tasks.

2. Denying the Legitimacy of Party Pluralism

When the post-war party pluralism was finally abolished, there were several attempts to dispute the legitimacy of the multi-party system as such. Such attempts contain nothing essentially new with regard to the arguments against parties and partyfactionalism expounded in the 19th century when the party system in the present-day sense of the word was established, or in the period after the October Revolution when a one-party Bolshevik dictatorship was introduced. These challenges are, however, very important and interesting because they represent a fundamental factor in Yugoslav political conditions.

The simplest reason put forward against party pluralism was by its nature an historic and political one and concerns the conduct of individual party leaders during the war. There were attempts to portrary the abolition of all the parties as a consequence of their betrayal of the country. Thus, the following explanation, for example, was given in November 1968:

> The question of our creating a multi-party system has from the very beginning never been raised in our country because all the leaderships of the bourgeois parties had on the whole compromised themselves by collaborating with the occupying forces or fled abroad and worked against our liberation movement. The popular masses came over to our side, fought together with us and accepted our program. Why should we now invent new parties? [47]

How convincing this explanation of the reasons why all political parties except one, were abolished depends on how reliable the historical facts on which it is based are. Factual proof is arrived at not only through documents, records and manuscripts but also through eyewitness accounts. One such account from 1944, which we have already quoted says:

> In Slovenia, the Liberation Front was organized early, on 27 April 1941, two weeks after the fall of Yugoslavia. The following parties joined it: the Communist and the Christian Socialist Party, the Sokol Organization, the Social Democratic Party, sections of the Slovene Peasant Party, of the Slovene Catholic Party, led by Dr. Anton Brecelj, and another ten or so political groups and organizations. . . . To speak about the greater or lesser influence of one party or another would be unjust. . . . In Croatia, the liberation movement consists only of the Communist Party, the Croatian Peasant Party and the Independent Democratic Party (which represents chiefly Serbs in Croatia). [48]

Since we have here a testimony from the war itself, it is obvious that it enjoys greater credibility than later accounts, given at a time when memories of the war and of the participation of individual bourgeois parties in the national liberation struggle had already begun to fade. In addition, certain practical aims and interests, demanding that the description and explanation of former historical events be adapted to current needs, probably also played a role. Therefore, a plausible explanation which would justify the abolition of party pluralism was necessary. Such an explanation was represented by the claim that only the CPY had taken part in the national liberation struggle and that for that reason a multi-party system could not be allowed: "It is clear that we do not approve of a multi-party system. In our country, only the Communist Party carried out the revolution and conducted the liberation war."[49] This also showed, however, that any fundamental change in the attitude toward an important political question, such as the question of party pluralism, also demanded a new explanation of the relevant historical facts, and even the destruction of the factual basis on which the original political attitude had rested.

The following attempt to deny the legitimacy of party pluralism, founded on the assertion that this pluralism has no raison d'être in a society constructing socialism, merits considerably greater attention.

> A multi-party system is needed where various parties at odds with one another have different programs on how different internal issues should be temporarily resolved but with the tendency to preserve that old system. Some of them have the old reactionary formulas in their program, others are a little more progressive, but all parties aim at preserving the old capitalist system.
>
> Our country, however, is not a capitalist country; here socialism is being built. A multi-party system has no raison d'être at all. That is why people coming from abroad have difficulty understanding this. When socialism has been built the Communist Party too will gradually disappear as a party, and our state is already gradually withering away, because the whole administrative process is being transformed down to the people.[50]

This is, in fact, an assertion that the multi-party system aims to protect the old order of things and that for this reason nothing essentially new can be achieved within its framework. This, however, is only partly true because in the contemporary multi-party system there exist socialist and even revolutionary parties which do not aim to preserve the old, capitalist system but which try by their participation in public life and parliament to pave the way for the construction of a socialist society. True enough, this is only one of the possibilities inherent in such a system and a barely feasible possibility at that. But this suffices to point out that a multi-party system as such is not a closed system preventing any possibility of a new, and even radical, change in the existing social order.

It is not only a question here, however, of assessing the openness of a multi-party system but also of re-examining the ideological tenet that there can be no socialism without a one-party system. This tenet practically amounts to the conviction that a society building socialism must have only a single program of social development, advocated by the ruling party, and that that program would be, in the nature of things, socialist.[51] Conversely, according to this conviction, socialism cannot be built if the existence of various parties is permitted.

It is interesting that we also come across a similar belief in the Soviet Union and other countries in Eastern Europe. The author of this idea was Lenin but it was Stalin who developed it and gave it its final form. He identified the political system of socialism with the dictatorship of the proletariat, and the dictatorship of the proletariat with the dictatorship of the ruling Communist Party. In Stalin's view, the dictatorship of the proletariat must be the *permanent* political order of society in which socialism is built and this dictatorship is not possible if it does not rely on one *permanent* leading political force. In the Soviet Union, this leading force could only be represented by the ruling Communist Party headed by Stalin himself. Or, as Stalin warned:

> Only the Party of the proletariat, only the Party of the Communists is capable of performing this role of principal leader in the system of the dictatorship of the proletariat. . . .
>
> Without the Party as the basic leading force, a lasting and firm dictatorship of the proletariat is not possible at all. . . .[52]

In other words, Stalin contested the existence of any other kind of political party, even of a workers' party, which would recruit their members chiefly from the ranks of workers. This stance of his exposed him to the criticism that the Soviet dictatorship of the proletariat was not in fact the dictatorship of the proletariat as a class but the dictatorship of one party which had only a minority of workers in its ranks. He shamelessly acknowledged the criticism to be well-founded and reduced the dictatorship of the proletariat to the dictatorship of one party:

> One should consider as the highest expression of the leading role of the party, for example, in our country, in the Soviet Union, in a

country of the dictatorship of the proletariat, the fact that our *soviets* and other mass organizations do not resolve a single important political or organizational question without Party directives. *In that sense,* it could be said that the dictatorship of the proletariat is, *in essence,* the 'dictatorship' of its vanguard, the 'dictatorship' of its Party.[53]

If we take Stalin's concept of the dictatorship of the proletariat a step further, we quickly see that it amounts to the dictatorship of the highest Party leadership, that is, of Stalin himself as its General Secretary. Stalin again:

> It is not possible to achieve and maintain the dictatorship of the proletariat without the Party, strong in its compactness and iron discipline. But iron discipline in the Party cannot be conceived without unity of will, without the complete and unconditional unity of action by all Party members.[54]

Since the thought and will of different people cannot be entirely equated without losing the spontaneity and individuality of every person, such total and unconditional unity of thought and action was possible only at the cost of absolute subjugation to the will of the highest leadership with Stalin at its head.

In fact, this absolute subordination of the rank and file to the will of the leadership, personified by the great leader and teacher, was a logical consequence of the abolition of the multi-party system which had even existed in the first few years after the October Revolution. While there was still free discussion and political competition in public life, the internal life of the Bolshevik Party too was under their influence.

> Destroying the multiparty system the Bolsheviks had no inkling of the consequences to themselves. They imagined that outside that system they would still remain what they had always been: a disciplined but free association of militant Marxists. They took it for granted that the collective mind of the party would continue to be shaped by the customary exchange of opinion, the give and take of theoretical and political arguments. They did not realize that they could not

ban all controversy outside their ranks and keep it alive within their ranks: they could not abolish democratic rights for society at large and preserve those rights for themselves alone.[55]

Hence, the Bolsheviks too, in depriving their political rivals and opponents of freedom of opinion, also deprived themselves of that same freedom. Had they continued to discuss freely and openly differences of opinion within their own ranks, this would have been a contagious example for non-Bolshevik parties which could not then be denied that freedom kept by the Bolsheviks for themselves. "No body politic," said Deutscher, "can be nine-tenths mute and one-tenth vocal. Having imposed silence on non-Bolshevik Russia, Lenin's party had in the end to impose silence on itself as well."[56]

After the Second World War, the ruling parties in the countries of people's democracies adopted this Bolshevik idea that socialism could only be built if party pluralism was replaced by a one-party system, which was based on a monolithic unity of thought and action. The belief was also accepted that only this ruling party could have a genuine socialist program. Few people publicly raised the crucial question: what should be done if the converse happens, that is, if the ruling party does not implement a socialist program, because it has either never seriously applied it or has ceased to do so in time, or because it has become corrupt and accepted, for example, a bureaucratic or state-capitalist program of social development? The CPY leadership provided the best confirmation of just how appropriate this question was when it began, after the publication of the Cominform Resolution in 1948, to claim that Stalin and the CPSU had given up the program for building socialism and that the Soviet Union could, therefore, no longer be called a socialist country. Moreover, basically the same question which was raised then was: "What is the attitude in the Soviet Union toward workers? How, then, can such a country be described as socialist in the full sense of the word?" The answer which followed was unequivocal:

They have not set off along the road of building genuine socialism but along the road of the worst kind of state capitalism, not relying on the workers below but on their own NKVD (State Security Service—now the KGB) and their armed forces. A caste is being created which is a burden to the countless working masses of those peoples. Or, is it really the socialist way, to solve the national question by resettling millions of people in Siberia and various deserts? This has nothing in common with socialism. These methods show that these people are not on the socialist path.[57]

This clearly confirmed that a one-party system as such is not a sufficiently reliable guarantee that the current policy of the ruling party will be socialist. Consequently, it is not possible, as is often done, to justify and defend the need for this system in the name of socialism. As the examples of the Soviet Union or Poland have shown, socialism is in serious danger if its construction is the monopoly of one party, since there are no gurarantees that the leadership of that party will resist all the temptations inherent in power.

To avoid any misunderstanding, this naturally does not mean that a multi-party system, particularly the one with several socialist alternatives, provides such a reliable guarantee. Far from it. A multi-party system provides certainly no absolute assurance that the policy of the party in power will always be socialist in everything. In contrast, however, to a one-party system, party pluralism, if not a closed system, offers a far greater opportunity of turning to public opinion and of lawful resistance to any corrupt policy and, above all, the opportunity of regular changes in power. Of course, there will always be those who say that a socialist society is built more easily if there is less resistance to overcome, and there will be less resistance if there is no opposition and no party contest, that is, if there is a one-party system. This is undoubtedly correct but it is also true to say that greater abuses of power are possible in such a case for the simple reason that the possibility of public control and criticism of the rulers is substantially limited, and because they who are in power, as a rule, are not afraid of having to pay for their mistakes in the policy which they pursue with the loss of their power. Thus there is less resistance but the possibility of very dangerous abuse of power is far greater and the best proof of this is the well-known extent of the loathsome violation of human freedoms, and even human lives, in the one-party systems such as fascism and Stalinism. We could, therefore, rightly draw the following lesson from our recent historical experience: "Never, absolutely never, should a single power in this world exist without an opposition and without opponents."[58] In this respect, not even a power which hides behind a program of socialist construction should be an exception.

There is, however, yet one more weighty reason against the multi-party system. This is the assertion that the multi-party system has an inherent tendency toward destruction, civil disorder and a return to the old ways. Moreover, this possibility of a return to the old ways was the main justification in the post-war years for using revolutionary coercion against any attempt to revive the multi-party system, since such a revival would lead to the destruction of the revolution's achievements. This admonition is contained in the following words:

> We are constantly criticized for not having a multi-party system; that a large number, in fact, the majority of our citizens are deprived of the opportunity to belong to a political organization and so forth. . . . But what would a multi-party system represent in our conditions and what does it really mean?
>
> A multi-party system means several parties and programs concerning social life and development. It means that the exponents of the revolution and the social transformation allow the organized destruction of the achievements of the revolution, for which blood has already been shed and for which armed battle has already been decided between the old and the obsolete and the new revolutionary forces which bring progress to social development. Which genuine and consistent revolution in history has of its own free will given its opponent his arms back to fight against the success of the revolution? Not a single one! The West does not want to understand this historical truth or else it does understand it, but wants to leads us onto thin ice . . . . Even some socialists in the West are asking us why don't we have a multi-party system. On the other hand, they like genuine socialism, but they cannot understand that for us, the way to socialism cannot be through a multi-party system but against it.[59]

At first glance, the true scope of this warning is unclear. If it takes into consideration the facts acknowledged earlier about the participation of individual bourgeois parties in the national liberation struggle, then this restriction on the free activity of individual parties could not refer to the Christian Socialists, the Social Democratic Party, sections of the Slovene

Catholic Party and the Slovene Peasant Party, or to the Croatian Peasant Party and the Independent Democratic Party, as it had been explicitly said that all of them had fought in the war on the same side as the CPY.[60] In addition, since the Yugoslav Republican Party, the People's Peasant Party, the Agrarian Party and several other groups and parties had joined the Popular Front while the battles for the country's libeation were still going on, this warning could not refer to them either. All this is on condition that these facts are still acknowledged.

If these facts are no longer borne in mind, however, then what this warning really implies is that to retain a multi-party system would mean a return to a situation of civil disorder and war. In other words, there is no civil peace and security, and, therefore, no socialism either if there are several parties. To all intents and purposes this amounts to a choice between a one-party system and civil war. Since the possibility of forming other parties in addition to the ruling one is based on the constitutional freedom of opinion and association as a *general* and *equal* right, the following warning could also be sounded: either there will be civil peace without freedom, or there will be freedom without civil peace and security, because uncontrolled freedom of opinion and association necessarily leads to a multi-party system, which in turn leads to civil war and counter-revolution.

It is interesting that this dilemma irresistibly recalls the similar choice with which Thomas Hobbes confronted his contemporaries when he pointed out that they have to choose between the state of nature, in which the liberty of every individual has no restraints, and the civil state, that is the state in which the individual renounces his rights and powers and absolutely subordinates himself to the sovereign power, that great Leviathan or that Mortal God "to which wee owe under the Immortall God our peace and defence."[61] The dramatic nature and weight of this dilemma lies in it, in fact, being a choice between insecurity in the state of nature, that is, the time of war "where every man is Enemy to ever man" and "wherein men live without other security than what their own strength, and their own invention shall furnish them withall,"[62] and security provided by the sovereign power, that is, the state which alone is capable, thanks to the absolute power at its disposal, of ensuring peace in political society. In other words, this is a choice between absolute freedom and extreme insecurity in the state of civil war, on the one hand, and absolute subordination and desirable security in the state of civil peace, on the other hand. In the present-day one-party system, this choice has been merely simplified, because the reasons for the emergence of civil disorder and war do not lie in unlimited individual freedom as such but in the freedom to associate in political parties, because the multi-party system is considered to be the main threat to civil peace and security. According to this idea, all citizens, except members of the ruling party, should waive the right to organize political parties in return for peace and security.

Lastly, in addition to the threat of civil war, there is another special reason which is sometimes quoted when the need to set up a multi-party system is challenged. It is the assertion that to establish several political parties would lead to the collapse of Yugoslavia as a multi-national state:

> Our measures are often not understood abroad, and for that reason the question is often asked as to why we do not have a multi-party system. The answer to this question becomes clearer when our country is seen as a country of many nationalities and when one bears in mind the situation at the time of the old Yugoslavia which, though formally unified under the Treaty of Versailles, was not a united state but a heterogenously composed conglomerate, held together only by force of arms and which collapsed as soon as war came. There were many parties then. Not all were allowed but there were some in Slovenia, in Croatia, in Serbia and in Montenegro. If those parties had wanted the support of the people, they first of all had to pursue the purely local policy of a nation and this prevented the setting up of a united state.

> Should we not start to form several parties, we would have to ask the question: What kind of parties would they be? If one was formed in Slovenia, for the Slovene nation, another in Montenegro, a third in Serbia, then in Macedonia and Croatia, it would mean having a disunited state which would again disintegrate. For these reasons, for these purely practical reasons, and not only reasons of principle we cannot allow such parties to be founded. Our aspiration is the unity of all.[63]

This statement asserts that there is a direct causal relationship between party pluralism and the possibility of the Yugoslav multi-national state disintegrating. It is true that in a multi-national state with party pluralism there is a tendency to form separate national parties for each nation, as, for example, the Croatian Peasant Party before the war, though usually there are parties which also rally members of various nations because certain socio-political and not national factors have been more crucial in the parties' foundation. In the same vein one should bear in mind that, as a rule, a one-party system in a multinational state is not free from this "sin" or tendency, either. It is possible, for example, for the ruling party as well to be organized as a special federation of national parties in individual federal units, for the formation of which not only ideological and political working class factors but primarily national ones are of crucial significance. If the ruling party in a one-party system is organized as a federation of national parties of each individual nation, one can expect that sooner or later, at least one of the national parties will start pursuing "a purely local policy of a nation." It must be admitted that, from time to time, leanings toward such a narrow national policy in Yugoslavia have existed but such phenomena have become apparent only after the fall of some republican leaders. Kardelj's war-time letter criticizing Andrija Hebrang's leanings toward Croatian separatism was not published until 1948:

> What is primarily at stake is that matters in Croatia will not go well as long as he is there. His whole mentality and character are such as to represent a constant tendency toward weakening Croatia's ties with Yugoslavia. This is demonstrated by specific instances but more particularly by the fact that we have to deal constantly with the same negative elements in Croatia. Firstly, at every turn Andrija Hebrang manifests his Croat nationalist bias.[64]

What is most interesting is that this was not the last example of nationalist chauvinism within the setup of the ruling party of a federal unit.

Despite these attempts to challenge the legitimacy of party pluralism and to justify the advantages and validity of a one-party system, the fact remains that this was not enough. Memories of the earlier forms of the party system had still not faded, and, some of the earlier statements about the characteristics of some one-party systems could not be easily forgotten. Thus, in the CPY document of July 1940 we find the one-party system equated with totalitarianism.[65] This was a logical consequence of the conviction previaling at the time that, in comparison with the multi-party system, the one-party system was less acceptable and justified and, therefore, its legitimacy debatable.

To avoid a possible critical comparison between the one-party system and party pluralism, the claim was soon resorted to that there were no great differences between the two. This, for example, was the purpose of the following explanation of the nature of our political system:

> Our entire system is based on such foundations, on such principles, that one cannot speak of a one-party system. We are a socialist country, not a centralized but a decentralized socialist country in both the economic and political respect. The direction of our policy is not determined by individual parties, those in power and those in opposition, by laying down certain directions in laws and elsewhere through a confrontation of views between these two elements. We have the Socialist Alliance of the Working People of Yugoslavia and all our citizens who work, all who do not live as parasites are its members. There are also trade unions, the League of Communists, young people's and women's and other social organizations and individuals. It goes without saying that the existence of some separate party is absurd because the conflict of different views is developed within the Socialist Alliance. If there is a conflict of views, there can be no question of a one-party system.[66]

Since the question of the nature of the elections had also been raised, this was demonstrated by the example of the way in which deputies were nominated and elected, which, according to these words, confirmed that a new form of a multi-party system existed in our country: "As you see, this is also a multi-party system, only in a new form. This is parliamentarianism, but at a higher level than in the West."[67] Only two years later, when the question was asked: "How do you view democratization: within the system of a single party or should it be expressed by a free difference of views? "—a similar answer was given:

> . . . I and all of us together do not believe that freedom of views can exist only in a multi-party system, but also in a one-party system, though our system is not a one-party system because our Socialist

Alliance of the Working People incorporates various groups, various
ex-followers of individual parties, etc. I believe free discussion is also
possible in a system such as ours, as well as in other socialist countries,
because the most democratic way is to accept the crystallized opinion of the majority.[68]

It should be said right away that the characteristics of the one-party
and multi-party systems have been well grasped in these two more or less
similar answers to foreign correspondents. Since a political party represents an association of like-minded individuals (hence a single party program and internal discipline which ensures this unanimity of views), it is
obvious that there cannot be confrontations and conflicts, between essentially different views in a system in which only one party exists and
rules. This conclusion is all the more awkward since, as it is very widely
held, free expression and conflict of views are identical with democracy
as such. If it was asserted that our new political order was genuinely democratic, then it had to be demonstrated that we also had freedom of expression and conflict of *different* views. As the assertion had already been
made, it was also easy to draw the conclusion that our system was not, in
fact, a one-party system where there was no such confict of opinion, but
really a new form of the multi-party system of which it could even be said
that it represented parliamentarianism at a higher level than in the West.
More than two decades had to pass, however, before Edvard Kardelj called
this new and higher form of pluralism, which cannot be described either as
a one-party or a multi-party system, the *pluralism of self-managing interests.*
This explanation would certainly be more convincing if more account
was taken of the fact that what is most important in answering the question
of whether a given system is one-party or multi-party, is the number of
legally recognized and existing parties and their mutual relations. This fact,
however, was neglected, in order to draw the conclusion subsequently that
free expression and the conflict of various political views alone are enough
for the existence of the so-called new form of the multi-party system. This
is, however, a task which goes beyond the scope of our research.
The contraction of the post-war party pluralism into a one-party system
also led to a certain confusion with respect to the meaning and scope of
the constitutional guarantee of freedom of political association. The question was raised as to whether freedom of association was an equal right

enjoyed by all citizens without exception. With the establishment of the one-party system there could no longer be a positive answer to this question since the equality of all citizens before the law is only possible if all citizens enjoy the freedom to associate in political parties or if this freedom is denied to all, without any exceptions. To put it in a nutshell, this freedom must be enjoyed by everybody or nobody at all. It seems that at the time when party pluralism was converted into party monism this reasoning was present and that there was a feeling that to some extent so-called non-party democracy would perhaps be the only principled and fair solution in accordance with the principle of legal and political equality. Since at this time all the bourgeois parties, as members of the Popular Front, had, on the whole, lost party individuality, justice required that there should be no exception to this. This was all the more evident because, in one way or another, the CPY had demanded from the coalition partners in the Popular Front that they cease customary party activity. It was, therefore, all the more awkward for it to seek from others what it did not agree to itself. Yet, as always, a "happy" solution was found on this occasion, too, according to which all the other parties had to become extinct straightaway while the CPY alone would exist a little longer as a separate organization and then also wither away gradually. The ultimate fate of all the parties would thus be the same, the only difference being that it would not be simultaneous.

We come across the first traces of this solution in 1951 in the following answer to a foreign journalist:

> To build socialism, ways have to be found which make it possible for it to be built as quickly and as easily as possible. When socialism has already been built, that is, when it has passed to a higher phase—communism—there is no question of any kind of parties or a one-party system: the state, moreover, withers away, and so does the role of the party and of the one-party system.[69]

This was explicitly confirmed in another answer to a foreign journalist six years later: "At our Sixth Congress, we provided the orientation for the withering away of the state and the Communist Party. This is, however, a process which will last for quite some time."[70] We also encounter basically the same thought in the League of Communists of Yugoslavia (LCY) program of 1958, which, true enough, does not refer to withering away but to the gradual disappearance of the leading political role of the LCY: "Taken in perspective, the leading political role of the LCY will disappear with the development and strengthening of the increasingly comprehensive forms of direct socialist democracy."[71]

The thesis about the gradual withering away of the ruling party after all the bourgeois parties have been dissolved represents the last act in the denial of the legitimacy of party pluralism and the justification of the historical necessity of the guiding role of the leading party. When the collective memory had more or less faded after some twenty years, it was no longer necessary to rake up the past in order to dispute the original party pluralism and justify the subsequent monism. It was even possible to reject explicitly the idea of the withering away of the Communist Party and the disappearance of its leading role, as the following statement bears out:

> As you know, at the Sixth Congress we spoke about the withering away of the state, but we did not speak about the withering away of the Party because that would have been premature. The withering away of the state is a lengthy process and it is implemented in the present stage with the growing participation in self-management. The withering away of the LCY, however, or the weakening of its role is out the question. What some of our friends in East European countries say about our wanting to reduce the Party's role to that of a mere educator isn't correct.[72]

3. The Constitutional and Legal Status of Party Pluralism

Older consitutions and legal systems based on them did not usually contain special provisions about political parties, nor did they define the nature of a given party system. A typical example is the American Constitution of 1787, passed at a time when the party system in the present meaning of the word had not yet been established. The Constitution does not even mention explicitly the freedom of association and the subsequent formation of individual parties was based on the right of the people peaceably to assemble, guaranteed in the First Amendment, and by other rights which are not, in fact, embodied in the Constitution but which the Ninth Amendment describes as having been retained by the people. More recent constitutions, as a rule, refer to the freedom of association and often other provisions as well, which determines the role of parties in the given political system and establish certain restrictions on the method and means of their struggle for power.

This second provision was made law in the legal system of post-war Yugoslavia. It was done on the eve of the first elections in the law on associations, meetings and public gatherings of 25 August 1944. (*Službeni List DFJ*, 65/45.) Article Two of this law provides for the existence of political parties (associations, which, depending on the sphere of their activity, could be political parties of autonomous regions, political parties of republics (on the territory of a federal unit) or federal political parties. An application to the relevant government body was enough for newly-formed or revived political parties actually to start work (Article 3), which was a much better solution for efficient party pluralism than the so-called prior approval. At least 50 voters had to sign the application to found or revive political parties of autonomous regions and republics, and at least 100 voters in the case of federal parties. The voters signing this application had to live in the areas where such parties operated. (Article 4) If the relevant Internal Affairs department had not ruled within 15 days from the time the application was submitted, it was assumed that the activity of the political party was not banned (Article 9, paragraph 2).

This was, at least according to the letter of the law, a very liberal system, which, nevertheless, contained one basic restriction. The relevant authority could ban the founding and activity of political parties which had a fascist or pro-fascist character or which provoked and fanned national, racial or religious inequality, hatred and dissent, or if the founders and persons leading the party, were proponents of such activity (Article 8, paragraph 1). Even greater confusion was caused by the provision according to which the relevant authority of an autonomous or federal unit could ban the activity of a federal political party if that activity threatened the equality and the unity of the said unit with other units (Article 8 paragraph 2). This created the possibility for some political parties to operate feely over the greater part of Yugoslav territory, while at the same time being banned from the territories of individual federal units. This provision, was in fact, directed against political parties which had not fully accepted the division of Yugoslavia into individual federal units, and the granting of federal unit status to individual historical provinces.

The party pluralism that had already been revived after the final liberation of the country was sanctioned on the basis of this law. Almost all of
the political parties took this opportunity to legalize their activity. By the
end of 1945, the Federal Ministry of Internal Affairs had ruled in favor of
the following parties either being revived or founded: the Democratic
Party (*Službeni List DJF*, 73/45), the Popular Front of Yugoslavia (77/
45), the Radical Party (78/45), the Yugoslav Republican Democratic
Party (86/45), the Socialist Party of Yugoslavia (88/45) and the Social
Democratic Party of Yugoslavia (97/45). The revival of the activity of the
People's Peasant Party (*Službeni List FNRJ*, 78/46) and of the Independent Democratic Party (7/47) was formally ratified after the first Constitution was passed on 31 January 1946. It is interesting to note that
some of the parties did not consider that *formal legalization* of their activity was also necessary. This shows their privileged position with regard
to the authorities of the day. The Croatian Republican Peasant Party, for
example, operated in Croatia, Bosnia and Hercegovina and Vojvodina
without having submitted an application to the Federal Ministry of Internal Affairs. Some confusion was also caused by the CPY which had not
been formally legalized because it believed that it did not have to submit
the appropriate application, as the other parties did, to the Federal Ministry of Internal Affairs. This created a paradoxical situation in which the
party in power was formally illegal with regard to the power which it
firmly wielded. At first this was justified by the fact that right up until
1948, the CPY remained for the most part a conspiratorial party, and
later, the leading, and in a certain sense, supra-constitutional, status of
this party was probably taken into account.

The status of party pluralism was further consolidated with the passing of the Constitution on 31 January 1946. Article 27 of the Constitution guaranteed the freedom of association, which, according to the interpretation of the time, also included the freedom to associate in different
political parties. This was also confirmed, among other things, by the subsequent law ratifying and amending the 25 August 1945 law on associations,
meetings, and other public gatherings (*Službeni List FNRJ*, 51/46), passed
on the basis of the new Constitution. The subsequent law took over almost to the letter all the important provisions of the 25 August 1945 law,
concerning the founding, registration and sphere of activity of political
parties (Articles 2, 3 and 4 were taken over to the letter from the previous

law). An essential difference concerned the conditions under which the founding and activity of political parties could be banned. Whereas the first law provided for the possibility of banning political parties of a fascist and pro-fascist character, in the second law this ban concerned parties bent on changing and destroying the constitutional structure for anti-democratic ends (Article 9). Other grounds for a ban—provoking and fanning national or religious inequality, hatred and discord, and endangering the equality and unity of a people's republic or autonomous province—essentially remained the same (Article 9).

Thus, even after the Constitution of 31 January 1946 was passed, party pluralism not only remained an unquestionable fact of the political life at the time but a possibility also guaranteed by the Constitution. Since all political parties, with the exception of the CPY, disappeared in time from the political scene the question was raised in those years whether the multi-party system and the freedom to associate in different political parties in post-war Yugoslavia was *legally* abolished, or whether, from the standpoint of the Constitution and the law, this was still a possibility which, for certain reasons, was no longer made use of. The answer to this question depends on the criteria which we apply. If we opt for a strictly legalistic approach, which is appropriate only to legal systems in which there is no great discrepancy between norms and reality, then we could conclude that the possibility of party pluralism continued to exist in post-war Yugoslavia.

The fact that immediately after the war, seven decisions were passed on the basis of which the activity of the pre-war parties was renewed and that these decisions were never *specifically* repealed points to such a conclusion. From a formal point of view, they are still in force. In addition, the law ratifying and amending the law on associations, meetings and other public gatherings, passed after the Constitution of 31 January 1946 came into force, specifically provided for the possibility of founding political parties. This law was valid right up until April 1965, that is, also after the Constitution of 7 April 1963 was passed. Since the new Constitution adopted almost word for word the provision from the Constitution of 31 January 1946, guaranteeing the freedom of association, it can be rightly assumed that, from the standpoint of practical application, its contents remained unchanged. This means that the right to form *different* political parties continued to be guaranteed. This is also confirmed, among other things, by the fact that after the new Constitution of 7 April 1963 was passed, one other party still existed besides the CPY. This was the HRSS which continued to publish its paper *Slobodni dom,* the last issue of which was published on 27 December 1963.

Certain attempts have, of course, been made to destroy any trace of such an interpretation of the constitutional provision on the freedom of association. This is particularly noticeable in the mutilated structure of the new Basic Law on the association of citizens of 4 April 1965 (*Službeni List SFRJ,* 16/65), which replaced the law on the ratification and amendment of the 25 August 1945 law on associations, meetings and public gatherings. While the old law had a separate section on political parties (associations), the new law referred to associations only. Since political parties could justly come under the general heading of associations, one could continue to believe that the freedom of association also includes the freedom to associate in political parties. Article 22 of the new law specifically provided for associations, founded according to previous regulations continuing to work in line with the provisions of this law.

As we have already indicated, such interpretations rests exclusively on a strictly legalistic approach. If, however, one starts from the fact that legal norms were not highly valued in post-war Yugoslavia because of the nature of the newly-established political order, then one should perhaps resort to legal realism. If one proceeds from the assumption that the law is primarily to provide the way in which bodies, and particularly the courts, which apply the law in individual cases, will act, then the answer to the question about the freedom to associate in *different* political parties would certainly be negative. As far as we know, starting from 1947, any attempt to continue the customary activity of political parties legalized earlier, or to found new ones, led to very unpleasant and even disastrous consequences.

The only exception was the CPY, which continued without letup or hindrance to expand its party activity. This raises the question of its special constitutional and legal status. We have already said that the CPY was never formally legalized because it did not submit the appropriate application to the Federal Ministry of Internal Affairs. Since it played a crucial role in the entire post-war development, despite this formal and legal defect in its position, it was, in Dragoljub Jovanović's words, that important constitutional "particle" not mentioned in the Constitution (constitutional "particle" is Lasalle's famous term).[73] It could be said therefore, that the CPY had a meta-legal, that is, supra-constitutional, status. This was finally

revealed when this special position of the CPY was enshrined in the fundamental principles of the Constitution, which represented the basic interpretation of the Constitution and the law as well as the activity of all and
each of their part. The role of the CPY, or the LCY, was established in the
following manner in the "Fundamental Principles" of the SFRY Constitution on 7 April 1963:

> The League of Communists of Yugoslavia, the initiator and organ-
> izer of the national liberation struggle and socialist revolution, has
> become, through the necessity of historical development, the organ-
> ized leading force of the working class and the working people in
> building socialism and in creating the solidarity of working people,
> and of the brotherhood and unity of the people.
> With its guidance of ideological and political work in conditions
> of socialist democracy and social self-management, the League of
> Communists is the prime mover of political activity aimed at pro-
> tecting and further developing the achievements of the socialist
> revolution and socialist social relations, and particularly at strength-
> ening socialist social and democratic awareness of the people (Funda-
> mental Principles, VI).

The leading role of the CPY thereby became permanent and overt, this being the most important feature of the one-party system.

The first example of such a constitutional solution was the Soviet Constitution of 1936, with Article 126 defining the position and role of the
ruling party as follows:

> The most active and most conscious citizens from the ranks of the
> working class and from other strata of workers are united in the All-
> Union Communist Party (Bolshevik), which represents the vanguard
> of the working people in its struggle to consolidate and develop the
> socialist order, and the leading nucleus of all workers' organizations
> both social and those at the state level.

This was the model of how the leading role won by the ruling party was
also *formally* legalized. The USSR Constitution of 7 October 1977 established the Communist Party of the Soviet Union (CPSU) as the "leading

and guiding force of Soviet society, the nucleus of its political system and of state and social organizations " (Article 6).

In the first post-war constitutions of the people's democracies in East European countries, including the Yugoslav Constitution of 31 January 1946, the ruling Communist Parties did not have this constitutional guarantee of the inviolability and longevity of their power because vestiges of party pluralism were still present to varying degrees. At the beginning of the 1950s, when the one-party system was finally entrenched, the constitutional position of the CPSU became an example which could no longer be disregarded when the constitutions then in force were fully or partly amended. The Czechoslovak Constitution of 11 July 1960 proclaimed the Communist Party, as the vanguard of the working class, the "leading force in society and in the State" (Article 4). In a similar manner, the Romanian Constitution of 1965 established the Romanian Communist Party as the "leading force of the whole of society" (Article 3).

We also find similar provisions in the recent constitutions of the so-called Third World. Article 5 of the Constitution of the Republic of Cuba, passed on 24 February 1976, for example, explicitly laws down: "The Communist Party of Cuba, the organized Marxist-Leninist vanguard of the working class, is the supreme leading force of society and state, which organizes and guides common efforts to achieve the lofty aims of the builiding of socialism and of moving toward a communist society." The Algerian constitution went even further when it openly decreed that the Front of National Liberation was the only party in the country (Article 95 of the 24 November 1976 Constitution of the Agerian Democratic and People's Republic). Article 97 of this Constitution also re-affirmed the vanguard and leading role of the party, so that the "decisive responsible functions at the state level are discharged by members of the Party leadership" (Article 102).

The most far-reaching step in decreeing party monism through the constitution was taken by the Constitutions of Albania and China. They laid down that the ideology of the ruling party was the only permissible and obligatory view of the world. According to the Albanian Constitution of 28 December 1978: "Marxism-Leninism is the ruling ideology in the People's Socialist Republic of Albania" (Article 3, Paragraph 2). The Chinese Constitution of 5 March 1978 also extended this ideology to the teaching of Mao Tse-tung: "The state upholds the leading position of

Marxism-Leninism and the teaching of Mao Tse-tung in all spheres of ideology and culture" (Article 14). The Chinese Constitution is exceptional in the socialist world in that it also *formally* binds every citizen "to support the leading role of the Chinese Communist Party " (Article 56). Or perhaps this is merely proof of sensible political realism and the sure knowledge that general support for the inviolable leading role of one party can only be exacted by law.

CONCLUDING REMARKS

It was not the purpose of this study of recent Yugoslav political history to lend weight to and justify one of the stances in the controversy surrounding the nature and role of the post-war party system but to refresh to some extent the memory of this not so distant but already forgotten period. People's and parties' memories are relatively short, particularly in times of great upheaval, when subsequent events supplant the events of earlier yerars in their memories. For the majority of readers today, even the older ones, the years from 1944 to 1949 were the period of the final victory over Hitler, the rehabilitation of the war-ravaged country and the split with Stalin. Hardly anyone today realizes that Yugoslavia emerged from the war with a kind of party pluralism and that this pluralism was legitimate at the time. Even less is known that this pluralism, that is, the possibility of associating into *different* political parties, has never *formally* been abolished, that is, no constitutional or legal provisions have been promulgated which would specifically prohibit that possibility. This lack of knowledge is not only a consequence of conscious suppression but also of a deep-rooted inclination to project the picture of the present-day state of affairs into the recent past preceding this situation in order that the period be thought of and presented only for the perspective of today's ideological needs and ruling interests.

The reality of that period, however, was essentially different. It could even be said that the attitude to the party system represented one of those convictions of the ruling forces in the country which, within a relatively short time, underwent a radical turn-about—from explicit acceptance of

212

party pluralism and justification of the existence of opposition parties to their complete rejection. On the eve of war, the CPY leaders had identified the one-party system with totalitarianism. When the national liberation war against the occupying forces was at its height, the CPY not only accepted the legitimacy of party pluralism but also acknowledged, to a great extent, particularly in the case of Slovenia, the equal participation of other parties in the national liberation struggle. The culmination of this tolerance of party pluralism was the solemn promise that when the war ended Communism would not be introduced, because in the political jargon of the time, it meant the Soviet system, that is, the dictatorship of the proletariat, which amounted in practical terms to the dictatorship of its vanguard—a communist party of the Bolshevik type. It seemed natural at the time that constant party rivalry should continue to exist within the political system of Democratic Federal Yugoslavia and that the ruling party could not have the exclusive right of shaping public opinion.

As the war neared its end, however, the question of sharing power was increasingly raised, the CPY leaders, following the example of the parallel consolidation of Bolshevik power after the October Revolution, gradually restricted and abolished the multi-party system. Different means were used for this purpose, force as well as guile. The legitimacy of the multi-party system and the freedom for the opposition to operate was also publicly acknowledged in words while in deed, the CPY accepted political opposition parties only as a temporary "bridge" for transferring the masses over to the side of the proletarian vanguard. At the same time a whole series of practical measures were taken through the acquired government machinery, including the judiciary, which prevented the revival of party organizations and the recruitment of followers, thwarted the activity of non-communist parties in individual areas (Bosnia and Hercegovina, Montenegro, Macedonia), and prevented the printing of opposition papers and the nomination of independent electoral lists. Political trials of individual opposition politicians also took place.

When the wings of post-war party pluralism had been clipped, the time came to reconcile public words with the action taken. From 1947 onwards, it was persistently emphasized that there could be no socialism without a one-party system, which in practice, amounted to the idea that in a society building socialism there mut be only *one* program of social development, represented by the ruling Communist party and that this program would naturally be a *socialist* one. In other words, the Bolshevik idea that socialism cannot be built if various, and especially opposition, parties are permitted to exist, was adopted.

The historical facts which we have listed, however, confirm that this viewpoint is untenable. In fact, the Russian Bolsheviks also bowed to this same idea at the end of the war. In 1921, as the party in power, they finally banned any organized opposition activity within the *soviets*. The banned parties included not only the so-called bourgeois parties, which had been physically liquidated earlier, but also former co-fighters and allies of the Bolsheviks—the Mensheviks and the Social Revolutionaries. In their basic orientation they were undoubtedly *socialist* parties, which, along with anarchits, also had the socialist transformation of Russian society as their aim. Even during the civil war, the Bolsheviks often threw them out of the *soviets* or restricted their participation by hook or by crook. But at that time, Lenin and Trotsky had always let it be know that, at the end of the civil war, they would be in a position to respect the rules of constitutionalism and hence allow opposition activity. When it seemed to them that they had become strong enough to establish a monopoly of their own power, they resolved to eliminate all possible rivals, including the Mensheviks and the Social Revolutionaries, who had very similar ideas with respect to the ultimate aims of the struggle. Party pluralism, therefore, in post-revolutionary Russia was not abolished to protect the socialist character of the new society but to perpetuate the Bolshevik monopoly of power.

The subsequent history of Stalinism demonstrated that this permanent concentration of power in the hands of one party was not a sufficient guarantee to preserve the socialist character of this new society. Moreover, such a monopoly, in fact, endangered and distorted the initial socialist achievements of the October Revolution and led post-revolutionary Russia into totalitarianism. The Soviet experience, therefore, confirms that the abolition of the multi-party system in the name of socialism or its defense cannot be justified.

After the Second World War, all the East European countries, the so-called people's democracies, also set off along this Bolshevik path. By the end of 1948, the complete hegemony of the ruling Communist parties had finally been established in those countries. In contrast to the Soviet Union, they retained a certain *illusion* of party pluralism, which was reflected in the existence in name only of some non-communist parties. Many of these parties even exist today, though their role has been reduced chiefly to that of a mere appendage to the ruling party.

The party system in Yugoslavia had a somewhat different fate. Intially, it came closest to the Bolshevik model, because not a single opposition party or group was permitted to survive. Later developments, particularly from 1950 onwards, showed a fundamental deviation from this model. At first pluralism was tolerated in literature and art, and later, a kind of pluralism also emerged in political thought. True enough, the latter was never *specifically* legalized but for the most part developed in the form of various interpretations of Marxism as the dominant ideology. Differences in political views were *tacitly* allowed but on condition that their proponents remained dispersed and did not organize themselves into more solid alliances and separate factions or parties. This was also the reason for this distinctive ideological and cultural pluralism not being correspondingly institutionalized.

In 1970, a new process of a deeper internal multiplication of various interests and views, based on the multi-national structure of the Yugoslav state community, began. Moreover, a firm shaping of these diverse, and at times even opposed, politial entities was also given a further fillip by relevent constitutional amendments which led to changes in the character of the Yugoslav Federation. Once pluralism was recognized with regard to understanding and representing one's own national interest (i.e., one's own federal unit) within the framework of a state community, it became more difficult to avoid the legitimate expression of various views on all other issues as well—for example, the relationship between the current policy and factual truth, the possibility of different analyses of controversial events from recent history, the attitude toward political views and their proponents, the relationship between politics and culture, limits to the freedom of creative expression, tolerance toward so-called political theater, and particularly the question of criteria in legal prosecution for so-called political offenses and penal policy for such offenses.

Ultimately, the legitimacy of the very expression—*pluralism*—which, as a synonym for the multi-party system was for a long time banished from current political jargon, was recognized. This recognition was given by Edvard Kardelj in his latest book,[1] not, of course, in the form of political or party pluralism but in the form of the *pluralism of self-managing interests.* But, the concept of pluralism itself, at least in words, thereby acquired official legitimacy. T' us the circle, started in 1941 with the formation of the Slovene Liberation Front as a special coalition of *essentially different* political parties was closed. Kardelj undoubtedly played a great role in the formation of this *pluralistic* Liberation Front, *and his last significant word was also pluralism.*

One should, however, remember that the word pluralism, readmitted by Kardelj to the official political vocabulary though in a more narrow and limited sense, was for a long time undesirable and that any mention of pluralism provoked opposition and criticism. In its original meaning pluralism belonged to another ideological tradition and could not serve to explain and justify the existing political system in Yugoslavia. True enough, relaxation in the face of other ideological influences in the building of a new political system, that is, the departure from the Bolshevik tradition and the Soviet model, began considerably earlier in Yugoslavia and thus several institutions characteristic of a state based on the rule of law (administrative dispute, codified administrative procedure, judicial control of constitutionality) were introduced into the power system. As far as the idea of pluralism was concerned, however, no concessions were allowed.

Thus, for example, at a scientific gathering in January 1966, the call by one of the participants to discuss pluralism in socialist democracy was rejected as politically unacceptable and scientifically unimportant. At the scientific gathering, "The Socialist Alliance and the Working Man," Stevan Vračar, professor at the Law Faculty in Belgrade, put forward in his written statement the idea that to confront pluralism as one of the basic characteristics of capitalist democracy and monism, as one of the basic features of socialist democracy, by reducing pluralism in the first instance to a multi-party system, and monism in the second, to a one-party system, was too simplistic.[2] On the contrary, according to Vračar pluralism cannot be understood independently of monism because they always exist and appear together. Monism always predominates in a modern society while pluralism is secondary.

Any social order, as well as its political system, is based on monism, and it is in line with this that the conditions for its survival are determined. The effect of certain factors or forces, above all of the mode of production and its agents, always predominates. Class-political forces and the system on which state power rests ensure domination through a series of factors and in a series of forms which have the same direction of activity while opposing forces become the proponents of pluralism. The fact that monism is fundamental and pluralism secondary is not seen in the simple opposition state—society, nor even in the particular formulation of political systems (for example, democratic or autocratic), or, in an even more restricted sense, of party systems (for example, one-party or two-party).[3]

In a bourgeois democracy, therefore, pluralism does not represent the predominant fact because, in the seemingly free play of various forces, only the ruling position of the bourgeoisie is strengthened, while among the citizens the illusion is created that they all participate equally in wielding power. In other words, the factual state of monism suits an explicitly developed pluralistic form. In socialism, particularly in the initial and formative phase of the socialist social order, the actual and formal and the organizational and institutional elements of monism become more evident. The harmony between form and content is much more apparent here than in bourgeois democracies. In a more developed, socialist democracy, Vračar goes on, pluralism is much more prominent but monism is not thereby abolished. Monism remains the predominant principle of the organization of society. These principles have been realized to a greater or lesser extent only in certain political systems and social orders, but the fact that monism represents the primary principle and pluralism the secondary one in all forms of the organization of society cannot be questioned.

At first glance, one could not expect these attitudes to be interpreted as a challenge to the official stance. The very assertion that there can be more pluralism in a more developed socialist society than in a post-revolutionary one is not incompatible with the prevailing interpretation of political development in socialism. True enough, at one point, Vračar says not even party pluralism should be excluded in some future and hypothetical societies, and goes on:

> Perhaps a kind of coalition of a communist and socialist party will gain power in the future, and the organizational and political independence of parties, even rivalry, according to the pattern ruling

versus opposition party remain in the era of socialism. Or perhaps in some socialist country, the former specifically one-party system will develop into a two or multi-party system, but on the foundations of powerful and stable socialism, for if a two or multi-party system has of itself not endangered but in fact strengthened the existence of capitalism, why should not the same also be possible in socialism? [4]

The hypothetical attitude thus presented was not incompatible with the publice attitude and policies of West European Communist parties at this time, even though, with regard to Yugoslav society, the author did not question the usual reasons against party pluralism.

This kind of deliberation about pluralism in socialist democracy, nonetheless, suffered ideological criticism and rebuttal, and this only because in his abstract and hypothetical reflections the author used the concept of pluralism as understood in the liberal political tradition. Criticizing this "borrowed concept," Najdan Pašić stressed that:

> to accept the orientation that we interpret our political system with the conceptual device borrowed from the West or somewhere else means, in fact, to capitulate to the difficulties of explaining the essence of the new social relations in the political sphere to capitulate in the face of unavoidable ideological barriers, which inevitably exist, in view of the fact that we are dealing here with relations and concepts originating from a different social reality and therefore, also expressing different social interests.[5]

Only ten years later, beginning with Kardelj's treatise, *Pravci razvoja političkog sistema socijalističkog samoupravljavanja* (Directions of the Development of the Political System of Socialist Self-Management), the pluralism of self-managing interests was not only to become legitimate but also one of the main concepts in explaining the political system, and Pašić was to become one of the most fervent interpreters of this concept.

Yet, if the idea of pluralism in a specific and truncated form, as the idea of "self-managing political pluralism" which supersedes the "political pluralism of the bourgeois state," was accepted by Yugoslav social science and official ideological thought, the idea of party pluralism in the context of the development of contemporary Yugoslav society was mentioned far less. It is worth noting, nevertheless, that at another learned gathering, the Conference on the General Problems of Responsibility, held in May 1968, one of the participants in the discussion, Andrija Gams, professor at the Law Faculty in Belgrade, stressed that political responsibility in our society could be established by "allowing the possibility to organize a legal, socialist, political opposition."[6] He thereby linked the problem of a legal opposition to the question of political responsibility, that is, to the creation of the possibility whereby "the one who calls to account is not identical with the one who must answer." The development of the Soviet Union immediately after the October Revolution, when several socialist parties existed, as well as the attitudes and the proclamations of some West European Communist parties also favored such a *socialist* but not bourgeois opposition. Gams, however, dissociated himself from this insofar as he said that our social and historical conditions were such that the question of an opposition could not be raised in the way "theoreticians of classical bourgeois constitutionality had done so or the way bourgeois democracies were doing." Such a socialist opposition, therefore, should on no account be "a party in the classical sense."[7]

If the confusion surrounding the choice between party pluralism and party monism has remained of peripheral interest for Yugoslav social science, for a section of the communist movement it has remained very much to the fore. According to the eminent former member of the Czechoslovak Communist Party, Jiri Pelikan, who held numerous political positions, from president of the International Student Union to Director of Television during the "Prague Spring" of 1968, but who left Czechoslovakia in 1970 opting for the fate of a political exile, the problem of democratic socialism without socialist party pluralism is difficult to resolve. In his political autobiography, translated in Yugoslavia, Pelikan writes:

> In brief, is it possible for communists to accept defeat at elections within a socialist society, or in a society on the road to socialism, as was the case in Czechoslovakia? If we assume this to be possible, we ask ourselves whether communists, though in a minority, would be ready to accept participation in the government or even to withdraw into opposition. In any case, I believe that such an alternative could have existed in Czechoslovakia because the other political parties

were also in favor of the Košice program of socialization, and not one of them, with the exception of a few minority factions, wanted to restore the pre-war capitalist republic. Since the problem of the pluralism of political parties and opposition within socialist society was not resolved in 1948, it was raised again in 1968 and this proved that genuine democratic socialism could not be achieved without resolving this problem and that we would always be exposed to the same degradations of power: centralization, bureaucratization, police state, depoliticization of the working class, étatism of the economy as was and had remained the case in the Soviet Union and other East European countries.[8]

If we turn again to the discussions of the problem of party pluralism in Yugoslavia, the acceptance of the term, pluralism, in most recent times, regardless of the way in which it is done, is yet more evidence of the existence of some more general legitimate ideas and institutions which are also a yardstick of the degree of democracy of any political system. Franc Šetinc went a step further than Kardelj in this respect when he said that

in our country, the Socialist Alliance means what a multi-party system means in other countries; it was in fact conceived as a barrier to the monopoly of decision-making. We do not have such an approach, we have neither two nor several parties; we have given the Socialist Alliance precisely that role in the system, but if the Socialist Alliance does not fulfill that role, if it is not the forum where numerous pluralist interests are expressed, then, naturally, this must lead to defects in the functioning of the political system as a whole.[9]

In other words, party pluralism, according to Šetinc, is an obstacle to political monopoly, and, as successor of the Popular Front in the post-war years, the Socialist Alliance should play a role similar to that of several political parties in some other systems.

Speaking in a similar vein as Šetinc, Aleksandar Grličkov stressed the need for a "dialogue between the League of Communists and other socialist forces." "At the Eleventh Congres," Grličkov asserted, "we pledged that we would open a dialogue between Communists and non-Communists, that is, with other socialist and self-management oriented forces, and we wanted to achieve this in the Socialist Alliance, as a front of all socialist forces."[10] Not much effort is needed to detect in all these public declarations about pluralism, about the Socialist Alliance, which should perform the role played by the multi-party system in other systems and about the dialogue between Communists and non-Communists, a certain similarity with the original proclamations and interpretations of the Popular Front after the war. With the disappearance of the traces of party pluralism from the political system and the Popular Front and with the transformation of the Popular Front into a monolithic organization and the transmission belt of the Communist Party after 1948, this original explanation of the nature of the Popular Front gradually faded from reality and people's consciousness. Some of the recent declarations about pluralism and dialogue quoted here remind one all the more that public declarations and promises made in the period which has been the subject of our investigation have not been implemented.

The acceptance of the "pluralism of self-managing interests" along with the simultaneous rejection of "political pluralism" shows, however, that the Bolshevik tradition of resolving the problems of political democracy and party pluralism has still not been completely abandoned. Besides some other traditional democratic influences, the share of this Bolshevik legacy in social development and the political system is still evident in many ways. Only the complete rejection of this Bolshevik legacy could confront us again with that same dilemma which arose in 1945, the dilemma of pluralism or monism. A genuine resolution of this dilemma can only come about if the constitutional freedom of association as a *common* and *equal* right, available to all citizens without discrimination, is applied in practice.

NOTES

Notes to Chapter I

1. For more about social movements, see Rudolf Heberle, *Social Movements*, New York, Appleton-Century Crofts, 1951, and Paul Wilkinson, *Social Movements*, London, Macmillan, 1972.

2. Ustavotvorni odbori Savezne skupštine i skupštine naroda, 10 December 1945-4 January 1946, Belgrade, Narodna Skupština FNRJ, s.a., pp. 23-24.

3. More on this in Dušan Živković's *Narodni Front Jugoslavije 1935-1945*, Belgrade, Institut za savremenu istoriju, 1979, pp. 71-107, and Ivan Jelić, "Osnovni problemi stvaranja Narodne Fronte u Jugoslaviji do 1941. godine," *Putovi revolucije*, 7-8/1966, pp. 71-100.

4. Živković, op. cit., pp. 79-80.

5. Ibid., pp. 103-104.

6. Ibid., pp. 96-97.

7. Ibid., p. 87.

8. Vladimir Simić, *Ideološki frontovi*, Belgrade, "Politika i društvo," 1937, pp. 32-43.

9. Ibid., p. 37.

10. Ibid., p. 39.

11. "Memorandum vodjstvu udružene opozicije—Beograd," published in *Sećanje na jednu diktaturu* by Dragoslav Smiljanić, Belgrade, "Rad," 1960, p. 156.

12. "VIII Demokratsko saopštenje prijateljima" published in Smiljanić, op. cit., pp. 154-155.

13. Branko Petranović, "Narodni front u političkom sistemu Jugo-slavije (1945-1949), *Istraživanja VIII,* Novi Sad, Institut za izučavanje istorije Vojvodine, 1979, p. 386.

14. Harold Laski, *A Grammar of Politics,* 4th ed., London, George Allen and Unwin Ltd., 1938, pp. 313-314.

15. Ernest Barker, *Reflections on Government,* Oxford, The Clarendon Press, 1942, pp. 284-311.

16. Ortega y Gasset, *The Revolt of the Masses,* London, Unwin Books, 1961, p. 58.

17. Aleksa Tomić, "Političke partije i strančarstvo, Njihova bit, funkcije i izopačenje," *Republika* of 15 January 1946.

18. Stalin, *Pitanja lenjinizma,* Belgrade, "Kultura," 1946, pp. 120-137.

19. Georg Lukács, "Taktik und Ethik," *Werke,* Neuwied und Berlin, Luchterhand, 1968, vol. 2, p. 73.

20. Ibid., p. 77.

21. Ibid., pp. 77-78.

22. Figures on the character and electoral strength of these parties in the interwar years are according to Ferdo Čulinović, *Dokumenti o Jugoslaviji,* Zagreb, "Školska knjiga," 1968.

23. *Zbornik dokumenata i podataka o narodnooslobodilačkom ratu jugoslovenskih naroda,* Belgrade, Vojnoistorijski institut Jugoslovenske narodne armije, 1956, vol. VI, book 5, pp. 185-189.

24. Giovanni Sartori, *Parties and Party Systems. A Framework of Analysis,* Cambridge, Cambridge University Press, 1976, book I, pp. 119-130.

25. Figures on the activity of the "Politika i društvo" Publishing Co-operative can be found in *Narodni Kalendar Napred* for 1940 and 1941. One aspect of the work of the "Politika i društvo" series was described by Aleksandar A. Miljković in "Biblioteka 'Politika i društvo' u istoriji naše sociologije sela," *Sociologija,* 4/1982, pp. 449-460.

26. "Naša prva reč," *Napred,* June 1938.

27. "Naš načelan stav o političkim, socijalnim i ekonomskim pitanjima," *Napred,* 3 January 1940.

28. *Rad zakonodavnih odbora Predsedništva Antifašističkog veća narodnog oslobodjenja Jugoslavije i Privremene narodne Skupštine DFJ,* 3rd April-25 October 1945, Belgrade, Prezidijum Narodne skupštine FNRJ, 1952, p. 518.

224 PARTY PLURALISM OR MONISM

29. "Izjava dr Dragoljuba Jovanovića, predstavnicima strane štampe," *Politika,* 29 September 1945, and "Izjava Jaše Prodanovića–za inostranu štampu," *Republika,* 27 November 1945.

30. *Glas,* 11 September and 6 October 1946.

31. *Politika,* 2 January 1946.

32. *Politika,* 24 April 1946.

33. Maurice Duverger, *Les partis politiques,* Paris, Armand Colin, 1951, pp. 340-344.

34. Sartori, op. cit., pp. 192-201; 217-238.

35. Jerzy Wiatr, "The Hegemonic Party System in Poland," *Mass Politics: Studies in Political Sociology,* eds. Erik Allardt, Stein Rokkan, New York, The Free Press, 1970, pp. 312-321.

36. Sartori, op. cit., p. 234.

37. *Zbornik dokumenata i podataka o narodnooslobodilačkom ratu jugoslovenskih naroda,* vol. VI, book 5.

38. Sartori, op. cit., p. 126.

39. Branko Petranović, *Politička i ekonomska osnova narodne vlasti u Jugoslaviji za vreme obnove,* Belgrade, Institut za savremenu istoriju, 1969, p. 92.

40. "Izjava Centralnog komiteta KP Jugoslavije povodom Rezolucije Informacionog biroa komunističkih partija o stranju u KPJ," *Borba,* 30 June 1948.

41. Staša Milijanović, "Godinu dana 'Republike' u Republici," *Republika,* 5 November 1946.

42. Vladimir Simić, "Istina o 'republikancima'," *Republika,* 25 June 1946.

43. "Kako je proglašena 'Obznana,' Izjava Republikanske stranke objavljena u 'Republici' 2. januara 1921'," *Republika,* 13 November 1945.

44. Branislav Miljković, "Narodni front i republikanci," *Republika,* 6 November 1945.

45. Jaša Prodanović, "Izmedju čekića i nakovnja," *Republika,* 18 December 1945.

46. Petranović, *Politička i ekonomska osnova narodne vlasti u Jugoslaviji za vreme obnove,* p. 162.

47. *Hrvatski glas,* 27 February 1946.

48. "Izborni proglas HRSS," *Politika,* 21 October 1945, and "Proglas članovima Demokratske stranke," *Politika,* 7 October 1945.

49.   Filip Lakuš, "Zašto Narodni front?," *Slobodni dom,* 20 February 1946.

50.   Branislav Miljković, "Narodni front i republikanci," *Republika,* 6 November 1945. More about socialist ideas at the time of the birth of the Republican Party, see Mihailo Ilić, *Ekonomsko-socijalni program Jugoslovenske republikanske stranke,* Belgrade, Moderna štamparija 'Vuk Karadžić," 1922.

51.   "Naš načelan stav o političkim, socijalnim i ekonomskim pitanjima," *Napred,* 3 January 1940. It may also be of interest to the readers that in its program, this group advocated that "it be made possible by law to *investigate the origins of wealth* (authors' italics) of public officials and public workers generally."

52.   Edvard Kardelj, *Put nove Jugoslavije. Članci i govori iz narodnooslobodilačke borbe 1941-1945,* Belgrade, "Kultura," 1946, p. 95.

53.   J. B. Tito, *Izgradnja nove Jugoslavije,* Belgrade, "Kultura," 1948, vol. II, book 2, p. 386.

54.   For further details see: Hugh Seton-Watson, *The Pattern of Communist Revolution: A History of World Communism,* London, Methuen, 1960; Andrew Gyorgy, "Satellite Parties in Eastern Europe," *Modern Political Parties,* ed., Sigmund Neumann, The University of Chicago Press, 1955; Francois Fejtö, *A History of the People's Democracies,* Harmondsworth, the Penguin Press, 1977; *Radnički i nacionalnooslobodilački pokreti,* Belgrade, Institut za medjunarodni radnički pokret, 1970, book II.

55.   Frano Cetinić, "Prijedlog za jednu kronologiju poljske krize," *Gledišta* 5-6/1981, p. 169.

56.   Patrice Gelard, *Les systèmes politiques des états socialistes,* Paris, Cujas, 1975, book II, pp. 660-663, 676-677.

Notes to Chapter II

1.   Although it has never been officially explained until now why this front was originally called *anti-imperialist* instead of *anti-fascist,* the real reason for this nomenclature is contained in the policy of the Comintern and in the well-known dependence of the CPY and of the Communist Party of Slovenia on the directives from Moscow. On 27 April 1941, fascist Germany was still considered "a friend" of the Soviet Union, because the "agreement of friendship," concluded between Molotov and

Ribbentrop, was still in force. Since at that time the foreign policy *interests* of the Soviet Union dictated utmost consideration towards Hitler and Germany, the Communist Party of Slovenia, as the disciplined executor of Moscow's directives, was not able to call the newly-created front *antifascist* but by the insufficiently clear attribute of "anti-imperialist," which in the Communist propaganda of that time chiefly referred to "English lords" and "French bankers." This conclusion is also confirmed by, among other things, the fact that right up until 22 June 1941, the CPY had never condemned fascist Germany as the aggressor and initiator of the Second World War, but maintained instead that the English and French imperialists *attacked* Germany, that is, that they, and not Germany, provoked and instigated the Second World War. The following quotation from the First of May proclamation of the CPY bears witness to this: "Seven months ago, the English and French imperialists attacked another imperialist power—Germany—in order to conquer her and to force her to capitulate and thus to secure their rule and continue without competition their pillage of colonies and semi-colonial peoples. . . . This imperialist war which was begun by the English and French imperialists, heavily affects both you and the entire working people of Yugoslavia."—Josip Broz Tito, "Radnom narodu Jugoslavije," (written in the second half of March 1940), *Sabrana djela,* Belgrade, "Komunist," 1978, vol. 5, pp. 56 and 58.

2. Metod Mikuž, *Pregled razvoja NOB u Sloveniji,* Belgrade, Military Publishing Institute of the Yugoslav People's Army, p. 102.

3. Edvard Kocbek, "Odgovori" (from the book by Boris Pahor and Alojz Rebula, "Edvard Kocbek, pričevalec našega časa," Trieste 1975), *Naši razgledi,* no. 9, 9 May 1975.

4. Ibid.

5. "Pozorište u zatvoru," interview by Bora Krivokapić with Joža Javoršek, *Ideje* 5/81, p. 126.

6. Ibid., p. 125.

7. Quoted from Živković, op. cit., p. 166.

8. Ibid.

9. Ibid.

10. Ibid., pp. 166-167.

11. Ibid., p. 167.

12. "Odgovori na deset pitanja inostranih novinara," Spring 1944, *Borba za oslobodenje Jugoslavije 1941-1945.* (until 9 May 1945), Belgrade, "Kultura," 1947, book I, vol. 1, pp. 194-195.

13. "Sporazum Komunističke partije Jugoslavije i Narodne seljačke stranke za borbu protiv okupatora," *Borba,* 28 October 1941, no. 5; quoted from *Istorijski arhiv KPJ,* Belgrade, History Department of the CPY Central Committee, 1949, vol. I, book 1, "Borba," 1941, p. 84.

14. "Narodnooslobodilacki odbori organi narodne vlasti," *Borba,* 18 November 1941, no. 15; quoted from *Istorijski arhiv KPJ,* vol. I, book 1, "Borba" 1941, p. 296.

15. War Office, Public Records Office, Minutes of Conference at Naples, 12 August 1944.

16. *Peti kongres Komunisticke partije Jugoslavije 21-28 jula 1948. Stenografske beleške,* Belgrade, "Kultura," 1949, p. 102.

17. V. I. Lenin, "Država i revolucija," *Izabrana dela,* Belgrade, "Kultura," 1960, vol. II, p. 248.

18. V. I. Lenin, "Proleterska revolucija i renegat Kaucki," *Izabrana dela,* vol. 12, p. 362.

19. J. Stalin, "K pitanjima lenjinizma," *Pitanja Lenjinizma,* p. 123.

20. Ibid., p. 129.

21. Ibid., p. 128.

22. Dragoljub Jovanović, "Privremena vlada izlazi pred svet," *Glas Jedinstvenog narodno-oslobodilačkog fronta Srbije,* no. 24, 13 March 1945, p. 1.

23. Dragoljub Jovanović, *Memoari,* manuscript in the SFRY archives, book VI, p. 142; quoted from Živković, op. cit., p. 116.

24. Jovan Marjanović, *Ustanak i narodnooslobodilački pokret u Srbiji 1941,* Belgrade, 1963, p. 209.

25. J. Stalin, "Osnove lenjinizma," *Pitanja lenjinizma,* p. 41.

26. Quoted from Živković, op. cit., p. 217.

27. Metod Mikuž, *Pregled zgodovine narodnooslobodilne borbe v Sloveniji,* Ljubljana, Cankarjeva založba, 1961, p. 232.

28. "Pozorište u zatvoru," *Ideje* 5/81, p. 126.

29. This declaration was signed by Edvard Kardelj, Boris Kidrič and Franc Leskošek for the Communist Party of Slovenia, by Jože Rus and France Lubej for the Sokol organization, and by Edvard Kocbek, Tone Fajfar and Marijan Brecelj for the Christian Socialists.—*Zbornik dokumenata i podataka o narodnooslobodilačkom ratu jugoslovenskih naroda,* vol. VI, book 5, pp. 185-189.

30. Kocbek, op. cit.

31. Ibid.

32. *Zbornik dokumenata i podataka o narodnooslobodilačkom ratu jugoslovenskih naroda,* vol. VI, book 5, pp. 190-194.

33. Edvard Kardelj's report to the Supreme Commander of the National Liberation Army and Partisan Detachments of Yugoslavia. Tito, on the attitude toward the Croatian Republican Peasant Party representatives of 14 August 1943, *Zbornik VII,* pp. 206-207; quoted from Petranović, "Narodni front u političkom sistemu Jugoslavije" (1945-1949), *Istraživanja VIII,* p. 313.

34. *ZAVNOH, Zbornik dokumenata 1943,* Zagreb, 1964, pp. 501-503; quoted from Petranović, op. cit., p. 313.

35. Archive of the Institute for the History of the Workers' Movement, Zagreb, CP Foundation, 34/2215; quoted from Živković, op. cit., p. 318.

36. Archive of the Institute for the Workers' Movement of Bosnia and Hercegovina, CP Foundation, no. 860; quoted from Živković, op. cit., pp. 343-344.

37. Archive of the Institute for the History of the Workers' Movement, Zagreb, CP Foundation, 26/215; quoted from Živković, op. cit., p. 390.

38. FNRJ Archive, Sava Kosanović Foundation, Proglas frakcije Dude Boškovića članovima i prijateljima SDS; quoted from Branko Petranović, *Političke i pravne prilike za vreme privremene vlade DFJ,* Belgrade, Institute of Social Sciences, 1964, p. 176.

39. Živković, op. cit., p. 322.

40. Archive of the Institute for the History of the Workers' Movement, Zagreb, CP, Foundation, 35/2337 (44); quoted from Živković, op. cit., p. 324.

41. Sreten Žujović-Crni, "Jedinstveni narodnooslobodilački front politička snaga naroda i zemlje," *Glas JNOFS,* 27 February 1945.

42. 28 January 1945, *Borba za oslobodenje Jugoslavije 1941-1945* (until 9 May 1945), Belgrade, "Kultura," 1947, book I, vol. 1, pp. 264-265.

43. "O Srbiji u Narodno-oslobodilačkoj borbi i o rezultatima te borbe," Speech at Kosmaj on 7 July 1945, *Izgradnja nove Jugoslavije,* book I, vol. 2, pp. 74-75.

44. "Speech at Bela Crkva on 7 July 1945," ibid., book I, vol. 2, p. 86.

45. "Makedonija u Jugoslaviji i perspektive njenog razvoja," Speech on the day celebrating the Macedonian people's uprising in Skoplje, 11 October 1945, ibid., book I, vol. 2, p. 162.

46. "Izjava o rezultatima izbora od 11. novembra 1945, data 16. novembra iste godine," ibid., book I, vol. 2, p. 222.

47. *Rad zakonodavnih odbora Predsedništva Antifašističkog veća narodnog oslobodenja Jugoslavije i Privremene narodne skupštine DFJ* (3 April-25 October 1945), p. 473.

48. FNRJ Archive, Presidium Foundation, file V, Comments on the list of deputies who could join the Anti-fascist Council of the National Liberation of Yugoslavia, signed Bc, probably an abbreviation of Bevc —Edvard Kardelj; quoted from Petranović, *Političke i pravne prilike za vreme Privremene vlade DFJ,* p. 140.

49. FNRJ Archive, Presidium Foundation, file V, Proposal to expand the Anti-fascist Council of the National Liberation of Yugoslavia with representatives of political parties and groups, signed BC, probably Bevc —Edvard Kardelj; quoted from Petranović, op. cit., p. 142.

50. *Demokratija,* 25 October 1945.

51. *Demokratija,* 1 November 1945.

52. *Rad zakonodavnih odbora Predsedništva Antifašističkog veća narodnog oslobodenja Jugoslavije i Privemena narodne skupštine DFJ* (3 April-25 October 1945), p. 295.

53. *Treće zasedanje Antifašistickog veća narodnog oslobodenja Jugoslavije. Zasedanje Privremene narodne skupštine,* 7-26 August 1945, Belgrade, FNRJ People's Assembly Presidium, s. a., p. 194.

54. The resignation of Milan Grol on 19 August 1945 from the post of vice-premier, Yugoslavia today (November 1945), *Jugoslovenski dokumenti* no. 7, private publication, printed at John Beelows Ltd. Gloucester.

55. Ibid.

56. Ibid.

57. *Demokratija,* 27 September 1945.

58. The resignation of Milan Grol on 19 August 1945 from the post of vice-premier, *Jugoslovenski dokumenti,* no. 7.

59. "Program Demokratske stranke. Neposredni i osnovni program," *Demokratija,* 27 September 1945.

60. Ibid.

61. "O slobodi," *Demokratija,* 18 October 1945.

62. "O apstinenciji opozicije," *Demokratija*, 27 September 1945.

63. Milan Grol, "Silom ili razlogom?" *Demokratija*, 25 October 1945.

64. *Treće zasedanje Antifašistickog veća narodnog oslobodenja Jugoslavije. Zasedanje Privremene narodne skupštine*, 7-26 August 1945, p. 302.

65. "Silom ili razlogom?" *Demokratija*, 25 October 1945.

66. J. B. Tito, "Situacija u Jugoslaviji," written in the middle of 1940, *Sabrana djela*, vol. 5, p. 129.

67. "Silom ili razlogom?." *Demokratija*, 25 October 1945.

68. Ibid.

69. "Rdjavi metodi," *Demokratija*, 8 November 1945.

70. "Silom ili razlogom?" *Demokratija*, 25 October 1945.

71. Ibid.

72. *Treće zasedanje Antifašistickog veća narodnog oslobodjenja Jugoslavije. Zasedanje Privremene narodne skupštine*, 7-26 August 1945.

73. "Dogadjaji i komentari," *Demokratija*, 1 November 1945.

74. "Dogadjaji i komentari," *Demokratija*, 18 October 1945.—Dragoljub Jovanović also testified to this: "How is it that the word "traitor" appears when Milan Grol is mentioned? During the Second World War and for several years after the liberation, that name was easily used. With my own eyes I saw on the front wall of the Novi Sad railway station the following slogan in large letters: 'Death to the Traitor Milan Grol.' It was written when Grol was leaving the government, after he had sent a very polite letter to Marshal Tito, a letter in which he spoke in terms of praise about the Premier but not about his associates, above all not Milovan Djilas. (After all, both he and Jaša Prodanović, were constantly squabbling with him, chiefly over the Montenegrin nation). That slogan was still there in February 1947 when I travelled to Sivac."—Dragoljub Jovanović, *Ljudi, ljudi*, book II, Belgrade, 1975, p. 34.

75. "Izborni zakon i izborna stvarnost," *Demokratija*, 27 September 1945.

76. Ibid.

77. *Zakodavni rad Predsedništva Antifašistickog veća narodnog oslobodenja Jugoslavije i Predsedništva Privremene narodne skupštine DFJ*, Belgrade, FNRJ People's Assembly Presidium, 1951, p. 627.

78. Ibid., p. 629.

79. Ibid., p. 628.

80. "Kutija bez liste," *Slobodni dom*, 31 October 1945.

81. See *Glas*, 11 September and 6 October 1945.

82. "Narodni front u političkom sistemu Jugoslavije (1945-1949)," *Istraživanja VIII*, p. 359.

83. Milovan Djilas, *Članci 1941-1946*, Belgrade, "Kultura," 1947, p. 233.

84. Ibid.

85. Ibid., p. 242.

86. Ibid., p. 243.

87. Ibid.

88. Quoted from *Demokratija*, 25 October 1945.

89. "Narodni front u političkom sistemu Jugoslavije (1945-1949)," *Istraživanja VIII*, p. 359.

90. "Rdjavi metodi," *Demokratija*, 8 November 1945.

91. "Silom ili razlogom?" *Demokratija*, 25 October 1945.

92. "Odgovori na pitanja novinara za Konferenciji s predstavnicima strane i domaće štampe," *Izgradnja nove Jugoslavije*, book I, vol. 2, p. 223.

93. A somewhat different opinion on the justification of the existence of the right to strike was presented by Gligorije Mandić and Nikola Jakšić, deputies of the Constituent Assembly, the FNRJ draft Constitution was discussed on 19 January 1946, of which more later.—*Zasedanje Ustavotvorne skupštine*, 29 November 1945-1 February 1946, Belgrade, FNRJ People's Assembly Presidium, s.a., p. 236.

94. "Izbori za Konstituantu,"—"Borba," 13 September 1945, *Izgradnja nove Jugoslavije*, book I, vol. 2, p. 223.

95. Ibid., p. 240.

96. *Ljudi, ljudi*, book II, p. 37.

97. "Odgovori na pitanja američkih novinara," *Izgradnja nove Jugoslavije*, book II, Belgrade, "Kultura," 1948, p. 198.

98. *Informativni priručnik o Jugoslaviji*, 1949, pp. 163-164.

99. "Ostvarimo socijalizam u našoj zemlji," *Izgradnja nove Jugoslavije*, book IV, Belgrade, "Kultura," 1952, pp. 279-280.

100. "Rdjavi metodi," *Demokratija*, 8 November 1945.

101. One need only recall that in Stjepan Radić's lifetime the CPY, following directives from Moscow, preached the breaking up of Yugoslavia, as a creation of Versailles, into independent national states, including, above all, an independent Croatia.

232 PARTY PLURALISM OR MONISM

102. Lovro Kranjec, "Naš najvažniji zadatak," *Slobodni dom*, 7 November 1945.

103. Filip Lakuš, "Zašto Narodni front," *Slobodni dom*, 20 February 1946.

104. Ibid.

105. Ibid.

106. Mile Glavaš, "Najvažniji zadaci naših mjesnih i kotarskih organizacija," *Hrvatski glas*, 8 May 1946.

107. *Slobodni dom*, 28 January 1949.

108. "Našim prijateljima," *Republika*, 8 November 1945.

109. "Izjava Jaše Prodanovića–za inostranu štampu," *Republika*, 27 November 1945.

110. Ibid.

111. Jaša Prodanović, "Izmedju čekica i nakovnja," *Republika*, 18 December 1945.

112. *Ljudi, ljudi*, book II, p. 240.

113. *Ustavotvorni odbori Savezne skupštine i Skupštine naroda*, 10 December 1945-4 January 1946, p. 632.

114. Ibid., pp. 632-633.

115. Edvard Kardelj, "Karakter, politika i zadaci Narodnog fronta Jugoslavije," *Put nove Jugoslavije*, pp. 79-112.

116. "Makedonija u Jugoslaviji i uslovi i perspektiva njenog razvoja," 11 October 1945, *Izgradnja nove Jugoslavije*, book I, vol. 2, p. 162.

117. *Slobodni dom*, 6 January 1946.

118. "Razgovor J. B. Tita s članovima Britanskog parlamenta i engleskim novinarima on 12 November 1945," *Izgradnja nove Jugoslavije*, book I, vol. 2, p. 214.

119. *Prvo redovno zasedanje Saveznog veća i Veća naroda*, 15 May-20 July 1946, Belgrade, the FNRJ People's Assembly, s. a., p. 547.

120. Ibid., p. 549.

121. Ibid., p. 552.

122. Ibid., pp. 552-553.

123. "Rdjavi metodi," *Demokratija*, 8 November 1945.

124. *Prvo redovno zasedanje Saveznog Veća i Veća naroda*, 15 May-20 July 1946, p. 577.

125. Ibid.

126. Ibid., p. 578.

127. *Treće redovno zasedanje Saveznog veća i Veća naroda*, 26 March-26 April 1947, Belgrade, FNRJ People's Assembly Presidium, s.a., p. 145.

128. "Imro Filaković isključen iz Hrvatske republikanske seljačke stranke," *Slobodni dom*, 7 August 1946.

129. *Rad zakonodavnih odbora Predsedništva Antifašističkog veća narodnog oslobodenja Jugoslavije i Privremene narodne skupštine DFJ* (3 April-25 October 1945), p. 496.

130. Ibid., p. 498.

131. Ibid., p. 502.

132. Ibid., p. 503.

133. Ibid.

134. This does not, however, mean that all traces of party pluralism in Slovenia were eradicated. Thus, in 1947, a group of Christian Socialists attempted to act as an independent force separate from the Popular Front. In 1946, the influence was also felt of some members of the Social Democratic Party in some parts of Slovenia (Celje, Trbovlje). "The forms of activity of the Social Democrats amounted to inciting the workers against Communists as spies of the Department of State Security, and to referring to the unfulfilled promises, given before the war, that the new government would introduce hygienic working conditions, flats and ensure equal remuneration."—Branko Petranović, "Gradjanske stranke u Jugoslaviji 1944-1948. i njihov karakter," *Istorijski glasnik*, 1969/I, p. 85.

135. Isaac Deutscher, *The Prophet Armed. Trotsky: 1879-1921*, New York and London: Oxford University Press, 1963, p. 287.

136. Ibid.

137. *Ljudi, ljudi*, book II, p. 241.

138. *Ustavotvorni odbori Savezne skupštine i Skupštine naroda*, 10 December 1945-4 January 1946, pp. 28-29.

139. Ibid., p. 29.

140. Ibid.

141. Ibid.

142. Ibid., p. 30.

143. Ibid., p. 33.

144. Ibid., p. 34.

145. Ibid., p. 35.

146. Ibid., p. 68.

147. *Prvo redovno zasedanje Saveznog veća i Veća naroda*, 15 May-20 July 1946, p. 502.

148. *Ustavotvorni odbori Savezne skupštine i Skupštine naroda,* 10 December 1945-4 January 1946, p. 76.

149. Ibid., p. 79.

150. *Prvo redovno zasedanje Saveznog veća i Veća naroda,* 15 May-20 July 1946, p. 432.

151. *Ustavotvorni odbori Savezne skupštine i Skupštine naroda,* 10 December 1945-4 January 1946, p. 62.

152. *Prvo redovno zasedanje Saveznog veća i Veća naroda,* 15 May-20 July 1946, p. 503.

153. Isaac Deutscher, *Trocki, Razoružani prorok,* Zagreb, "Liber," 1976, book 2, ch. II, pp. 103-104.

154. *Treće redovno zasedanje Saveznog veća i Veća naroda,* 26 March-26 April 1947, p. 434.

155. *Četvrto redovno zasedanje Saveznog veća i Veća naroda,* 24-29 November 1947, Belgrade, FNRJ People's Assembly Presidium, s.a., pp. 9-10.

156. "Narodni front u političkom sistemu Jugoslavije (1945-1949)," *Istraživanja VIII,* p. 367.

157. Deutscher, op. cit., p. 518.

Notes to Chapter III

1. Philip Selznick, *The Organizational Weapon, A Study of Bolshevik Strategy and Tactics,* Illinois, The Free Press, 1960, pp. 126-128.

2. Duverger, op. cit., pp. 383-386. Petranović also writes about the same thing, though in a different way, when he asserts that the "CPY proceeded from the assumption that the previous political formations could be more easily destroyed by political methods than by frontal attacks," *Politička i ekonomska osnova narodne vlasti u Jugoslaviji za vreme obnove,* p. 142.

3. Hannah Arendt, *The Origins of Totalitarianism,* New York, Meridian Books, 1958, pp. 366-367.

4. In October 1946, J. B. Tito, who was then President of the Popular Front of Yugoslavia, when asked by an American journalist whether he was also General Secretary of the CPY replied: "I am the Premier and a Communist. In the Government I do what every Communist does, that is, I aspire to have our people build their country and a better social system.

It is of little importance whether I have this or that function in the Communist Party because my main function is—Premier and Supreme Commander of the Yugoslav Army . . . ." *Izgradnja nove Jugoslavije,* vol. II, book 2, p. 197.

5. "Izjava Centralnog komiteta KP Jugoslavije povodom Rezolucije Informacionog biroa kommunističkih partija o stranju u KPJ," *Borba,* 30 June 1948.

6. Kardelj, *Put nove Jugoslavije,* p. 111.

7. "Izborni proglas Narodne seljačke stranke," *Politika,* 3 October 1945.

8. "Osnovna organizaciona načela Narodnog Fronta Jugoslavije," Articles 2 and 3.

9. Filip Lakuš, "Zašto Narodni front?" *Slobodni dom,* 20 February 1946.

10. *Prvi kongres Narodnog fronta Jugoslavije,* Split, "Slobodna Dalmacija," 1945, pp. 45-46 and 68.

11. *Politika,* 7 October 1945.

12. Ibid., 15 September 1945.

13. Ibid., 23 September 1945.

14. "Izjava Mite Stanisavljevića," *Novosti,* 9 November 1945.

15. *Politika,* 23 September 1945.

16. Quoted from David Shub, *Lenin, A Biography,* Harmondsworth, Penguin Books, 1966, p. 117.

17. Jaša Prodanović, "Na velikoj prekretnici," *Republika,* 6 November 1945.

18. *Republika,* 18 December 1945.

19. Lukács, "Geschichte und Klassenbewusstsein. Studien über Marxistische Dialektik," *Werke,* vol. 2, pp. 439-440.

20. Jakov Blažević, "Narodni sudovi moraju biti izraz demokratske volje naroda," *Arhiv za pravne i društvene nauke,* 1-2/1945, pp. 94-95.

21. Jaša Prodanović, "Nezavisnost sudjenja," "Smenjivanje sudija," "Izmirenje dva člana Ustava," *Republika,* 7, 14 and 21 January 1947.

22. Jaša Prodanović, "Sud i sudije," *Republika,* 6 November 1945.

23. Milivoje Č. Marković, "Sud i sudije. Razmišljanje povodom jednog članka," *Novosti,* 13 November 1945.

24. *Ustavotvorni odbori Savezne skupštine i Skupštine naroda,* p. 68.

25. Branko Petranović, "Vodjstva gradjanskih stranaka i njihova

politika za vreme rata i revolucije naroda Jugoslavije," *Politički život Jugoslavije 1914-1945,* Belgrade, Treći Program Radio Beograda, 1973, p. 529.

26. *Slobodni dom,* 9 April 1948.

27. *Prvi kongres Narodnog fronta Jugoslavije,* p. 11.

28. "Listovi RSS," *Demokratija,* 25 October 1945.

29. "Zašto izlazimo," "Jovan M. Jovanović, the founder of "Novosti," "Izjave Mite Stanisavljevića," *Novosti,* 9 November 1945.

30. "Obaveštenje Redakcionog odbora prijateljima, pretplatnicima i čitaocima *Republike,*" *Republika,* 16 October 1956, and "Pretplatnicima i suradnicima 'Slobodnog doma,'" *Slobodni dom,* 26 December 1963.

31. *Ustavotvorni odbori Savezne skupštine i Skupštine naroda,* p. 33.

32. *Politika,* 27 July 1946.

33. "Jedno rešenje Narodne skupštine Srbije," *Republika,* 30 July 1946.

34. *Politika,* 13 August 1946. After Jovanović's expulsion from the Party, the Agrarian Party and the People's Peasant Party merged again into the United Agrarian Party at the "Unification Congress." *Politika,* 28 October 1946.

35. Milentije Popović, "Povodom izjave Glavnog odbora Narodne seljačke stranke o pristupanju Jedinstvenom narodnooslobodilačkom frontu Srbije," *Borba,* 26 February 1945.

36. Kardelj, *Put nove Jugoslavije,* p. 96.

37. See reports on the trial of Dragoljub Jovanović in *Borba,* 2, 4, 5, 8 and 9 October 1947.

38. D. L., "Povodom presude špijunu i izdajniku Dragoljubu Jovanoviću," *Borba,* 11 October 1947.

39. It is, of course, not really necessary to remind our readers that Seton-Watson and Clissold, leaving aside their political and diplomatic careers and activities, are well-known historians and researchers of the conditions in Eastern Europe and Yugoslavia. Seton-Watson had recently co-edited his father's correspondence with the Yugoslavs under the title, *R. W. Seton-Watson i Jugosloveni. Korespondencija 1906-1941.* Zagreb, Zagreb University, Institute of Croatian History, 1976. His book *Nations and States. An Enquiry into the Origins of Nations and the Politics of Nationalism,* London, Metheun, 1977, has also been translated into Serbo-Croatian.

40. Dragoljub Jovanović, *Socijalizam i seljaštvo,* Belgrade, "Politika i društvo," 1941, p. 54. See also *Narodna seljačka stranka. Osnovna načela, Program. Statut,* Belgrade 1940.

41. *Socijalizam i seljastvo*, p. 56.
42. Ibid., p. 9.
43. Tito, *Izgradnja nove Jugoslavije*, vol. II, book 2, p. 123.
44. "Povodom programa Demokratske stranke g. Grola," *Politika*, 17 September 1945.
45. "Izborni zakon i izborna stvarnost," *Demokratija*, 27 September 1945.
46. *Zakonodavni rad Predsedništva Antifašistickog veća narodnog oslobodjenja Jugoslavije i Predsedništva Privremene narodne skupštine*, 19 November 1944-27 October 1945, pp. 993-994.
47. "Saopštenje udruženih opozicionih stranaka od 20 Septembra 1945," *Demokratija*, 27 September 1945.
48. Petranović, *Političke i pravne prilike za vreme privremene Vlade DFJ*, p. 189.
49. *Rad zakonodavnih odbora Predsedništva Antifašističkog veća narodnog oslobodjenja Jugoslavije i Privremene narodne skupštine DFJ*, 3 April-25 October 1945, p. 707.
50. Ibid., pp. 328-329.
51. Jovan Djordjević, "Ustavotvorna skupština i novi izborni sistem," *Arhiv za pravne i društvene nauke*, 3-4/1945, pp. 123-124.
52. Djilas, "Značaj novih političkih zakona i namjere reakcije," *Članci 1941-1946*, pp. 231-236.
53. Dragoljub Jovanović, "Opozicija nekad i sad," *Politika*, 26 September 1945.
54. *Službeni list DFJ*, no. 83, 28 October 1945.
55. Živojin Ristić, *Izborni zakoni Srbije*, Belgrade, Belgrade University, Law Faculty, 1935, pp. 120-121.
56. *Zakonodavni rad Predsedništva Antifašističkog veća narodnog oslobodjenja Jugoslavije i Predsedništva Privremene narodne skupštine*, 19 November 1944-27 October 1945.
57. "Kutija bez liste," *Demokratija*, 1 November 1945.
58. "Postavljanjem 'kutije bez liste' osujećen je manevar opozicije apstinencijom," *Politika*, 28 October 1945.
59. Boris Kidrić, *Sabrana dela*, Belgrade, "Kultura," 1959, book II, p. 412.
60. A brief report by the Federal Electoral Commission was published in the daily press and in *Službeni list DFJ*, No. 92, 27 November 1945.

With regard to the election results in Serbia, which are also the most interesting ones, *Borba,* 14 November 1945, contains a review of the election results in each region and district, but there are gaps in this review and not all of the electoral districts are listed. *Novosti,* 18 November, carried more details on how individual parties in the Popular Front fared in the elections.

61.   Lukács, "Früschriften 1919-1922," *Werke,* vol. 2, p. 101.

Notes to Chapter IV

1.   *Zakonodavni rad Predsedništva Antifašističkog veća narodnog oslobodjenja Jugoslavije i Predsedništva Privremene narodne skupštine DFJ* (19 November 1944-27 October 1945), p. 944.

2.   *Treće zasedanje Antifašističkog veća narodnog oslobodjenja Jugoslavije. Zasedanje Privremene narodne skupštine,* 7-26 August 1945, p. 183.

3.   *Rad zakonodavnih odbora Predsedništva Antifašističkog veća narodnog oslobodjenja Jugoslavije i Privremene narodne skupštine DFJ* (3 April-25 October 1945), Belgrade, Presidium of the FNRJ National Assembly, 1952, p. 525.

4.   *Treće zasedanje Antifašističkog veća narodnog oslobodjenja Jugoslavije. Zasedanje Privremene narodne skupštine,* 7-26 August 1945, p. 373.

5.   Ibid., p. 374.

6.   *Rad zakonodavnih odbora Predsedništva Antifašističkog veća narodnog oslobodenja Jugoslavije i Privremene narodne skupštine DFJ* (3 April-25 October 1945), p. 526.

7.   *Treće zasedanje Antifašističkog veća narodnog oslobodjenja Jugoslavije. Zasedanje Privremene narodne skupštine,* 7-26 August 1945, p. 387.

8.   Ibid., pp. 386-387.

9.   *Rad zakonodavnih odbora Predsedništva Antifašističkog veća narodnog oslobodjenja Jugoslavije i Privremene narodne skupštine DFJ* (3 April-25 October, 1945), p. 526.

10.   *Treće zasedanje Antifašističkog veća narodnog oslobodjenja Jugoslavije. Zasedanje Privremene narodne skupštine,* 7-26 August 1945, p. 395.

11.   Ibid., p. 396.

12.   Ibid., p. 376.

13.   Ibid., p. 377.

14. Coke's *Reports,* Pt. XII, 65, (1608).

15. *Rad zakonodavnih odbora Predsedništva Antifašističkog veća narodnog oslobodjenja Jugoslavije i Privremene narodne skupštine DFJ* (3 April-25 October 1945), p. 524.

16. *Treće zasedanje Antifašističkog veća narodnog oslobodjenja Jugoslavije. Zasedanje Privremene narodne skupštine,* 7-26 August 1945, pp. 381-382.

17. Ibid., p. 383.

18. Montequieu, *L'Ésprit des Lois,* Paris, Garnier Frères, s.a., Book XI, Chapter VI, p. 143.

19. K. Marx-F. Engels, "Debate o slobodi štampe i o publikovanju rasprava u staleškog skupštini," *Dela,* Belgrade, "Prosveta," 1968, Vol. 1, pp. 226-227.

20. *Prvo redovno zasedanje Saveznog veća i Veća naroda,* 15 May-20 July 1946, Belgrade, FNRJ National Assembly, pp. 501-502.

21. Ibid., p. 501.

22. Ibid., p. 502.

23. The institution of people's prosecutors was provided for in Article 22 of the Law on the Public Prosecutors ("FNRJ Official Gazette," 60/46), which stated: "To make it possible for the people to participate in implementing the tasks of public prosecutors, public prosecutors are assisted by people's prosecutors as voluntary associates. The people's prosecutors are elected by citizens at their meetings in economic enterprises, official bodies, institutions, in the streets and housing estates of large cities, in villages and municipalities."

24. Ibid., p. 496.

25. Ibid., p. 507.

26. Ibid.

27. Ibid., pp. 507-508.

28. *Treće redovno zasedanje Saveznog veća i Veća naroda,* 26 March-26 April 1947, pp. 142-143.

29. Ibid., pp. 143-144.

30. Ibid., p. 169.

31. Ibid., p. 143.

32. Jakov Blažević, "Narodni sudovi moraju biti izraz demokratske volje naroda," *Arhiv za pravne i društvene nauke,* nos. 1-2/1945, p. 95.

33. *Ustavotvorni odbori Savezne skupštine i Skupštine naroda,* 10 December 1945-4 January 1946, p. 241.

34. Ibid., p. 508.
35. Ibid., p. 501.
36. Ibid., p. 502.
37. Ibid.
38. Ibid., p. 620.
39. Ibid., p. 622.
40. Ibid.
41. Ibid., p. 631.
42. Ibid.
43. Ibid., p. 633.
44. Ibid.
45. J. B. Tito, "Odgovori na pitanja novinara na Konferenciji s predstavnicima strane i domaće štampe," *Izgradnja nove Jugoslavije,* Book I, Vol. 2, p. 223.
46. *Zasedanje Ustavotvorne skupštine,* 29 November 1945-1 February 1946, p. 236.
47. Ibid., pp. 346-347.
48. Ibid., p. 540.
49. Ibid.
50. This provision of the Agreement says literally: "The new government will publish a declaration which will contain the basic principles of democratic freedoms and guarantees for their implementation. Personal freedom, freedom from fear, freedom of religion and conscience, freedom of speech, the press, assembly and association will be especially stressed and guaranteed as will the right to property and private initiative,"–"DFJ Official Gazette," 3/51.
51. Dragić Joksimović, "Obrazloženje predloga Zakona o slobodi od straha," *Zakonodavni rad Predsedništva Antifašističkog veća narodnog oslobodjenja Jugoslavije i Predsedništva Privremene narodne skupštine DFJ* (19 November 1944-27 October 1945), p. 994.
52. *Rad zakonodavnih odbora Predsedništva Antifašističkog veća narodnog oslobodjenje Jugoslavije i Privremene narodne skupštine DFJ* (3 April-25 October 1945), p. 571.
53. Ibid., p. 573.
54. Ibid., p. 572.
55. Ibid., p. 573.
56. *Treće zasedanje Antifašističkog veća narodnog oslobodjenja*

Jugoslavije. Zasedanje Privremene narodne skupštine, 7-26 August 1945, p. 603.

57. Ibid., p. 288.
58. Ibid., p. 293.
59. Ibid., p. 291.
60. Ibid., p. 293.
61. Ibid.
62. Ibid., p. 294.
63. Ibid., p. 285.
64. Ibid., pp. 603-604.
65. Ibid., p. 309.
66. Ibid., p. 310.
67. *Rad zakonodavnih odbora Predsedništva Antifašističkog veća narodnog oslobodjenje Jugoslavije i Privremene narodne skupštine DFJ* (3 April-25 October 1945), p. 429.
68. *Treće zasedanje Antifašističkog veća narodnog oslobodjenja Jugoslavije. Zasedanje Privremene narodne skupštine*, 7-26 August 1945, p. 286.
69. *Treće redovno zasedanje Saveznog veća i Veća naroda*, 26 March-26 April 1947, p. 259.
70. Ibid.
71. Ibid., p. 260.
72. Ibid., p. 261.
73. *Treće zasedanje Antifašističkog veća narodnog oslobodjenja Jugoslavije. Zasedanje Privremene narodne skupštine*, 7-26 August 1945, p. 362.
74. Ibid., p. 353.
75. Ibid.
76. *Rad zakonodavnih odbora Predsedništva Antifašističkog veća narodnog oslobodjenje Jugoslavije i Privremene narodne skupštine DFJ* (3 April-25 October 1945), p. 458.
77. Ibid.
78. Ibid., p. 466.
79. *Treće zasedanje Antifašističkog veća narodnog oslobodjenja Jugoslavije. Zasedanje Privremene narodne skupštine*, 7-26 August 1945, p. 348.
80. *Rad zakonodavnih odbora Predsedništva Antifašističkog veća narodnog oslobodjenje Jugoslavije i Privremene narodne skupštine DFJ* (3 April-25 October 1945), p. 465.

81.   Ibid., p. 460.

82.   Ibid., p. 466.

83.   V. I. Lenin, "Dopuna preambule Krivičnog zakonika RSFSR i Pisma D. I. Kurskom," *Dela,* Belgrade, Institute for the International Workers' Movement, 1976, Vol. 35, p. 231.

84.   Ibid., pp. 231-232.

85.   Until the first FNRJ Constitution was passed on 31 January 1946, general acts of the federal units' representative bodies were called decisions.

86.   *Politika,* 25 January 1945.

87.   Ibid., 4 February 1945.

88.   *Rad zakonodavnih odbora Predsedništva Antifašističkog veća narodnog oslobodjenje Jugoslavije i Privremene narodne skupštine DFJ* (3 April-25 October 1945), p. 489.

89.   Ibid.

90.   *Treće zasedanje Antifašističkog veća narodnog oslobodjenja Jugoslavije. Zasedanje Privremene narodne skupštine,* 7-26 August 1945, p. 354.

91.   *Zakonodavni rad Predsedništva Antifašističkog veća narodnog oslobodjenje Jugoslavije i Predsedništva Privremene narodne skupštine DFJ* (19 November 1944-27 October 1945), p. 173.

92.   *Četvrto redovno zasedanje Saveznog veća i Veća naroda,* 24-29 November 1947, p. 172.

93.   Ibid., p. 141.

94.   Ibid., p. 156.

95.   Ibid., p. 172.

Notes to Chapter V

1.   "Protiv rovarenja reakcionara," speech at Titova Korenica at the celebration of Uprising Day, 27 July 1946, *Izgradnja nove Jugoslavije,* book II, p. 118.

2.   Ibid.

3.   "Odgovori na pitanja američkih novinara, 14 oktobra 1946," *Izgradnja nove Jugoslavije,* book II, p. 198.

4.   "Rezolucija Drugog kongresa Narodnog fronta Jugoslavije," *Drugi kongres Narodnog fronta Jugoslavije,* Belgrade, a Yugoslav Popular Front Publication, 1947, p. 51.

5. Ibid.
6. Josip Broz Tito, "Narodni front kao opštenarodna politička organizacija," *Drugi kongres Narodnog fronta Jugoslavije*, p. 14.
7. Ibid.
8. Ibid., p. 15.
9. Ibid.
10. Ibid.
11. "Pismo CK SKP (b) od 27 marta 1948 drugu Titu i ostalim članovima CK KPJ," *Pisma CK KPJ i pisma CK SKP (b)*, Belgrade, 1948, pp. 33-36.
12. Moša Pijade, "O projektu Programa Komunističke partije Jugoslavije," *Peti kongres Komunističke partije Jugoslavije*, 21-29 July 1948, p. 823.
13. "Izjava Centralnog komiteta KP Jugoslavije povodom rezolucije Informacionog biroa komunističkih partija a stanju u KPJ," *Borba*, 30 June 1948.
14. *Peti kongres Komunističke partije Jugoslavije*, p. 574.
15. J. B. Tito, *Borba za oslobodjenje Jugoslavije*, book I, vol. I, p. 195.
16. *Peti kongres Komunističke partije Jugoslavije*, p. 574.
17. J. B. Tito, "Politički izveštaj," *Treći kongres Narodnog fronta Jugoslavije*, Belgrade, Popular Front Federal Board, 1949, p. 8.
18. "Programska deklaracija," ibid., p. 103.
19. "Statut Narodnog fronta Jugoslavije," ibid., p. 107.
20. Dragoljub Jovanović, *Ljudi, ljudi*, book II, p. 115.
21. "Godinu dana 'Republike' u Republici," *Republika*, 5 November 1946.
22. Archive of the Yugoslav workers' movement, Report of the CC of the CP of Serbia, 1947. Quoted from Branko Petranović, *Politička i ekonomska osnova narodne vlasti za vreme obnove*, p. 162.
23. Dragoljub Jovanović, *Ljudi, ljudi*, book II, p. 115.
24. *Republika*, 31 July 1956.
25. Ibid.
26. Ibid.
27. *Politička i ekonomska osnova narodne vlasti u Jugoslaviji*, p. 161.
28. *Slobodni dom*, 9 January 1946.
29. *Hrvatski glas*, 11 June 1946.
30. In all, twelve issues were published between 27 September and 7 November 1945.

31. *Hrvatski glas,* 1 November 1946.

32. Ibid., 8 May 1946.

33. *Politička i ekonomska osnova narodne vlasti u Jugoslaviji za vreme obnove,* p. 161.

34. "Razgovor predsjednika Izvršnog odbora HRSS a talijanskim novinarom," *Slobodni dom,* 9 April 1948.

35. "Pristaše HRSS sela Jarmine čestitali su Maršalu Titu imendan," "Proslava imendana Maršala Tita u Desniću," *Slobodni dom,* 27 March 1946.

36. "Savjetovanje pristaša HRSS u Zagrebu i Karlovcu," *Slobodni dom,* 13 September 1950.

37. Ibid.

38. "IV plenarni sastanak predstavnika HRSS," *Slobodni dom,* 18 October 1950.

39. "Politička izveštaj Franje Gažija," ibid.

40. "Rezolucija o tekučim zadacima Narodnog fronta Jugoslavije," *Slobodni dom,* 1 February 1950.

41. *Politička i ekonomska osnova narodne vlasti u Jugoslaviji za vreme obnove,* p. 101.

42. *Slobodni dom,* 18 February 1954.

43. Ibid., 14 April 1955.

44. Ibid., 8 May 1958.

45. Ibid., 1 May 1961.

46. Branko Petranović, "Narodni front u političkom sistemu Jugoslavije (1945-1949)," *Istraživanja VIII,* p. 386.

47. J. B. Tito, "Demokratija znači svestrano ispoljavanje i afirmaciju čovekove ličnosti," interview given to the French weekly "Paris Match," *Borba,* 14 November 1968, p. 4.

48. J. B. Tito, *Borba za oslobodjenje Jugoslavije 1941-1945,* book I, vol. I, pp. 194-195.

49. J. B. Tito, "Odgovori na pitanja grupe američkih novinara," 11 March 1952, *Borba za socijalističku demokratiju,* Belgrade, "Kultura," 1955, book VI, p. 17.

50. J. B. Tito, "Odgovori na pitanja urednika indijskog socijalističkog lista 'Navšakti,'" 9 November 1951, *Borba za socijalističku demokratiju* (26 June 1950 to the end of 1951), Belgrade, "Kultura," 1953, pp. 455-456.

51. "Gathered in the Popular Front are all those who wish to implement popular program, a program having as its aim the implementation of socialism. Consequently, if one wishes to implement a program, it is the Popular Front program. But, if someone wants to implement another program, outside the Popular Front, then it isn't a socialist program but a program hostile to socialism, and, naturally, we shall not allow such a program at the elections."—J. B. Tito, "Ostvarimo socijalizam u našoj zemlji," 18 February 1950, *Izgradnja nove Jugoslavije* (January 1949-June 1950), Belgrade, "Kultura," 1952, pp. 279-280.

52. J. Stalin, "K pitanjima lenjinizam," Pitanja lenjinizma, pp. 128-129.

53. Ibid., p. 129.

54. "O osnovama lenjinizma," *Pitanja lenjinizma,* p. 81.

55. Isaac Deutscher, *The Prophet Unarmed,* Oxford University Press, 1959, p. 16.

56. Ibid.

57. J. B. Tito, "Govor na Drugom kongresu Saveza sindikata Jugoslavije," 9 October 1951, *Borba za socijalističku demokratiju* (26 June 1950 to the end of 1951), Belgrade, "Kultura," 1953, pp. 399-400.

58. Dobrica Ćosić, *Vreme smrti,* Belgrade, "Slovo Ljubve," 1979, vol. 1, p. 332.

59. J. B. Tito, "Borba komunista Jugoslavije za socijalističku demokratiju," 3 November 1952, *Borba za socijalističku demokratiju,* Belgrade, "Kultura," 1955, pp. 330-331.

60. J. B. Tito, *Borba za oslobodjenje Jugoslavije 1941-1945,* book I, vol. 1, pp. 194-195.

61. Thomas Hobbes, *Leviathan,* edited by C. B. MacPherson, Penguin Books, ch. 17, p. 227.

62. Ibid., ch. 13, p. 186.

63. J. B. Tito, "Iz razgovora s urednikom kanadskog lista 'Ottawa Journal'," 6 May 1953, *Borba za mir i medjunarodnu saradnju* (1953), Belgrade, "Kultura," 1956, pp. 62-63.

64. *Peti kongres Komunističke partije Jugoslavije,* Belgrade, "Kultura," 1948, pp. 126-127.

65. J. B. Tito, "Situacija u Jugoslaviji," written in mid-July 1940, *Sabrana djela,* Belgrade, Publishing Center "Kommunist," vol. 5, p. 129.

66. J. B. Tito, "Iz razgovora sa učesnicima seminara Edi Šervuda,"

18 July 1954, *Borba za mir i medjunarodnu saradnju* (1953), Belgrade, "Kultura," 1956, p. 202.

67. Ibid., p. 203.

68. J. B. Tito, "Iz razgovora sa direktorom pariskog lista 'Le Monde'," 30 April 1956, *Borba za mir i medjunarodnu saradnju* (1956-1957), Belgrade, "Kultura," 1959, pp. 40-41.

69. J. B. Tito, "Odgovori na pitanja indijskog socijalističkog lista Navšakti," 9 November 1951, *Borba za socijalističku demokratiju* (26 June 1950 to the end of 1951), Belgrade, "Kultura," 1953, pp. 437-438.

70. J. B. Tito, "Intervju predstavniku američke televizijske kompanije CBS," 20 June 1957, *Borba za mir i medjunarodnu saradnju* (1956-1957), Belgrade, "Kultura," 1959, p. 356.

71. *Program Saveza komunista Jugoslavije,* Belgrade, "Kultura," 1958, p. 235.

72. J. B. Tito, "Privredna reforma je revolucionaran posao koji se mora izvršiti," 20 November 1966, *Borba za mir i medjunarodnu saradnju* (20 October 1966-1 October 1967), Belgrade, Belgrade Publishing and Printing Firm, "Kultura" editorial board, 1972, p. 59.

73. *Ustavotvorni odbori Savezne skupštine i Skupštine naroda,* 10 December 1945-4 January 1946, p. 27.

Notes to Concluding Remarks

1. Edvard Kardelj, *Pravci razvoja političkog sistema socijalističkog samoupravljanja* (Directions of the Development of the Political System of Socialist Self-Management) Belgrade, "Kommunist," 1977.

2. Stevan Vračar, "Pluralizam u socijalističkoj demokratiji," *Socijalistički savez i radni čovek,* Belgrade, "Socijalizam," 1966, pp. 87-99.

3. Ibid., p. 98.

4. Ibid., p. 97.

5. Ibid., p. 168.

6. "Savetovanje o opštim problemima odgovornosti," *Arhiv za pravne i društvene nauke,* 1-2/1969, pp. 143-147.

7. Ibid., p. 146.

8. Jiri Pekikan, *Praško proljeće,* Zagreb, "Globus," 1982, pp. 75-76.

9. Franc Šetinc, "Slovenija i zajedništvo," *NIN,* 24 October 1982.

10. Aleksandar Grličkov, "Dijalog i društvena kritika danas," *Politika,* 14 February 1981.

BIBLIOGRAPHY

Books and Articles:

Arendt, Hannah, *The Origins of Totalitarianism,* New York, Meridian Books, 1958.

Authoritarian Politics in Modern Society: The Dynamic of Established One-Party States, eds. Samuel Huntington, Clement Moore, New York, Basic Books, 1970.

Avakumović, Ivan, *The History of the Communist Party of Yugoslavia,* Aberdeen, Aberdeen University Press, 1964, vol. 1.

Bilandžić, Dušan, *Historija SFRJ,* Zagreb, "Školska knjiga," 1978.

Borkenau, Franz, *European Communism,* New York, Harper, 1953.

Daniels, Roberts, *The Nature of Communism,* New York, Vintage Books, 1962.

Deutscher, Isaac, *Trocki,* Zagreb, "Liber," 1975-1977, books I-III.

Duverger, Maurice, *Les Partis politiques,* Paris, Armand Colin, 1951.

Djilas, Milovan, *Članci 1941-1946,* Belgrade, "Kultura," 1947.

Djordjević, Jovan, "Ustavotvorna skupština i novi izborni sistem," *Arhiv za pravne i društvene nauke,* 3-4/1945.

Fejtö, Francois, *A History of the People's Democracies,* Harmondsworth, Penguin Books, 1977.

Gelard, Patrice, *Les systemes politiques de états socialistes,* Paris, Cujas, 1975.

Goati, Vladimir, "Socijalni pokret—pokušaj definisanja koncepta," *Politička sociologija,* Belgrade, "Mladost," 1977.

Gyorgy, Andrew, "Satellite Parties in Eastern Europe," *Modern Political Parties*, ed., Sigmund Neumann, Chicago, University of Chicago Press, 1955.

Heberle, Rudolf, *Social Movements*, New York, Appleton-Centrury-Crofts, 1951.

Hunt, R. N. Carew, *The Theory and Practice of Communism*, Harmondsworth, Penguin Books, 1963.

Huntington, Samuel, *Political Order in Changing Society*, New Haven, Yale University Press, 1968.

Ilić, Mihailo, *Politički i pravni članci*, Belgrade, "Politika i društvo," 1946.

Ionescu, Ghita, *The Politics of the European Communist States*, London, Macmillan, 1967.

Jelić, Ivan, "Osnovni problemi stvaranja Narodne fronte u Jugoslaviji do 1941. godine," *Putovi revolucije*, 7-8/1966.

Jovanović, Dragoljub, *Socijalizam i seljaštvo*, Belgrade, "Politika i društvo," 1941.

─────. *Ljudi, ljudi*, Belgrade, published by the author, 1973, 1975, books I-II.

Kardelj, Edvard, *Put nove Jugoslavije. Članci i govori iz narodnooslobodilačke borbe 1941-1945*, Belgrade, "Kultura," 1946.

─────. *Sećanja*, Belgrade, "Radnička štampa," 1980.

─────. *Pravci razvoja političkog sistema socijalističkog samoupravljanja*, Belgrade, "Kommunist," 1977.

Kidrič, Boris, *Sabrana dela*, Belgrade, "Kultura," 1959.

Kocbek, Edvard, "Odgovori" (from the book by Boris Pahor and Alojz Rebula "Edvard Kocbek, pričevalec našeg časa," Trieste, 1975), *Naši razgledi* no. 9, 9 May 1975.

Krivokapić, Boro, "Pozorište u zatvoru: Razgovor sa Jože Javoršekom," *Ideje*, 5/1981.

Lenin, V. I., *Izabrana dela*, Belgrade, "Kultura," 1960.

Lukacs, Georg, *Etika i politika*, Zagreb, "Liber," 1972.

─────. *Povijest i klasna svijest*, Zagreb, "Naprijed," 1970.

Lukić, Radomir, *Političke stranke*, Belgrade, "Naučna knjiga," 1966.

Macropolitical Theory, Handbook of Political Science, eds. Fred Greenstein, Nelson Polsby, Reading, Massachusetts, Addison-Wesley, 1975, vol. 3.

Mikuž, Metod, *Pregled zgodovine NOB v Sloveniji*, Ljubljana, "Cankarjeva založba," 1960, 1961, books I-II.

————, "Donesek k zgodovini razvoja Osvobodilne fronte ob njeni tridesetletnici," *Jugoslovenski istorijski časopis*, 3-4/1971.

Milanović, Djordje, "Počeci i prvi uspesi u razvoju Narodnog fronta u Vojvodini tokom 1935 i 1936. godine," *Istraživanja I,* Institute for the History of Vojvodina, 1971.

Narodna seljačka stranka; Osnova načela, Program, Statut, Belgrade, 1940.

Narodni front i komunisti: Jugoslavija, Čehoslovačka, Poljska 1938-1945, Belgrade, Institute of Contemporary History, 1968. *Istorijski zapisi* 3-4/1959.

Pelikan, Jiri, *Praško proljeće,* Zagreb, "Globus," 1982.

Petranović, Branko, "Gradjanske stranke u Jugoslaviji 1944-1948 i njihov karakter," *Istorijski glasnik,* I/1969.

————, "Vodjstva gradjanskih stranaka i njihova politika za vreme rata i revolucije naroda Jugoslavije," *Politički zivot Jugoslavije 1941-1945,* Belgrade, Third Program of Belgrade Radio, 1973.

————, *Političke i pravne prilike za vreme privremene vlade DFJ,* Belgrade, Institute of Social Sciences, 1964.

————. *Politička i ekonomska osnova narodne vlasti i Jugoslaviji za vreme obnove,* Belgrade, Institute of Contemporary History, 1969.

————, *Istorija Jugoslavije 1918-1978,* Belgrade, "Nolit," 1980.

————, "Narodni front u političkom, sistemu Jugoslavije (1945-1949)," *Istraživanja VIII,* Novi Sad, Institute for the Study of the History of Vojvodina, 1979.

Pijade, Moša, *Izabrani govori i članci 1941-1947,* Belgrade, "Kultura," 1947.

Political Opposition in One-Party States, ed., Leonard Shapiro, London, Macmillan, 1972.

Political Parties and Political Development, eds. Joseph LaPalombara, Myron Weiner, Princeton, Princeton University Press, 1966.

"Politički život Jugoslavije 1941-1945," *Treći program* 1973.

Pregled istorije SKJ, Belgrade, "Kultura," 1963.

Radnički i nacionalno-oslobodilački pokreti, Belgrade, Institute for the International Workers' Movement, 1970, book II.

Ribar, Ivan, *Politički zapisi,* Belgrade, "Prosveta," 1948-1959, books I-IV.

Sartori, Giovanni, *Parties and Party Systems. A Framework for Analysis,* Cambridge, Cambridge University Press, 1976, book I.

"Savetovanje o opštim problemima odgovornosti," *Arhiv za pravne i društvene nauke,* 1-2/1969.

Selznick, Philip, *The Organizational Weapon, A Study of Bolshevik Strategy and Tactics,* Illinois, The Free Press, 1960.

Seton-Watson, Hugh, *The Pattern of Communist Revolution: A History of World Communism,* London, Methuen, 1960.

Shub, David, *Lenin: A Biography,* Harmondsworth, Penguin Books, 1966.

Simić, Vladimir, *Ideološki frontovi,* Belgrade, "Politika i društvo," 1937.

Skilling, Gordon, *The Governments of Communist East Europe,* New York, Crowell, 1966.

Smiljanić, Dragoslav, *Sećanja na jednu diktaturu,* Belgrade, "Rad," 1960.

Socijalistički savez i radni čovek, Belgrade, "Socijalizam," 1966.

Stalin, J., *Pitanja lenjinizma,* Belgrade, "Kultura," 1946.

Škerl, France, "Vloga in pomen Osvobodilne fronte slovenskega naroda (1941-1943)," *Prispevek za zgodovino delavskega gibanja,* 1-2/1966.

Tito, J. B., *Izgradnja nove Jugoslavije,* Belgrade, "Kultura," 1948, vols. I-II.

————, *Sabrana djela,* "Kommunist," 1978.

Wiatr, Jerzy, "The Hegemonic Party System in Poland," *Mass Politics: Studies in Political Sociology,* eds. Erik Allardt, Stein Rokkan, New York, The Free Press, 1970.

Wilkinson, Paul, *Social Movements,* London, Macmillan, 1971.

Živković, Dušan, *Narodni front Jugoslavije 1935-1945,* Belgrade, Institute for Contemporary History, 1978.

Printed Records:

Treće zasedanje Antifašističkog veća narodnog oslobodjenja Jugoslavije. Zasedanje Privremene narodne skupštine, 7-26 August 1945, Belgrade, Presidium of the FNRJ National Assembly, s.a.

Zakonodavni rad Predsedništva Antifašističkog veća narodnog oslobodjenje Jugoslavije i Predsedništva Privremene narodne skupštine DFJ, 19 November 1944-27 October 1945, Belgrade, Presidium of the FNRJ National Assembly, 1951.

Rad zakonodavnih odbora Predsedništva Antifašističkog veća narodnog oslobodjenja Jugoslavije i Predsedništva Privremene narodne skupštine, 3 April-25 October 1945, Belgrade, Presidium of the FNRJ National Assembly, 1952.

Zasedanje Ustavotvorne skupštine, 29 November 1945-1 February 1946, Belgrade, FNRJ National Assembly, s.a.

Ustavotvorni odbori Savezne skupštine i Skupštine naroda, 10 December 1945-4 January 1946, FNRJ National Assembly, s.a.

Zasedanja Narodne Skupštine FNRJ, 1946-1949, FNRJ National Assembly.

Prvi kongres Narodnog fronta Jugoslavije, Split, "Slobodna Dalmacija," 1945.

Drugi kongres Narodnog fronta Jugoslavije, Belgrade, Yugoslav People's Front Publication, 1947.

Treći kongres Narodnog fronta Jugoslavije, Belgrade, Popular Front Federal Committee, 1949.

Peti kongres Komunističke partije Jugoslavije, Belgrade, "Kultura," 1948.

Službeni list DFJ, odnosno FNRJ, 1944-1949.

Dokumenti o Jugoslaviji, ed. Ferdo Čulinović, Zagreb, "Školska knjiga," 1968.

Dokumenti o razvoju narodne vlasti, ed. Leon Geršković, Belgrade, "Arhiv za pravne i društvene nauke," 1948.

Istorija socijalističke Jugoslavije, eds. Branko Petranović and Čedomir Štrbac, Belgrade, "Radnička štampa," 1977, books I-III.

Newspapers:

Politika
Borba
Glas
Demokratija
Novosti
Hrvatski glas
Republika
Slobodni dom

INDEX

EAST EUROPEAN MONOGRAPHS

The *East European Monographs* comprise scholarly books on the history and civilization of Eastern Europe. They are published under the editorship of Stephen Fischer-Galati, in the belief that these studies contribute substantially to the knowledge of the area and serve to stimulate scholarship and research.

1. *Political Ideas and the Enlightenment in the Romanian Principalities, 1750–1831.* By Vlad Georgescu. 1971.
2. *America, Italy and the Birth of Yugoslavia, 1917–1919.* By Dragan R. Zivjinovic. 1972.
3. *Jewish Nobles and Geniuses in Modern Hungary.* By William O. McCagg, Jr. 1972.
4. *Mixail Soloxov in Yugoslavia: Reception and Literary Impact.* By Robert F. Price. 1973.
5. *The Historical and Nationalist Thought of Nicolae Iorga.* By William O. Oldson. 1973.
6. *Guide to Polish Libraries and Archives.* By Richard C. Lewanski. 1974.
7. *Vienna Broadcasts to Slovakia, 1938–1939: A Case Study in Subversion.* By Henry Delfiner. 1974.
8. *The 1917 Revolution in Latvia.* By Andrew Ezergailis. 1974.
9. *The Ukraine in the United Nations Organization: A Study in Soviet Foreign Policy. 1944–1950.* By Konstantin Sawczuk. 1975.
10. *The Bosnian Church: A New Interpretation.* By John V. A. Fine, Jr., 1975.
11. *Intellectual and Social Developments in the Habsburg Empire from Maria Theresa to World War I.* Edited by Stanley B. Winters and Joseph Held. 1975.
12. *Ljudevit Gaj and the Illyrian Movement.* By Elinor Murray Despalatovic. 1975.
13. *Tolerance and Movements of Religious Dissent in Eastern Europe,* Edited by Bela K. Kiraly. 1975.
14. *The Parish Republic: Hlinka's Slovak People's Party, 1939–1945.* By Yeshayahu Jelinek. 1976.
15. *The Russian Annexation of Bessarabia, 1774–1828.* By George F. Jewsbury. 1976.
16. *Modern Hungarian Historiography.* By Steven Bela Vardy. 1976.
17. *Values and Community in Multi-National Yugoslavia.* By Gary K. Bertsch. 1976.
18. *The Greek Socialist Movement and the First World War: the Road to Unity.* By George B. Leon. 1976.
19. *The Radical Left in the Hungarian Revolution of 1848.* By Laszlo Deme. 1976.
20. *Hungary between Wilson and Lenin: The Hungarian Revolution of 1918–1919 and the Big Three.* By Peter Pastor. 1976.

21. *The Crises of France's East-Central European Diplomacy, 1933–1938.* By Anthony J. Komjathy. 1976.

22. *Polish Politics and National Reform, 1775–1788.* By Daniel Stone. 1976.

23. *The Habsburg Empire in World War I.* Edited by Robert A. Kann, Bela K. Kiraly, and Paula S. Fichtner. 1977.

24. *The Slovenes and Yugoslavism, 1890–1914.* By Carole Rogel. 1977.

25. *German-Hungarian Relations and the Swabian Problem.* By Thomas Spira. 1977.

26. *The Metamorphosis of a Social Class in Hungary During the Reign of Young Franz Joseph.* By Peter I. Hidas. 1977.

27. *Tax Reform in Eighteenth Century Lombardy.* By Daniel M. Klang. 1977.

28. *Tradition versus Revolution: Russia and the Balkans in 1917.* By Robert H. Johnston. 1977.

29. *Winter into Spring: The Czechoslovak Press and the Reform Movement 1963–1968.* By Frank L. Kaplan. 1977.

30. *The Catholic Church and the Soviet Government, 1939–1949.* By Dennis J. Dunn. 1977.

31. *The Hungarian Labor Service System, 1939–1945.* By Randolph L. Braham. 1977.

32. *Consciousness and History: Nationalist Critics of Greek Society 1897–1914.* By Gerasimos Augustinos. 1977.

33. *Emigration in Polish Social and Political Thought, 1870–1914.* By Benjamin P. Murdzek. 1977.

34. *Serbian Poetry and Milutin Bojic.* By Mihailo Dordevic. 1977.

35. *The Baranya Dispute: Diplomacy in the Vortex of Ideologies, 1918–1921.* By Leslie C. Tihany. 1978.

36. *The United States in Prague, 1945–1948.* By Walter Ullmann. 1978.

37. *Rush to the Alps: The Evolution of Vacationing in Switzerland.* By Paul P. Bernard. 1978.

38. *Transportation in Eastern Europe: Empirical Findings.* By Bogdan Mieczkowski. 1978.

39. *The Polish Underground State: A Guide to the Underground, 1939–1945.* By Stefan Korbonski. 1978.

40. *The Hungarian Revolution of 1956 in Retrospect.* Edited by Bela K. Kiraly and Paul Jonas. 1978.

41. *Boleslaw Limanowski (1935–1935): A Study in Socialism and Nationalism.* By Kazimiera Janina Cottam. 1978.

42. *The Lingering Shadow of Nazism: The Austrian Independent Party Movement Since 1945.* By Max E. Riedlsperger. 1978.

43. *The Catholic Church, Dissent and Nationality in Soviet Lithuania.* By V. Stanley Vardys. 1978.

44. *The Development of Parliamentary Government in Serbia.* By Alex N. Dragnich. 1978.

45. *Divide and Conquer: German Efforts to Conclude a Separate Peace, 1914–1918.* By L. L. Farrar, Jr. 1978.

46. *The Prague Slav Congress of 1848.* By Lawrence D. Orton. 1978.

47. *The Nobility and the Making of the Hussite Revolution.* By John M. Klassen. 1978.

48. *The Cultural Limits of Revolutionary Politics: Change and Continuity in Socialist Czechoslovakia.* By David W. Paul. 1979.

49. *On the Border of War and Peace: Polish Intelligence and Diplomacy in 1937–1939 and the Origins of the Ultra Secret.* By Richard A. Woytak. 1979.

50. *Bear and Foxes: The International Relations of the East European States 1965–1969.* By Ronald Haly Linden. 1979.

51. *Czechoslovakia: The Heritage of Ages Past.* Edited by Ivan Volgyes and Hans Brisch. 1979.

52. *Prime Minister Gyula Andrassy's Influence on Habsburg Foreign Policy.* By Janos Decsy. 1979.

53. *Citizens for the Fatherland: Education, Educators, and Pedagogical Ideals in Eighteenth Century Russia.* By J. L. Black. 1979.

54. *A History of the "Proletariat": The Emergence of Marxism in the Kingdom of Poland, 1870–1887.* By Norman M. Naimark. 1979.

55. *The Slovak Autonomy Movement, 1935–1939: A Study in Unrelenting Nationalism.* By Dorothea H. El Mallakh. 1979.

56. *Diplomat in Exile: Francis Pulszky's Political Activities in England, 1849–1860.* By Thomas Kabdebo. 1979.

57. *The German Struggle Against the Yugoslav Guerrillas in World War II: German Counter-Insurgency in Yugoslavia, 1941–1943.* By Paul N. Hehn. 1979.

58. *The Emergence of the Romanian National State.* By Gerald J. Bobango. 1979.

59. *Stewards of the Land: The American Farm School and Modern Greece.* By Brenda L. Marder. 1979.

60. *Roman Dmowski: Party, Tactics, Ideology, 1895–1907.* By Alvin M. Fountain, II. 1980.

61. *International and Domestic Politics in Greece During the Crimean War.* By Jon V. Kofas. 1980.

62. *Fires on the Mountain: The Macedonian Revolutionary Movement and the Kidnapping of Ellen Stone.* By Laura Beth Sherman. 1980.

63. *The Modernization of Agriculture: Rural Transformation in Hungary, 1848–1975.* Edited by Joseph Held. 1980.

64. *Britain and the War for Yugoslavia, 1940–1943.* By Mark C. Wheeler. 1980.

65. *The Turn to the Right: The Ideological Origins and Development of Ukrainian Nationalism, 1919–1929.* By Alexander J. Motyl. 1980.

66. *The Maple Leaf and the White Eagle: Canadian-Polish Relations, 1918–1978.* By Aloysius Balawyder. 1980.

67. *Antecedents of Revolution: Alexander I and the Polish Congress Kingdom, 1815–1825.* By Frank W. Thackeray. 1980.

68. *Blood Libel at Tiszaeszlar.* By Andrew Handler. 1980.

69. *Democratic Centralism in Romania: A Study of Local Communist Politics.* By Daniel N. Nelson. 1980.

70. *The Challenge of Communist Education: A Look at the German Democratic Republic.* By Margrete Siebert Klein. 1980.

71. *The Fortifications and Defense of Constantinople.* By Byron C. P. Tsangadas. 1980.

72. *Balkan Cultural Studies.* By Stavro Skendi. 1980.

73. *Studies in Ethnicity: The East European Experience in America.* Edited by Charles A. Ward, Philip Shashko, and Donald E. Pienkos. 1980.

74. *The Logic of "Normalization:" The Soviet Intervention in Czechoslovakia and the Czechoslovak Response.* By Fred Eidlin. 1980.

75. *Red Cross. Black Eagle: A Biography of Albania's American Schol.* By Joan Fultz Kontos. 1981.

76. *Nationalism in Contemporary Europe.* By Franjo Tudjman. 1981.

77. *Great Power Rivalry at the Turkish Straits: The Montreux Conference and Convention of 1936.* By Anthony R. DeLuca. 1981.

78. *Islam Under the Double Eagle: The Muslims of Bosnia and Hercegovina, 1878–1914.* By Robert J. Donia. 1981.

79. *Five Eleventh Century Hungarian Kings: Their Policies and Their Relations with Rome.* By Z. J. Kosztolnyik. 1981.

80. *Prelude to Appeasement: East European Central Diplomacy in the Early 1930's.* By Lisanne Radice. 1981.

81. *The Soviet Regime in Czechoslovakia.* By Zdenek Krystufek. 1981.

82. *School Strikes in Prussian Poland, 1901–1907: The Struggle Over Bilingual Education.* By John J. Kulczychi. 1981.

83. *Romantic Nationalism and Liberalism: Joachim Lelewel and the Polish National Idea.* By Joan S. Skurnowicz. 1981.

84. *The "Thaw" In Bulgarian Literature.* By Atanas Slavov. 1981.

85. *The Political Thought of Thomas G. Masaryk.* By Roman Szporluk. 1981.

86. *Prussian Poland in the German Empire, 1871–1900.* By Richard Blanke. 1981.

87. *The Mazepists: Ukrainian Separatism in the Early Eighteenth Century.* By Orest Subtelny. 1981.

88. *The Battle for the Marchlands: The Russo-Polish Campaign of 1920.* By Adam Zamoyski. 1981.

89. *Milovan Djilas: A Revolutionary as a Writer.* By Dennis Reinhartz. 1981.

90. *The Second Republic: The Disintegration of Post-Munich Czechoslovakia, October 1938-March 1939.* By Theodore Prochazka, Sr. 1981.

91. *Financial Relations of Greece and the Great Powers, 1832–1862.* By Jon V. Kofas. 1981.

92. *Religion and Politics: Bishop Valerian Trifa and His Times.* By Gerald J. Bobango. 1981.

93. *The Politics of Ethnicity in Eastern Europe.* Edited by George Klein and Milan J. Reban. 1981.

94. *Czech Writers and Politics.* By Alfred French. 1981.

95. *Nation and Ideology: Essays in Honor of Wayne S. Vucinich.* Edited by Ivo Banac, John G. Ackerman, and Roman Szporluk. 1981.

96. *For God and Peter the Great: The Works of Thomas Consett, 1723–1729.* Edited by James Cracraft. 1982.

97. *The Geopolitics of Leninism.* By Stanley W. Page. 1982

98. *Karel Havlicek (1821–1856): A National Liberation Leader of the Czech Renascence.* By Barbara K. Reinfeld. 1982.

99. *Were-Wolf and Vampire in Romania.* By Harry A. Senn. 1982.

100. *Ferdinand I of Austria: The Politics of Dynasticism in the Age of Reformation.* By Paula Sutter Fichtner. 1982

101. *France in Greece During World War I: A Study in the Politics of Power.* By Alexander S. Mitrakos. 1982.

102. *Authoritarian Politics in a Transitional State: Istvan Bethlen and the Unified Party in Hungary, 1919–1926.* By William M. Batkay. 1982.

103. *Romania Between East and West: Historical Essays in Memory of Constantin C. Giurescu.* Edited by Stephen Fischer-Galati, Radu R. Florescu and George R. Ursul. 1982.

104. *War and Society in East Central Europe: From Hunyadi to Rakoczi— War and Society in Late Medieval and Early Modern Hungary.* Edited by János Bak and Béla K. Király. 1982.

105. *Total War and Peace Making: A Case Study on Trianon.* Edited by Béla K. Király, Peter Pastor, and Ivan Sanders. 1982

106. *Army, Aristocracy, and Monarchy: Essays on War, Society, and Government in Austria, 1618–1780.* Edited by Wayne S. Vucinich. 1982.

107 *. The First Serbian Uprising, 1804–1813.* Edited by Wayne S. Vucinich. 1982.

168. *PNA: A Centennial History of the Polish National Alliance of the United States of North America.* By Donald E. Pienkos. 1984.
169. *The Slovenes of Carinthia.* By Thomas M. Barker and Andreas Moritsch. 1984.
170. *The Saga of Kosovo: Focus of Serbian-Albanian Relations.* By Alex N. Dragnich and Slavko Todorovich. 1984.
171. *Germany's International Monetary Policy and the European Monetary System.* By Hugh Kaufmann. 1985.
172. *Kiril and Methodius: Founders of Slavonic Writing.* Edited by Ivan Duichev. 1985.
173. *The United States and the Greek War for Independence, 1821-1828.* By Paul C. Pappas. 1985.
174. *Joseph Eötvös and the Modernization of Hungary, 1840-1870.* By Paul Bödy. 1985.
175. *Jewish Leadership during the Nazi Era: Patterns of Behavior in the Free World.* Edited by Randolph L. Braham. 1985.
176. *The American Mission in the Allied Control Commission for Bulgaria, 1944-1947: History and Transcripts.* Edited by Michael M. Boll. 1985.
177. *The United States, Great Britain, and the Sovietization of Hungary, 1945-1948.* By Stanley M. Max. 1985.
178. *Hunyadi: Legend and Reality.* By Joseph Held. 1985.
179. *Clio's Art in Hungary and in Hungarian-America.* By Steven Bela Vardy. 1985.
180. *Slovakia 1918-1938: Education and the Making of a Nation.* By Owen V. Johnson. 1985.
181. *Ilija Garasanin: Balkan Bismarck.* By David MacKenzie. 1985.
182. *Medieval Buda: A Study of Municipal Government and Jurisdiction in the Kingdom of Hungary.* By Martyn C. Rady. 1985.
183. *Eastern Europe in the Aftermath of Solidarity.* By Adam Bromke. 1985.
184. *Istvan Tisza: The Liberal Vision and Conservative Statecraft of a Magyar Nationalist.* By Gabor Vermes. 1985.